RE

"*Beyond the Tango* proves that with knowledge and commitment couples can successfully navigate just about every marital challenge. Susan McKeown has done a terrific job of weaving her vast personal and professional experience with expert references, compassion, empathy, and humor into a practical, step-by-step guide to a happy, fulfilling, long lasting marriage. This is a must-read for couples at every stage of their relationships."

LINDA SAUNDERS PAQUETTE, JD

****

"Relationships are like a dance, but the tempo quickens, and the steps seem to be ever changing. This remarkable book gets it! *Beyond the Tango* addresses real issues for real couples in ways that invite growth, stability, and a pathway to deeper connections with less stress and more joy."

PAUL S. BOYNTON, Author of *Begin with Yes* and *Be Amazing*

****

"This new book by Susan McKeown is a sequel to *Beyond the First Dance* and continues to explore the nature of our most intimate relationships. Using dance to explain our interactions is quite lovely. The chapters are self-contained and helpful with bullet points and references that are on target and easy to understand. Every marriage and long-term relationship can be strengthened by the pearls of wisdom imparted through this book. I highly recommend it."

TERESA PONN, MD FACS

****

"Susan McKeown has written a guide to marriage and family, drawing not only on her personal and professional experiences but a thorough reading of noted, experienced authors on the related topics. This is an excellent read for marrieds of all ages, but particularly those planning on a marriage. There are invaluable insights here. Should be required reading."

JAMES F CONWAY JR., MD

****

"Susan's passion for advising couples on building happy marriages comes through in every chapter and on every page. Her guidance, practical tips, and exercises are sure to interest couples who are eager to hear from a knowledgeable source, a skilled writer, and, most of all, a distinctive voice that is understanding and supportive."

KATHY FORTIN, Published author, Dartmouth College MALS

****

We highly recommend this book to anyone who is married and recommend reading it right away! The book is easy to read, humorous, and gives great insight and advice in a down to earth way. There have been many times during our three-year marriage and now parenthood that we think back on Susan's stories and teachings-with a relatable laugh or "Ah ha" moment after using her advice and seeing how it supports our marriage.

DUKE AND KRISTIN LOGAN (APRN)

****

"Using her experience of over 40 years conducting marriage workshops as well as her own 50 years of marriage, Susan McKeown presents an approach to dealing with the many challenges couples face in married life. I found myself nodding in agreement with her throughout reading the book. *Beyond the Tango* is a wonderful primer for newlyweds and should be kept as a reference book for their future lives together."

JOHN J. BUCHINO, M.D., Emeritus Professor of Pediatrics,
University of Louisville, Louisville, KY

****

"All the ingredients for a good enough marriage come to mind in reading *Beyond the Tango*. The most important decision one makes in their life is who to choose for a mate. This book reads like a novel and allows the reader to soak up all the necessary ingredients for a fulfilling, long term relationship. Susan shares her own life experiences both personal and professional to help couples who strive for a healthy, happy marriage. Let the dance go on."

DEEDEE SOUZA, MSW, LICSW

****

Whether you are looking for a guide to long-term relationships or help on specific topics such as parenting, loneliness, sexuality, or spirituality, this book is for you. Susan draws from her own experience, wisdom of experts, and examples from movies and books in this thorough and engaging description of the joys and struggles of relationships. The result is applicable information, insight, and inspiration. I highly recommend *Beyond the Tango*.

REV. DR. DAVID B. REYNOLDS,
Licensed Psychotherapist and Minister

****

Beyond the Tango, a wonderful guide to keeping your marriage loving and healthy, takes readers through the stages of marriage and its inevitable challenges in a clear, easy to access format that addresses a wide range of strategies and topics, including parenting, finances, intimacy, and even solitude. Susan McKeown provides a wealth of citations for further reading and exploration, along with concrete steps to take for improved communication and self-understanding. After 50 years of marriage, McKeown has plenty of experience to draw on. The stories she shares from her own marriage, full of honesty and humor, form the heart of this indispensable book.

KATHERINE TOWLER
Author of *The Penny Poet of Portsmouth*

****

"In *Beyond the Tango* Susan reminds couples that a long-term marriage, like dance, takes practice. With sound advice and quick-step exercises *Beyond the Tango* guides couples through issues that arise in all relationships with humor, personal anecdotes, and research. I recommend keeping this book handy as a reference during the all different stages of your marriage."

MARCY LYMAN

****

"Beyond the Tango" is more than just a guide; it is a caring and lively marriage companion offering practical, useful advice in nurturing and preserving any committed relationship so as to better handle the inevitable challenges to staying on the dance floor."

PAUL K. CASEY, MA, JD and KATHLEEN L. CASEY, MA.
Presenters in Marriage Preparation Programs for the
Archdiocese of Baltimore for 20 years." Ellicott City, MD

****

"Brava! Susan McKeown has done it again with her well-presented work: *Beyond the Tango.* Susan has made good, doubled down even, on the hopeful promise she made on her wedding night to write a book for married couples! This book continues the great recipes, if you will, presented in her earlier book: *Beyond the First Dance: A Guide for Couples to Think Beyond Their Wedding Day.* The chapters are filled with practical, real-life roadmaps for any couple who wants to better their marriages in order to lead happier, healthy lives. Susan graciously and generously shares her own marriage to Patrick as a model to navigate both the smooth and rough terrains of married life. It is an excellent resource for couples.

PAUL ASHTON, PSY.D.,D.MIN.

****

Beyond the Tango

A Guide to a Thriving Marriage while Juggling Careers, Kids, and Chaos

Susan McKeown
APRN, CPS, MFA

BEYOND THE TANGO: A GUIDE TO A THRIVING MARRIAGE WHILE JUGGLING CAREERS, KIDS, AND CHAOS

PROJECT MANAGER: Jessie Ranew
INTERIOR LAYOUT AND JACKET DESIGN: Nicole Sturk

To my husband, Patrick, for knowing and supporting my dreams and to our four children, Katie, Eileen, Daniel, and Matthew who provided me with enough experiences to keep me both humble and proud. I love you all.

Contents

Section I: Line Dancing

These busy, juggling years are quite a contrast to the Tango!

Section II: Twist and Shout

Are you moving fast, yet feeling like you are going nowhere?

Introduction

Still in my mind's eye is the elderly couple who were a fixture on our college campus. He walked with his shoulders slightly stooped and she beside him, matronly and plump, with a white bun atop her head, wisps of hair framing her soft, pretty face. He was a professor of economics, and she was his wife of fifty years. Every day they walked hand in hand across the quad. They were a familiar sight to me and my boyfriend, Patrick, as we hurried to our classes. Their obvious love and devotion embodied the rewards of a long and happy marriage. I idealized married love as a young college student, picturing my future role as a loving wife with a nursing career and a station wagon full of kids. What was their secret?

I met Patrick at a Christmas dance my sophomore and his junior year in college. We were standing next to each other in line to get a soda. He started up a conversation and asked if I wanted to sit down. Three hours later, we had learned about each other's siblings, parents, summer jobs, and that we only lived 17 miles apart back home in Connecticut. Well, that's convenient, I thought! We exchanged Christmas cards, but that was it. A year later, I saw him at a crowded basketball game over Christmas break; he said he would be returning to school the following September. Unbeknownst to me, he was in a construction accident at his summer job and missed a year of school. Meanwhile, we each had developed serious relationships. However, that interaction hinted that we could meet up at the start of school in nine months, and it motivated us to cool things with our significant others and be available when we returned.

Our senior year involved a lot of walking, talking, eating meals together, and spending as much time together as we could. By Thanksgiving, we had severed our other relationships and by Christmas we were mad about each other. When Patrick and I became engaged, we were as full of hope, excitement, and optimism as any two people in love. We married the year after graduation and looked forward to our life together. I continued to ponder the elements of a long and loving marriage.

We were fortunate that both sets of parents had been married thirty years, so that was a good model. But they, of course, were so busy working, raising, and educating kids, neither set of parents looked they were on "The Love Boat." I wanted a true happily ever after. How does one build that emotion into a marriage, not only to prevent divorce, but to be genuinely happy?

Prior to our wedding in 1971, Patrick and I had attended a seminar for engaged couples. We were eager to check this obligation off our to-do list because all we cared about was getting married. We were too young and naïve to believe we needed the information they were sharing; our love would carry us through, and life would be grand. We had not yet realized that the professor and his wife had *learned* how to face challenges, not been spared them.

When we arrived at the bridal suite on our wedding night, we were starving. We indulged ourselves with room service. As we ate our soup and ham sandwiches, I told Patrick that I planned to write a book about marriage. Patrick loves to tell that story—who would ever think of that, or mention it, on their wedding night? My intention was not to intimidate him but rather to reflect how much I respected marriage and was looking forward to our life together. I envisioned a long, loving, and romantic relationship; the way I thought marriage should be. I figured I would learn a lot on this journey, and I wanted to pass it on. One week after our honeymoon, Patrick came home from work and presented me with a blank journal to start writing. And write I did.

My early entries were often written during periods of stress. However, in between my entries, I was quite happy. Patrick never read any of my notes, but he noticed the timing of my journal writing. He commented that, after I died, anyone reading them would think I was very unhappy. I could see his point, so I began dating my writings. These musings helped me process issues at different points in our marriage. Eventually, I began to include what I was learning from reading and from observing others.

One Sunday, five years after our wedding, our pastor announced that the new Engaged Couples' Program needed married couples as group leaders. Having had a few years experiencing the reality of marriage and life with our first child, we felt we had something to offer. We had no idea how much we would learn.

In the early days of the program, we acted as facilitators for a group of four or five couples. When we were leaving to go to the program, we were usually squabbling about something, likely having to do with running late. Getting the babysitter settled and gathering our materials always took longer than we planned. By the time we arrived, we were not happy with each other. It seemed hypocritical to teach these enthusiastic, passionate couples about how to build a happy marriage.

There were several written exercises on communication for the couples to complete. Since Patrick and I were not speaking to each other, we worked right along with them. When finished, the couples exchanged their papers to discuss their answers privately. We did the same. By the end of the evening, we liked each other again. It turned out that addressing important topics, rather than ignoring them, provided a valuable lesson for us, as well as the couples. While they learned ways to build healthy habits early into their relationship, Patrick and I received continuing education that improved our marriage.

Over time, I realized that many of these engaged couples had placed attending this program last on their to-do list, as had we. For many couples, once they are engaged, the focus shifts to intense wedding planning with little time spent in exploring their relationship. With so much expense, energy, and effort already invested in the wedding, they are unlikely to alter their plans, even if they have concerns about their decision to marry.

It seemed these couples could benefit from information and discussions before their engagement, while they were still dating. Hence, my dream of writing about marriage became a reality with my first book, *Beyond the First Dance; A Guide for Couples to Think Beyond their Wedding Day.* The book is intended for seriously dating couples to contemplate what is important in choosing a mate, red flags to watch for, and talking points before marriage.

In addition to the impetus I had from working with the couples, there were several other factors that motivated me to embark on writing about marriage. I have been a pediatric nurse practitioner (PNP) for over forty years and was employed at the same clinic for my entire career. In my role, I made home visits to all the newborns in our practice and followed my patients in clinic throughout their childhood and adolescence. My position allowed me to work intimately with the same families for three generations and witness firsthand the impact a disruptive relationship has on couples and their children.

In my work as a PNP, every periodic exam included providing health-promotional information to the parents. In the field of pediatrics, it is referred to as anticipatory guidance. The purpose is to teach parents about the next stage of their child's development, as awareness and information increases confidence and a more positive outcome. The same principle applies to marriage. Knowing what to expect and having the skills to address issues can *prevent* couples from becoming derailed by difficult situations. I have witnessed marriages that have survived the birth of an infant with severe disabilities and the loss of children from cancer, suicide, drug overdose, and accidents. How do couples endure these tragedies and keep their marriage intact? Establishing healthy habits and support systems early in a marriage can make a critical difference in securing their relationship.

For eighteen years, I have co-facilitated a family support group with Patrick for adult family members dealing with a loved one who suffers with substance use disorder (SUD). This disease ruptures family relationships like few other conditions. If a marriage does not have the underpinnings needed to withstand such a disruption, the dissolution of the marriage can be another fallout of this disease.

The novelist Pat Conroy wrote a compelling piece on the ending of his marriage titled, "The Anatomy of Divorce," where he called divorce "the death of a small civilization." Sounds dramatic, right? Having lost six sisters-in-law through divorce myself, I find it is an accurate description. These divorces involved both sides of our family, forever impacting 12 adults and 14 children. They also affected all the aunts, uncles, cousins, and grandparents who loved them and were part of their lives. With the termination of these six marriages, we never saw most of these in-laws again. We also witnessed the divorce of close friends with whom we had enjoyed a long friendship. What might have prevented these heartbreaking events? I wanted greater insight to share with couples early in their relationship.

Several years ago, I heard Dr. Vincent J. Felitti speak on the landmark study, *Adverse Childhood Experiences* (ACE). This research of 17,421 adults living with chronic relapsing illnesses, (e.g., diabetes, chronic liver disease, obstructive pulmonary disease, obesity, cardiovascular, and SUD) revealed the significant relationship between the experiences of childhood trauma and adult morbidity. As a Certified Prevention Specialist (CPS), I use this study as the basis of much of my advocacy work on matters of mental health and substance misuse. Separation and divorce of parents are among those experiences that cause trauma for a child and have an impact on a child's adult life. And as a CPS, I have learned that it is always easier to prevent problems than it is to try to fix them after the fact.

These experiences have also taught me that marriage is not for everyone. Nor is having children. Both vocations require love, commitment, and endurance. There should be more support for people who choose to remain single and for those who choose not to have children. For those who choose marriage and parenthood, however, the decision should be taken seriously. Couples should have their eyes wide open and be willing to learn and grow.

While I strongly advocate for the preservation of marriage and the prevention of divorce, there are exceptions. When a spouse or children are exposed to physical, emotional or sexual abuse, domestic violence, *untreated* mental illness, alcoholism, or substance abuse, the detrimental effects can be overwhelmingly destructive to their long-term wellbeing. If these conditions are not aggressively addressed, I believe there needs to be a safe exit strategy.

During the early years, many couples find that the quality of their relationship declines as their marriage faces challenges: money, sex, careers, religion, in-laws, raising children, and division of household labor top the list. When faced with these issues, keeping marriage a priority is a task many couples find daunting. This is the time when couples often consider calling it quits.

After raising children and looking ahead to their retirement years, couples who are not emotionally intimate often decide to stop pretending. "Gray Divorce" is the term used by Dr. Susan Brown from Bowling Green University to describe the fastest growing group experiencing divorce. My generation, the Boomers, are those born between 1946 and 1964. Roughly one in three Boomers is unmarried, mostly because of divorce. We are the first generation that has increased its divorce rate, resulting in the least stable marriages in American history.

Preventing the pain of divorce for couples and their children is the driving force and goal of this book.

Prevention is primary, so this book examines the importance of adopting healthy habits *early* in your relationship to ensure your marriage will not only survive but thrive. Learning to prevent indifference, the ultimate relationship killer, from permeating your marriage provides a strong protective factor. Effective communication skills, along with love and commitment, can shield your partnership from the difficulties that happen in every marriage. To that end, I raise some long-term challenges early in the hopes that you will learn the skills to deal with them if they should arise.

The metaphor of dance is used throughout my writing. I believe the fancy footwork required to master a variety of dances compares well with the flexibility and skills needed to achieve a lifelong, healthy, and happy marriage. You and your partner do not have to like dancing to recognize that continually stepping on each other's toes or twirling in opposite directions is not going to have a good outcome. This behavior is uncomfortable, irritating, and over time can become unbearable, making some couples just stop dancing.

Patrick and I have never taken formal dance lessons, but we can be found on the dance floor at every wedding we attend. We have learned to keep dancing. Just as lessons could help a couple become more accomplished dancers, couples willing to learn new skills can become adept at their marriage. Every dance has its unique moves. To learn a variety of dances requires determination, flexibility, and commitment, as does marriage. The tango involves dramatic, synchronized steps. The passion of this early dance morphs into the sequenced pattern of line dancing, when you and your partner stand next to each other with little physical contact. Couples may often feel like they are in the line dancing stage when they need to work at staying in sync. The twist and shout dance allows for independent moves, demanding physical stamina, but can be very sensual when coordinated with your partner. Likewise, your marriage will require endurance to maintain and strengthen your physical and emotional intimacy while juggling your other responsibilities.

There will be different dances throughout your married life, some intimate and exciting, some energetic, some solo, some even lonely at times. There needs to be a balance of both independence and intimacy, while continually learning new steps to stay in sync. Life can be very hectic in one sense, yet it often feels mundane to many couples who find the daily routine a chaotic monotony. Everyone else's life can mistakenly look so much more exciting. Your ability to connect during these years will take deliberation. Communicating your individual needs, hopes, and desires, and prioritizing these together is critical for emotional intimacy, the hallmark of a satisfying union.

The early and the middle years of marriage are challenging for couples. Not addressing issues head-on is often the reason for divorce by the eighth year. The earlier a couple develops effective communication skills and adopts healthy habits, the greater the likelihood their marriage will thrive.

One exercise Patrick and I introduce to the engaged couples is to have them each define a good marriage. They are asked to think of a couple whom they know personally that has a strong relationship. We give each of them a small card, cut to the size of a credit card that will fit easily into their wallet. Separately, they write on their own card those traits they feel model a relationship they would like for their own marriage. Qualities like a sense of humor, trust, respect, faith, caring, friendship, honesty, integrity, and fun are often mentioned. These reflect the core values they want to instill in their own relationship. We suggest they use this card as a personal roadmap to evaluate how they are living up to their definition of a strong marriage.

On several occasions, Patrick and I have run into couples who have pulled out the wrinkled and worn card from their wallets. If you have not done this exercise, you might find it worthwhile. No one should define what a good marriage is for you, but you should each be able to define that for yourself. If you leave the house in the morning with an exchange of profanities and then glance at your card and see "respect," it may inspire a moment of contemplation. Talking about the issue *together* when you get home, along with an apology, could salvage not only an evening, but also help you arrive at a better way to handle tough topics. The next time you can address a difficult topic without anger or contempt.

Evaluation is an important part of any project and your marriage is no different. You may find it helpful to ask yourself a couple of questions over the course of your life together, like "What is it like to be married to me?" and "How would I like to be married to me?" Honest answers can give you an interesting perspective on your marriage.

I have written this book from my personal and professional experience in a heterosexual relationship. However, the principles discussed can have universal application, and it is my hope that this book benefits all couples committed to marriage. My hairdresser, who has been with his partner for over 20 years, stated matter-of-factly after reading my first book, "Anyone who thinks a gay marriage is any different from a heterosexual one ought to live in our house for 24 hours." I believe his comment reflects that this book is relevant for anyone seeking an emotionally healthy, long-term, and loving marriage.

There remains a universal human desire to have one relationship where we know that we are loved unconditionally and that there is someone who always has our back. A strong and loving marriage can meet these needs. For those who seek it, marriage remains an important commitment that benefits a couple, their children, and society.

The demise of a marriage is seldom the result of a single factor. The causes are many, including financial issues, differences in values and temperament, in-laws, parenting, religious beliefs, infidelity, poor communication, alcoholism, substance abuse, sexual incompatibility, and unaddressed mental health concerns. How can couples prevent these and other factors from escalating to the point of divorce? Knowing yourself, taking responsibility for meeting your own needs, commitment to your partnership, respect for your spouse, and healthy communication skills can all make a critical difference.

The chapters are meant to follow the general flow of married life. Research related to marriage and parenting are used throughout the book. Dr. John Gottman is mentioned in several chapters, as he has conducted extensive bioresearch in his "love lab" in Seattle, Washington and is considered the guru on the study of marriage. As most couples have children, many chapters address the additional realities of raising a family. With or without children, however, this book is intended to strengthen your relationship as a couple to handle the challenges life will present.

At the end of each chapter, there are steps to consider building into your relationship. Adopting healthy habits early, and correcting unhealthy ones, can prevent tough issues from destroying your marriage. References cited are also listed at the end of each chapter. May this book offer support, encouragement, and skills to enhance your marriage and parenting experiences and make your journey a rewarding one. Now, onto the dance floor!

WORKS CITED

Brown, Susan Ph.D. *The Journals of Gerontology*: Series B, Volume 67, Issue 6, November 2012, Pages 731–741,*https://doi.org/10.1093/geronb/gbs089;* October 18, 2012

Conroy, Pat. "The Anatomy of Divorce." *Atlanta Magazine*, November 1, 1978 *https://www.atlantamagazine.com/great-reads/anatomy-of-a-divorce.*

Felitti, Vincent M.D. "Adverse Childhood Experiences." *American Journal of Preventive Medicine,* June, 2019, Volume 56, Issue 6, Pages 774–786 *https://www.ajpmonline.org/article/S0749-3797(19)30143-6/fulltext.*

SECTION I

Line Dancing

The dance of the early years of marriage

"A successful marriage requires falling in love many times, always with the same person."

MIGNON MCLAUGHLIN

Line Dancing

Line Dancing is characterized by a repeated sequence of steps performed in a straight line. The "Electric Slide" and the "Macarena." are popular at weddings. The dancers have little physical contact and change direction many times during a sequence. In the end, they can face any of the four walls.

Throughout this dance, you are trying to pay attention to all the steps and keep moving without stumbling, looking foolish, or facing the opposite direction. Facing the wrong wall is often how couples feel at this stage. They ask questions like "What are we doing?" "Am I in the right place?" "Are we headed in the right direction?" and "Are we in this together?"

In the early years of your marriage, your relationship requires accommodating many new aspects of your life: launching your careers, buying your first home, and perhaps having a baby and adjusting to parenthood. Learning new dance steps is the metaphor for continually adopting healthy habits that will serve as a foundation for a partnership that will endure and grow. Sustaining your relationship will take some fast and fancy foot work! Are you ready?

CHAPTER 1

Knowing Yourself

"To know yourself, you must sacrifice the illusion that you already do."

VIRONIKA TUGALEVA

Many factors are critical to the growth, intimacy, and longevity of a marriage. There are few, however, that will have greater influence than *knowing yourself.* Having this insight is an evolving and lifelong process. Recognize and name what you feel. Think about and understand why you feel the way you do. The ability to know yourself and communicate your needs and desires to your spouse is the epitome of emotional intimacy. Self-knowledge will affect not only the well-being and growth of your marriage but may well affect its survival.

The feelings you have regarding issues and situations are not right or wrong, good or bad. They are your feelings. They are your spouse's feelings. They are personal. It is the willingness to expose your vulnerability that will build the emotional intimacy on which a long, loving, and trusting relationship is built. Since you will each grow throughout your marriage, sharing yourself is an ongoing process. Without introspection, you are apt to expect your partner to be a mind reader. Most married couples would admit they are poor mind readers, especially in the early years of their relationship. The reason is not because your spouse does not care or deliberately wants to annoy you. The real reason is because your spouse does not yet understand many things about you. Your emotions are unknown to your partner. You and your spouse do not view life the same way. Each of you has your own personality and temperament. Your countless childhood experiences, both good and bad, are different from your spouse.

Your medical and genetic histories are unique. To expect your spouse to understand you without clearly communicating your emotions is an unrealistic expectation, likely to leave you frustrated.

When we became engaged, I found newspaper clippings on my bureau about the cost of living for a family in the United States. I knew these were "love notes" from my father. They reflected his worry about our financial situation and how we would support a family. At the time, Patrick had a low-paying job as a state employee. My father figured I would probably get pregnant right away and be a stay-at-home mom. Daddy thought Patrick's income surely would not be adequate to cover our expenses. I appreciated his concern but felt my optimism would win out. I was confident that Patrick would become a teacher, and I would practice as a nurse, and we would do fine. Daddy was not so sure. If I had not been confident, his worry would have unnerved me. I knew I was marrying the right man.

Patrick was unable to serve in the military due to a medical deferment, but as an immigrant he wanted to serve our country in some capacity. We decided to do a year of volunteer work. My poor father. Our low income was a concern enough and now we were giving up our jobs completely! Four months after we were married, we moved to Texas for a year in VISTA (now AmeriCorps) doing volunteer work 1,500 miles from home. What we wanted was adventure. What we learned was partnership and self-reliance.

The importance of knowing myself was made evident to me when we crossed the Texas border. Looking across the terrain, I surely knew I was not in New England. I suddenly thought of not being home for the holidays with family. I was overcome with sadness and tears started rolling down my cheeks. Patrick could not imagine what suddenly made me so sad. He was focused on the adventure, and I was homesick.

Our adventure began following our weeklong orientation in Dallas. After receiving our assignment, we headed to Georgetown on a Sunday afternoon. At that time, it was a small, sleepy town. We were greeted by graffiti on the brick wall of a building in the town square that read, "Welcome to Eagle Territory." We were curious, as it did not seem like a town that would have a gang. We were too new to Texas to know that it represented the local religion—football. That was only the first of many things we were going to learn.

We were told we would be staying at the Blake Hotel for three weeks until we secured our own housing. That sounded like a nice arrangement. In this two-story town, no hotel stood out, so we pulled into a mom-and-pop store to ask directions. The clerk scratched her head, commenting "Blake Hotel, Blake Hotel, I have heard of it. Let me look it up in the phone book." That seemed very strange given the size of the town. Then she looked up and said, "Oh, it's right around the corner." We looked at each other in amazement. No need to drive, we could just walk over and check in. Rounding the building, we eyed a two-story, dilapidated house with a weathered sign announcing, "Blake Hotel $2.00 a night for a double." As we were taking in the scene, the front door banged open and an intoxicated man stumbled out, swung around the post, and fell into the rusted glider on the front porch. Well I'll be, we are spending our first few weeks in a flophouse. Daddy would be so proud! And he would never find out.

That year we discovered it was a good thing we liked each other, because our friendship was all we had. For the first three months, we did not have a radio or a television, and we never had a phone. We were forced to talk to each other, a lot! In retrospect, it was an enormously valuable experience. Without the influence of in-laws, family members, and friends, we had to figure out things on our own. We learned a lot about ourselves and each other.

Knowing yourself and communicating to your spouse takes practice. Recognize when you feel happy, sad, content, irritable, angry, or calm, and figure out what triggers these feelings. This awareness can allow you to channel, avoid, and control the negative emotions and revive and enjoy the positive ones. Then you, rather than your emotions, are in control. Sharing this insight with your spouse increases your emotional intimacy.

Recognize that you will discover things about your spouse that you will never quite understand. An issue that does not bother you at all may be something that your spouse finds upsetting. Something that delights or saddens your partner may not be anything that crosses your mind. Yet, when an experience has an emotional effect on your spouse, positive or negative, it can have an impact on your marriage. Learning these things about each other and sharing with each other are what enriches a marriage. Start now, as it is an ongoing dance.

Steps:

- Take the time for introspection.
- Identify what you are feeling.
- Figure out what triggered the emotion in you.
- Share with your spouse. Don't expect them to mind read.
- Ask for what you need.
- Recognize what you find upsetting and minimize those triggers.
- Learn what makes you feel calm, happy, joyful, and repeat!

CHAPTER 2

Trying to Change Your Spouse

"To love someone is to strive to accept that person exactly the way he or she is, right here and now."

FRED ROGERS

During the early years of marriage, many couples go through a period of trying to change their spouse. This seems to occur around the third or fourth year, or maybe for the duration of the marriage for some of us slower learners. We all try it. It doesn't work!

In his book, *The Science of Happily Ever After*, Dr. Ty Tashiro talks about the traits a spouse possesses as a strong predictor of success in a healthy, romantic relationship. He notes that *personality* and *values* are the strongest, and negative traits are most often constant across a lifetime. While it is hoped that we all will experience personal growth in our relationships, couples should not count on these basic qualities changing.

A few years into marriage, many couples notice a change of rhythm. Do not be surprised if there are moments when each of you silently asks, "What was I thinking?" In a *Psychology Today* article, Licensed Clinical Social Worker (LCSW) Michele Werner-Davis uses this question to typify this stage of marriage. Marriage, like other developmental periods of life, has stages. The pace of your life has picked up speed since the honeymoon. Work and financial responsibilities may seem to erase the romance of the tango years.

In a study titled "Marital Happiness and Psychological Well-Being Across the Life Course," researchers reported findings that indicate marriage satisfaction begins to decline around the fourth year. By this time, life has settled into a daily schedule of working, rustling up an evening meal, watching some television, and then dropping into bed, only to awaken the next morning and repeat the same routine. Weekends can be busy catching up on household chores that have piled up during the week and squeezing in time to see family and friends. This is when couples may question, as the classic Peggy Lee song asks, "Is That All There Is?"

Learning how to maintain and grow intimacy during these busy years is key to a satisfying marriage. However, there are certain realities that often prove challenging. Now, you know the strengths and weaknesses of your partner better. Some of them may take you by surprise, and you may realize you do not always like what you find.

Harville Hendrix, author of *Getting the Love You Want*, explores the psychology of the love relationship and the stages couples experience as they progress from the infatuation stage of "romantic love" to the conscious stage of "reality love." You may have expectations for each other that do not match reality. Hendrix notes that when a couple makes a commitment, the period of the power struggle begins. This is when, he states, "some aspect of their partner's character or a personality trait that was once thought highly desirable, is beginning to annoy them."

During this stage, I learned that Patrick did not possess some of the traits I assumed he had. When I first met his family, his father was installing kitchen cabinets and his married brother was remodeling a bathroom. I presumed the handyman trait was in the genes. Patrick did not seem interested in these undertakings, but I thought it was because he did not yet have anything of his own to fix. My thinking was wrong.

Traits, like being a handyman, are not ones I had given much thought to while dating, nor should they be a deal breaker for a marriage. But when expectations about your partner do not match reality, it can pose a problem. When living in an apartment, we called the landlord to handle a dripping faucet or heating issue. Owning our own home, however, would prove to be a different matter.

The first hint occurred when we had been married for four years and living in an apartment. I was seven months pregnant with our first child, and we were decorating the nursery. Looking at the stack of children's books, I thought that a bookshelf under the window would be perfect. I made a request (in my gentlest tone!) that he take a woodworking class and make one. I offered to paint it. I thought this would be a basic project and could boost his confidence for when we became homeowners.

He attended the course every Wednesday evening for six weeks. Finally, it was the night of the last class, and I nested on the couch waiting for him to arrive home with this last addition to the nursery. Imagine my surprise when he walked in carrying two handfuls of small wooden pieces. He explained that the class had not worked out the way he hoped. After making a few wrong cuttings, he decided to scrap the bookshelf and cut out six bird shapes. I would have asked about the instructor, but I was speechless. He went on to suggest that I could paint them and hang them as a mobile for the baby.

By the next week, after shaking my head in exasperation, I chose six bright colors, painted each wooden bird, and wired them over the bassinette. Being a birdwatcher, Patrick had taken time to cut out six different shapes, which I had not noticed. When he looked at my handiwork and saw that I had painted the cardinal blue, he was speechless. I was as clueless about birds as he was about woodworking. I hung them as they were and bought a bookshelf at a yard sale.

It took me longer than I care to admit accepting the fact that home projects were not Patrick's strength. I continued to make requests. Even simple tasks seemed to conspire against him. The breaking point came after ten years. Like I said, some of us are slow learners! Moving into our new home, I asked him to hang a pineapple knocker on the front door. Wouldn't you know it, right where it had to be centered was a knot under the painted door, making it impossible to hang. He was understandably frustrated, and it was not a pretty scene. The four-letter words were dropping like rain, as he cursed about how he hated "this stuff" and that "nothing was standard." Right then, I *finally* accepted what I should have years earlier, that his abhorrence for such projects was not going to change, and I vowed to stop making these handyman requests.

It would have been easy to envy women married to a handy husband. Yet, I noted that some of them complained their husbands spent too much time in the workshop. Other friends have said, "You're lucky, my husband thinks he can fix anything and doesn't want me to call anyone." One time, our friend Al attempted to fix a minor toilet problem. He enjoys such projects about as much as Patrick, but he wanted to tackle it. Things went from minor to major and $400 later with a cracked toilet, he finally surrendered.

Patrick, of course, had his own frustrations with me. On the fourth night after our honeymoon, he had to wonder, "What was I thinking?" when he arrived home from work expecting dinner. (Remember, back then women were expected to cook!) Mom had cooked when I lived at home. While in college, and later working at the hospital, I ate in the cafeteria. After the honeymoon, I realized I had no skills. Sure, we had gotten some cookbooks for wedding presents, but they were still packed away. The first night I made hotdogs. The second night I made hamburgers. The third night I heated Dinty Moore canned stew. The fourth night I cried. I had completed my repertoire. Patrick managed to hide his shock and disappointment as we made scrambled eggs. He said we would figure it out. I decided to get some recipes from my patients. With every home visit to give a vitamin B shot to an elderly woman, I asked for a recipe. They were delighted to help this young bride. I still remember the one pot hamburger stroganoff and the pork chop/rice dish that were gourmet delights to us.

Patrick would say that my happy disposition, so appealing while we were dating, is a ruse for my inattention. I start chores or projects, not completing one before moving on to the next, leaving a trail of clutter, often for him to clean up. If he made a dollar every time he tripped over my kicked-off shoes, we could have paid off the mortgage years earlier. Funny how those characteristics, so cute while you are dating, can grow into irritating quirks.

When we were able to change our thinking and focus on qualities we appreciated, we came to have more realistic expectations. Patrick was a willing partner in household chores and caring for the kids, freeing me up to do other things. I learned to do the simpler projects myself and hire someone for the more skilled ones, and life became a whole lot easier. Handyman Fred does not know how many arguments he saved. Seeing him pull up in front of the house and fasten on that tool belt was like hearing "Pachelbel's Canon" on our wedding day.

I recall one Saturday, I decided to wallpaper the bathroom. I needed uninterrupted time, without tending to the kids or fixing meals. Patrick took the children all day and ordered a pizza for dinner. This allowed me to immerse myself in the project, completing the wallpapering and stenciling a border. I was thrilled! Most household chores are rarely completed in a finite period. Laundry, groceries, meals, and housework are repetitive tasks that are never done. I found it incredibly rewarding to see results from the day's efforts, and I relished that feeling every time I went into the bathroom. Patrick and I had found some new dance steps that day and they worked for both of us. It was a different dance than I expected, but we finally got into sync. Today, it is not unusual to see many of the traditional roles reversed; the wife outside mowing the lawn and gardening while the husband is inside doing the housework.

As it turned out, Patrick loves gardening and landscaping. He has beautified our yard beyond my imagination. Three years ago, he decided some bushes and a fence needed to be replaced. You can only guess my surprise when he got on YouTube and then headed to the lumber store. Armed with posts and bags of cement, he completely re-designed that section of the yard. It was amazing to witness what happened when I stopped pushing and he found his own motivation and discovered what he could accomplish.

Couples often become disillusioned by the routine of their everyday life. A sense of frustration may leave you feeling that others' lives are more fulfilling. It is important throughout your marriage not to compare yourselves with other couples. No one's marriage is as perfect as it may appear to you. Our human condition prevents that from ever being so. Keeping a healthy perspective and focusing on the traits that first attracted you to your mate can help change your outlook. Whenever something needed fixing, I reminded myself of Patrick's spontaneity and acts of kindness as I dialed up Handyman Fred. The work got done, and we were still on the dance floor together.

Over the course of your marriage, you want to accept each other's idiosyncrasies and find the roles for which you are best suited. "Each to his own trade" is a good motto to adopt. It is all part of the dance you are learning.

Steps:

- Show patience and kindness. They build confidence and support growth.

- Focus on your spouse's strengths and show appreciation for those qualities.

- Avoid nagging. Say what is bothering you without demeaning your spouse.

- Recognize the difference between annoyances/disappointments (e.g. not being handy) and serious deal breakers.

- Define the roles that work best for you as a couple, not on stereotypes or other people's opinions.

- Do not compare your marriage to anyone else's; focus on making your marriage stronger.

- Correct your own irritating habits. It is another way of saying "I love you."

WORKS CITED

Hendrix, Harville Ph.D. *Getting the Love You Want.* New York: Henry Holt and Co., 1988.

Kamp, Dush, CM, Taylor MG, Kroeger RA. "Marital Happiness and Psychological Well-Being Across the Life Course." *Family Relations*, April 2008 57 (2): 211-226.

Tashiro, Ty, Ph.D. *The Science of Happily Ever After.* Harlequin Enterprises Limited, Ontario, Canada, 2014.

Werner-Davis, Michele. "The Marriage Map." *Psychology Today.* February 18, 2009. https://www.psychologytoday.com/us/blog/divorce-busting/200902/the-marriage-map.

CHAPTER 3

Guarding Against Indifference

"Don't worry when I fight with you, worry when I stop because it means there's nothing left for us to fight for."

UNKNOWN

Love and hate may seem like opposite emotions that could describe the beginning and end of a marriage. The word hate, meaning to loathe or despise, is often used erroneously as a synonym for anger. Love and anger, however, can represent another emotion that is healthy for marriage—passion. You will have times when you feel angry with one another, but that emotion can reflect your frustration about wanting things to be better. When channeled effectively, anger can help infuse energy into your relationship.

I believe the opposite of love is *indifference*. There is no passion with indifference. Indifference is a dead-end. It is reflected in statements like "I don't care," "I don't care about you, your feelings, or us," or "I don't want to work on resolving our issues or healing our relationship." This attitude has caused the demise of friendships, family relationships, and is fatal to marriages.

You may have moments when you feel like you hate your life. Stress, fatigue, and dealing with the daily chaos of home and work may make you want to run away. Money, sex, religion, in-laws, household chores, jobs, and parenting create plenty of ammunition for conflict. When you have arguments about these issues, they can evoke feelings of anger. Your ability to tackle these will determine how you, as a couple, come out on the other side of these emotional discussions. What is important is that negative emotions do not become chronic. Over time, the unwillingness to address difficult issues can lead to resentment, an ingredient lethal to a marriage. Do not be afraid of disagreements. Be afraid of *not* having them. Avoidance can provide the fertile ground for indifference to take seed. Care enough to jump into the fray and address the issue.

A 2012 UCLA study by Thomas Bradbury and Benjamin Karney, both psychology professors at the Relationship Institute, followed 172 couples for over a decade. They noted a difference in the meaning of "commitment" between couples who remained married and those who divorced. In their study, "78.5 percent were still married after 11 years, and 21.5 percent were divorced. The couples in which both people were willing to make sacrifices for the sake of the marriage were significantly more likely to have lasting and happy marriages." They were willing to compromise, work on developing better communication, and become more effective at solving problems. The other 21.5 percent of couples indicated they were committed to the relationship when things were going well, but they were not so willing to do the work when conflicts arose. They were divorced by the end of the study. Their definition of commitment did not include the hard work required to address the tough topics.

When a couple's only conversation focuses on the day's to-do list, their marriage can feel like a job rather than a relationship. The passion of the tango feels like a distant blur, and the line dance of activity without intimacy has taken over their lives. There is not much passion and romance in this litany, but this is often the reality of daily life for many married couples. The goal here is not making the to-do lists your only conversation. Connecting with each other during the daily chaos is vital. For some couples it is a short, loving text or a quick phone call during the day to breaks the tedium. For Patrick and me, it has been our daily teatime.

The whistling tea kettle was a fixture in Patrick's Irish home. His mother could brew a perfect cup of tea that I always looked forward to when I visited during our dating days. After we were married, we decided it was a tradition we wanted to carry forward. Afternoon tea became our special time to touch base, that is until we stopped paying attention. Like many decisions in marriage, it was not a conscious one. Our quiet afternoon ritual became complicated when children arrived and it slowly evaporated. When we neglected carving out teatime, we both felt the disconnect. We were not hearing about the highs and lows of each other's day. The lack of connection felt empty; an emotion that can become the breeding ground for indifference. Neither of us wanted to forego the ritual so we waited until after the kids were in bed. The whistling tea kettle was our call to calmness and connection.

The decisions in marriage which have the greatest impact are often not the momentous ones. They are often mundane. Foregoing teatime does not sound like a big deal. For us, it was. Be alert to the impact that stress is having on your marriage. Guard against letting the strains of your marriage become so great that you no longer care. When things are not going well, and you lack the energy to work on your relationship, your marriage is at a dangerous crossroads. Remember, it is easier to prevent something than it is to fix it later. Indifference is a marriage killer. Pay attention. Recognize the warning signs early and be proactive in keeping passion alive. Guarding against indifference may be one of the most critical dance lessons of your marriage.

Steps:

- Build a routine into your day for connecting with each other.

- Channel your anger, but don't be afraid of disagreements

- Infuse some pizazz into your marriage, like a surprise note in a pocket or a text.

- A quiet candlelight dinner at home can make a mundane evening romantic.

WORK CITED

Bradbury, Thomas, Benjamin Karney, and Dominik Schoebi. "Here is what real commitment to your marriage means." *Newsroom UCLA*. http://newsroom. ucla.edu/releases/here-is-what-real-commitment-to-228064.

CHAPTER 4

Counseling with Confidentiality

"You can't change anyone else, but people do change in relationship to your change."

JACK CANFIELD

Throughout this book, I make several references to seeking help from a skilled counselor. Including this professional as a lifeline can provide critical support when you experience a communication roadblock. This person should become one of the team of professionals you likely already have in your life: a car mechanic, electrician, plumber, dentist, doctor, lawyer, and banker. Having connections with these experts is considered good planning.

Do you have to see these specialists every week? Not likely, but think of it as if your car gets stuck; you want to be able to pick up the phone and call someone you trust, who knows you, your car, and can get you back on the road. It may take a few visits, but then you are up and running. That is what a personal counselor should be, someone who knows you and knows your situation. You do not have to start at square one at each visit, but rather you are able to pick up where you last left off and address what is going on right now.

You will go through periods in your life when you need some objective input for solving a problem. As the bumper sticker says, "shit happens," and problems can consume your mental and emotional energy. Sometimes an issue is your own doing. Sometimes it is another person's doing. Whatever the source, it is important to figure out a plan and deal with it, especially when those issues affect your marriage.

While close friends or colleagues may be a good sounding board, are they really the best people to consult? It might be wiser to consider a professional, who can provide objectivity and expertise. There are several reasons for doing so:

- A good counselor does not solve your problems but helps you to discover options and solutions for yourself. They can look at all sides of an issue and offer insight that you may be unable to see.

- Family and friends care about you, which often results in biased opinions. Even if they happen to have a professional license, they have an emotional connection to you that is likely to interfere with objectivity.

- Long after you have dealt with your issue, your friend will remember the difficulties you experienced. Their knowledge and memory of events can affect future interactions with you and your loved one.

- Having a comfortable and trusting relationship with a counselor allows you a place where you can take your angst and deposit it. By not burdening your family, co-workers, and friends, you are allowed an opportunity to escape. You can then go to work without well-meaning colleagues inquiring every day how you are doing. Every family gathering would not have to center on your problems. When you have an opportunity to socialize with friends, it's nice to laugh and have fun hearing about *their* life without having to talk about yours.

- A counselor is bound by professional confidentiality and has the qualifications to be an objective listener. They are familiar with the raw emotions you may be experiencing and are trained to deal with those feelings. They do not lose sleep over your problem, like friends or family would. This is what professionals are trained and paid to do.

- You will learn new skills to use in future situations.

Some people bristle at the idea of talking to a stranger. While some men have sought counseling on their own, my experience working with families and parenting groups is that it is often more difficult for men to seek help about personal issues. Women generally are more comfortable opening up and discussing situations in their lives, so counseling does not seem as foreign to them. Men may be used to handling problems on their own or feel that they should be able to fix an issue. They may view seeking help as a sign of weakness. When it comes to your marriage, the benefits will far outweigh any discomfort involved.

When deciding to hire any professional, you should interview them to see if they meet your needs. On the back of most insurance cards there is a number for behavioral health. The Mental Health Parity and Addiction Equity Act passed in 2008 allows the same coverage for counseling as for other conditions included in your plan. Calling that number will give a list of providers. You can then choose the gender and location you prefer and set a time for a brief interview. Do not be afraid to ask for an initial meeting before you get into the nitty-gritty of the issues. Remember, you are the consumer seeking a service, so do not hesitate to shop around until you connect with someone you are comfortable with. Then, you can set up a time for an in-depth appointment.

It is unhealthy to let your problems fester. As with an infection, treatment is needed. If a nagging issue does not receive the needed attention, it becomes like a pebble in your shoe and affects every step of your dance routine. Trying to handle it alone can consume physical, emotional, and mental energy that negatively impacts your marriage. Conversely, unloading stress frees up your energy and allows you to attend to the people and activities that are important in your life.

If you happen to be blessed with a supportive spouse, a word of caution. Talking only with your mate can sometimes cause more problems than it helps. For one thing, you may each have different concerns. Your dialogue may cause your partner to have a more negative or pessimistic view of the situation. Without meaning to, you can create a cesspool rather than a lifeboat. If the concern is something you are both experiencing, like issues with finances or children, talking about it incessantly may preclude any new ideas that could help you deal with the problem in a proactive way.

When our four children were teenagers, I learned that continually talking with Patrick about my worries and frustrations only served to amplify his concerns. After all, living in the same household, he was aware of the issues. He really did not benefit from hearing it regurgitated by me. I found having a professional counselor was beneficial, not only for me, but for our marriage. I could share concerns, get an objective perspective on issues, and learn new ways of addressing situations in a more constructive way. I would occasionally invite Patrick to join me if I felt it would be beneficial to the situation. This allowed us to enjoy our date nights with a moratorium on discussing the children.

Counseling can, and should, be viewed as a critical resource in your marriage. While it is beneficial for both of you to engage in seeking help, if one is resistant, do not let that stop the other from seeking support. Remember, one is better than none. While you cannot change your mate's behavior, you can gain new insight and skills. Avoid nagging and go alone. Someone must lead on the dance floor and who cares which one it is? It is only important that at least someone is working to change the dance when needed. Try it and see if your marital dance does not become smoother.

Steps:

- Make a counselor part of your support team.

- Choose a professional you are comfortable with and trust.

- Consider individual *and* marriage counseling to address personal *and* marital concerns.

- Refrain from using family, friends, and colleagues as a sounding board.

- Plan fun and problem-free respite time individually and as a couple.

CHAPTER 5

Contemplating Having Children

"Parenting is not for sissies. You have to sacrifice and grow up."

JILLIAN MICHAELS

Marriage itself is a major life transition as you discover your own dance as a couple. The discussion about having children should take place before marriage. Couples may delay talking about this important topic for fear their partner may feel differently. One may be hesitant about the responsibilities but come around with encouragement from a supportive spouse. If one feels strongly about having children and the other is adamantly opposed, this requires open, honest discussion with respect, caring, and good listening.

If you both want children but could not become pregnant, have you discussed your thoughts on adoption or infertility treatment? Have you talked about how many children you would like? If you feel that you are at a crossroads, employing the help of a counselor is a wise decision. One spouse should never trick or coerce the other into parenthood. If one of you is not on board, the tasks of parenting can fall squarely on the spouse who pushed forward, compounding resentment in the years ahead.

Becoming a parent is not for everyone. Your life is no longer centered on you and your spouse. You are taking on the responsibility for another person, one who will be depending on you for their very existence. For many years, parenting is a one-way street, requiring you to give to someone who does not yet know how to give back. Couples who become parents believing it will make them happier have a misconception of what is entailed. While parenting can be a rewarding job, it can also be arduous and humbling. Parenting, like marriage, is for the committed, not the timid. During these line dancing years, you will come to realize that two of the most important roles you will have in your life are those of spouse and parent. These roles will affect your physical, emotional, spiritual, financial, and social well-being. A proactive, positive, and preventive stance can bode well for your parenting experience.

The time alone before children gives you the chance to enjoy each other as adults and lovers. Patrick and I are grateful for the four years we had together before having our first baby. We had the opportunity to get to know each other and adjust to life as a couple. That first year in VISTA, we had to figure out things on our own. During the next three years, we earned advanced degrees, traveled, and saved for a house before welcoming our daughter. It was a time of great freedom that we did not get to fully experience again until retirement. The other three children were born over the following twelve years, each a full-term pregnancy with no complications. We are aware how fortunate we were, as we witnessed many couples experience difficult situations.

The consideration to start a family, and when, brings a whole new dimension to your relationship. How do you know when you are ready to become parents? There is no right way to decide to have a baby. Feeling confident in your marriage and wanting to share your love can be strong signs of the willingness to take on a new life. In a *Business Insider* article, psychologist Carl Pickhardt shared several important considerations. He refers to the importance of having a strong support system, a good work ethic, confirmed self-care, and the desire to nurture another human being as important points to evaluate your readiness.

Your willingness to work hard and stay focused, often with less sleep and more distractions, bodes well for success in parenting. Feeling ready to take on the responsibilities for nurturing a new life, versus running away from boredom, can help you accept the emotional demands of parenting. Are there health issues that should be addressed before becoming pregnant? This vocation requires partnership. There will be new demands that affect your sleep, your work schedule, your freedom to come and go as you please, and new financial obligations.

Your ability to connect and share your questions and concerns will strengthen your partnership as you embark on this unknown journey.

While life is never perfect, having a stable relationship, a strong faith, confidence in each other, and a steady income will provide a good foundation for your new family. There are couples who have a "save the marriage" baby, and it seldom works out well. A weak marital foundation should not be expected to successfully support the demands of parenting.

An article in *The Washington Post* says that while parenting "gives people a sense of purpose and meaning, as well as lifelong social connections . . . it doesn't appear to bring American parents more happiness." The research cited data from 13 countries showing American parents are 12 percent unhappier than non-parents, which placed the U.S. last on the parental happiness scale. The study finds the lack of U.S. policies supporting the family is likely a fundamental cause. The absence of social support increases the cost and the amount of stress and anxiety that parents feel. I observed this when working with young families. Issues related to parental leave, lack of paid sick and vacation days, high cost of childcare, and inflexible work schedules affected my families. The study also cautions that it is the lack of a social safety net, *not* their children, that causes stress and unhappiness for parents.

The expense of raising a child is a consideration for a couple contemplating parenthood. An article in *USA Today* states that, according to the U.S. Department of Agriculture, in 2018 a middle-income American family is likely to spend $233,610 to raise a child to age eighteen, not including college. When we started our family, the figure was $180,000, and we found that staggering. Instead of being totally overwhelmed, we decided to look at the undertaking like the proverbial "eating the elephant, one bite at a time." Education, consistent employment, and good health are important assets in taking on this responsibility. Like marriage, go into parenthood with your eyes wide open and a strong desire to meet the challenge. A deep faith was also an important factor for us.

Most couples assume they will be able to have children when *they* decide to start a family. What does it mean for a couple when that does not happen? Our friend Sarah became pregnant much earlier than anticipated. She and her husband Chris had to rethink their education and careers goals, along with their housing plans, given the complexities of having a baby so soon. Since many of their friends were "free" for several more years, it was a challenge for them not having the spontaneity to catch a movie, go out to dinner, or enjoy a weekend away whenever they chose. This was a stressful time early in their marriage, but they altered their dance steps. Sarah delayed grad school for a few years and worked the evening shift part time to help save on childcare. They were able to successfully work through that period with good communication and strong support for each other.

What if you are unable to conceive or carry a pregnancy to term? What would this mean to your marriage? Are you emotionally and financially able to seek fertility counseling? Would you opt for any medical procedures that may be recommended? And what if that does not result in the hoped-for pregnancy or ends in repeated miscarriages? Would you both agree on adoption? The answers are hard to know until you experience such a situation, but one that requires serious discussion and a strong foundation.

Infertility is a painful reality for many couples. Stress results when a couple wants to start a family and, month after month, pregnancy does not happen. For a couple in their twenties, one year with regular intercourse without a pregnancy is considered a reason to look at possible medical causes. For couples in their mid-to-late thirties, six months without conception is considered reason to investigate. Due to their age, older couples have time constraints about exploring the cause and initiating treatment. The reason may be due to a physical issue for either spouse. Scheduling sex in order to conceive can be unromantic and extremely taxing on a marriage.

In a 2016 study, author Dr. Tami S. Rowen of the University of California-San Francisco reported that "couples with infertility have significantly more anxiety, depression, and stress." She also notes that "women seem to be more affected than men in their sexual life and they have greater tendency to classify the marital relationship as bad when the couple fails to conceive."

In an article in *The Atlantic*, couples shared their experience around infertility issues. One woman wrote "infertility is isolating, painful, and discouraging." As others start their families, infertile couples find that "vacations, career changes, moves, and even dinner plans" are affected, as they live month to month. When some so-called simpler procedures do not result in a pregnancy, couples often look to in-vitro fertilization (IVF). They express hope they will "beat the odds and come out [of the procedures] with more than just a mountain of debt." The article refers to the high level of divorce with IVF, based on a 2014 study of Danish couples.

Although treatment can be extremely expensive, this was not listed as a primary factor for marital disruption. The causes cited were related to "loss of their dreams and expectations ... stillborn births and miscarriages ... [and] unresolved grief." Janet Takefman, psychologist for the Reproductive Center at McGill University, notes in a *SLATE* article "that infertile couples have a lower divorce rate." She attributes this to a couples' ability and willingness in "'fighting a crisis together and learning how to cope quickly with something traumatic.'" She concludes, "'If you survive that, you'll be in good standing for the rest of your marriage.'"

Miscarriages are traumatic events for couples desperately hoping for a child. Some people who have not had this devastating experience have been known to minimize the emotional impact on a couple, thinking there could not be an attachment so early in a pregnancy. This is not the case. A miscarriage is a loss. Minimizing the pain can cause harm to the couple and with friends who do not understand the degree of hurt. Grief counseling and marital therapy can help a husband and wife deal with this loss and keep their marriage intact.

These issues around conception are difficult events to prepare for, as they are usually not anticipated and, therefore, not talked about earlier. Strengthening your communication skills, by being willing to express your feelings and listen openly to your spouse, are essential when facing these intimate, emotionally charged topics. Talk about the possible scenarios and what support you would seek if these issues should arise in your marriage.

Steps:

- Discuss having children early in your relationship. Are you on the same page?

- Communicate your hopes and fears in starting a family.

- Talk about how to respond to inquiring in-laws and friends.

- Discuss handling an ill-timed pregnancy.

- What are your thoughts and feelings if you could not conceive?

- Explore your opinions and emotions on IVF and adoption.

WORKS CITED

Bodenner, Chris. "When Infertility Threatens a Marriage." *The Atlantic*. October 26, 2016. https://www.theatlantic.com/notes/2016/10/when-infertility-threatens-marriage/505436/.

Doyle, Kathryn. "Infertility can take the fun out of women's sex lives." *Reuters*.

May 25, 2016. https://www.reuters.com/article/us-health-infertility-women-sex/infertility-can-take-the-fun-out-of-womens-sex-lives-idUSKCN0YG2TS.

Firth, Shannon. "Study: Infertile Couples 3 Times more likely to divorce." *USnews.com*. January 31, 2014. https://www.usnews.com/news/articles/2014/01/31/study-infertile-couples-3-times-more-likely-to-divorce.

Lebowitz, Shana. "A Psychologist says Four Factors Determine Whether You're Ready to Have a Kid—but Most People just Focus on One." *Business Insider*. May 5, 2017. https://www.businessinsider.com/how-to-know-if-youre-ready-to-have-a-kid-2017-5.

Picchi, Aimee. "Raising a child costs $233,610. Are you financially prepared to be a parent?" *USA Today*. February 26, 2018. https://www.usatoday.com/story/money/personalfinance/ 2018/02/26/raising-child-costs-233-610-you-financially-prepared-parent/357243002/.

Richards, Sarah Elizabeth. "When Sex Becomes a Chore." *SLATE*. April 12, 2010. https://slate.com/human-interest/2010/04/a-new-study-shows-how-infertility-affects-a-couple-s-sex-life.html

Swanson, Ana. "Many parents will say kids made them happier. They're probably lying." *The Washington Post*. July 6, 2016. https://www.washingtonpost.com/news/wonk/wp/2016/07/06/many-americans-will-tell-you-having-kids-made-them-happier-theyre-probably-lying/.

CHAPTER 6

Building Reserves

"When the well runs dry, we know the worth of water."

BEN FRANKLIN

You know the fuel light in your car that indicates if you are running low on gas? My first car, a Volkswagen beetle, had a handy lever under the dashboard that could be pulled when the car ran out of gas. It would drop in enough reserve to get to the nearest gas station. I often think what a useful device it would be for our marriage if there were gauges telling us when we are sleep deprived, energy depleted from over commitment, or stressed due to credit card bills. Since these gauges do not exist, the next best thing is realizing when your reserves are down. You could then make lifestyle choices to replenish your tank and avoid depletion.

Even in the best marriages, there will be stressful periods that tax your fortitude. The cause may be the loss of a job, a change of career, an accident, an unexpected expense, a sick child, or an aging parent. Often no one is responsible for these situations, they just happen. To hope that your life will be free of difficulties and setbacks is unrealistic. It is good to know that adversity happens to everyone, and it helps to be prepared when your turn comes.

Times of transition represent some of the greatest stress that couples experience. This is especially true after the birth of the first child, as Dr. Gottman and Nan Silver note in their study with newlywed couples, where 67 percent went through a dramatic decline in marital satisfaction. I certainly witnessed this in my decades doing newborn home visits. The difference with couples who successfully navigate challenges is the relationship they had prior to the birth. Did they have emotional intimacy and friendship? Did they have the habit of connecting with each other daily? Such bonding creates a bridge that helps couples through turbulent times.

One of our turns with adversity came as a three-headed life transition when Patrick and I had been married for four years. When our first child was one month old, Patrick suffered a serious back injury during his summer job. The initial treatment involved complete floor rest, as our mattress was not firm enough. The hope was that the injury would heal without surgery. When he could be upright, he was instructed to avoid anything that rotated the spine. This resulted in not being allowed to vacuum, rake, sweep, or shovel, all chores he had willingly done. Then, of course, there was a baby who needed constant care, and he was unable to even pick her up.

Financially, things were equally challenging. The workman's compensation was based on his summer job, not his teaching career, where he was paid two-thirds of his regular week's pay. He was known to comment how "three-thirds stunk; two-thirds was a killer!" Having just had the baby, I was on unpaid maternity leave. We had gone from two full-time incomes to a fraction of one income for three of us. Also, during this time, we purchased and moved into our first home.

As the months dragged on, Patrick experienced little physical improvement. His orthopedic doctor rightly observed that both of us were getting depressed at the lack of progress. With restricted activities, life was not much fun, especially as we adjusted to being first time parents. With our sex life pretty much at a standstill, we were grateful that our relationship was not solely dependent on that aspect; but it was challenging. My stress was reflected in a Sunday evening phone call to his doctor the night before spinal surgery to inquire about the risk of impotence. He reassured me, and I slept better that night.

The procedure, while successful, required many weeks recuperation. The experience was physically, emotionally, and financially draining. I recall saying to Patrick, "don't let me ever tell you that you do not do anything around here, because now that you can't, I realize how much you do." From shoveling throughout that winter to taking out the garbage, it was one chore after another for me. His job was to lie on the floor and go swimming at the YMCA, an activity he despised, even more so during those cold, miserable January days. He did, however, manage to muster a sense of humor that was aided by visits from our friends. The reassurance that our situation would improve, along with a strong faith that we both share, and playing with the baby, helped us maintain a positive attitude through this nine-month ordeal. Our daily connection was our teatime, where we talked about better days ahead.

While Patrick was recovering, I asked his surgeon if he would be willing to speak to our Nurse Practitioner Association on pediatric orthopedic conditions. He kindly agreed and suggested that we ride together. On coming to the house to pick me up, he checked in on Patrick before we sped off to the meeting in his sports car. I realized during that half-hour car ride how circumstances and stress can affect one's judgment. As the doctor had left his wife and four kids at home and revved up his sports car, I think he enjoyed getting out too. If I had not liked, respected, and loved Patrick so much, I might have suggested he keep on driving and take me away from the drudgery. I did not suggest it and neither did he, but I appreciated how a spouse could feel emotionally vulnerable and want to escape when circumstances overwhelm.

Financially, things were so tight that when the car needed an oil change, I took a free class at the local tech school to do it myself. That gesture made a lasting impression on Patrick. He often shared this when speaking with the engaged couples. The incident made him realize that I was a partner who had his back (no pun intended!). The events of those nine months gave us insight into the incredible importance of partnership.

Similar incidents, like the one I have described here, occur in every long-term relationship, and will have an impact on your marriage. Being prepared with strong "legs of support" can provide the stamina needed to stay on the dance floor. The sooner you build these legs into your partnership, the more likely you will withstand life's unforeseen challenges.

Physical:

- Are you only getting five to six hours of sleep a night, planning to catch up on the weekend?

- Do you keep putting off your annual physical exam until you have more time?

- Are you continually grabbing fast food instead of preparing healthy meals?

- Are you delaying exercise until your schedule lightens up?

- Are you staying physically active with outings you both find fun?

Keeping physically healthy is necessary to deal with the pressures of everyday life, but it is critical when you are experiencing periods of increased stress. Getting seven to eight hours sleep every night and at least thirty minutes of exercise daily, will change your metabolism, help keep your weight in control, and pump endorphins into your depleted system. Remember your annual check-up because other people are depending on you. If there should be an unexpected health challenge, a healthy body is better able to heal.

Emotional:

- Are you inflexible about your schedule?

- Are you obsessive about how things must be done?

- Do you allow time every day for solitude, meditation, or prayer?

- Are you projecting an attitude of hope and optimism?

- Do you know what restores you? An outing, classical music, a museum?

- When was the last time you two sat together, relaxed and talked?

- What ritual can you build into your daily schedule for a touch point?

Being rigid about how things must be done can add unnecessary stress when you're faced with crises. Rearranging your priorities can save a lot of energy. Taking breaks for some solitude with no distractions, even for a few minutes, can provide invaluable breathing space, creating emotional reserves. Constant complaining about how bad a situation is can rob you of valuable energy needed for healing. Being able to support each other with some degree of optimism can be an invaluable gift you can give to each other, allowing you to look ahead to better days.

Financial:

- Do you pay your bills first, hoping there will be some left for savings?

- Do you have an emergency fund?

- Are you maxing out your credit cards?

- Are you spending money on unnecessary items?

- Is your sick and vacation time at work used up?

- Do you have disability insurance to deal with the unexpected?

Pay yourself first when your paycheck arrives by putting money in your emergency account. This provides a cushion that will be there for an unexpected expense without adding more stress to an already difficult situation. Feeding this account may mean cutting down expenses in another area. You may not be going out to eat as often, but entertaining at home can allow you to socialize with friends less expensively. Going to the theatre can be replaced with a romantic evening at home, with a candlelight dinner followed by Netflix and popcorn. Needing time away from the job when an emergency occurs will add more anxiety if there is little or no paid time off. Keep some sick leave and vacation time banked at work to draw on when needed. While life insurance is sensible, having disability insurance is often inexpensive and more practical during your early, childless years.

Social:

- When was the last time the two of you had friends over for an evening or met up with old high school or college pals?

- How about planning an activity separately for a relaxing lunch with a friend or a hike with a buddy?

- Do you keep putting off extending invitations for friends to come over, waiting for things to be less chaotic or your house to be neater?

Know that things will never be perfect. Do it anyway! Planning regular get-togethers with other couples can give a real boost to your endorphins. Getting together with a friend can help you through some gloomy days.

Spiritual:

- Are you connected to a church, synagogue, mosque, or other spiritual community?

- Do you dedicate time in the week when you and your family worship together?

- Do you allow for daily solitude or meditation?

Having the faith that your situation will improve is invaluable to your outlook. An hour of worship, particularly during times of stress, listening to a well delivered sermon, and taking time for prayer or meditation, can do much to revitalize a discouraged spirit and instill hope. Strengthening these legs will provide strong prevention tools to deal with life's challenges and keep you on the dance floor.

Steps:

- Schedule a regular exam with your primary care provider.

- Incorporate exercise into your day

- Plan downtime to relax.

- Pay your bills on time and attack your debt.

- Keep some vacation and sick time banked at work.

- Plan get-togethers with friends.

- Build in time to renew your spiritual self.

- Recognize when you are running on empty and address it.

WORK CITED

Gottman, John M., and Nan Silver. *The Seven Principles for Making Marriage Work*. New York: Crown Publishing, , 1999.

CHAPTER 7

Establishing Support Systems

"Be strong enough to stand alone, smart enough to know
when you need help, and brave enough to ask for it."

MARK AMEND

The last chapter addressed ways in which you could internally strengthen your marriage by attending to self-care: physically, emotionally, financially, socially, and spiritually. This section widens your support circle to include external aspects of your life. When life takes you on an unanticipated detour, having alternate paths available can prevent your marriage from being swept off the dance floor.

When I was studying nursing in college, I learned about "collateral circulation." This is a medical term that describes a situation in which the body sets up alternate pathways for blood flow to prevent permanent damage to an organ. For example, when a clot forms in a coronary artery and prevents a vital part of the heart from receiving adequate blood supply, the body then builds a network of blood vessels that circumvents the clot, supplying the necessary oxygen. This collateral circulation allows the heart to continue to function, albeit through a different route. Collateral circulation can serve as a metaphor for how a couple can survive the unexpected, sometimes devastating, events which can occur in any marriage.

When do you develop these alternate routes? Since prevention is always an asset, you are wise to build these support systems into your life and strengthen them over the course of your marriage. The relationships you develop with extended family, close friends, neighbors, and co-workers are the collateral circulation that can provide strength in times of strife. These bonds will sustain you as you deal with the unexpected and regain your balance. Just as your daily, healthy lifestyle choices increase the likelihood of good health as you age, the support systems you establish enhance the probability of a positive outcome for your marriage.

Some of the difficult times will happen in the natural order of life, such as the loss of your parents. Other episodes will occur at unexpected times and cause a major upheaval. These events, however, do not have to destroy your marriage. Each of you will need to regroup and identify what the event means to all aspects of your relationship. This process does not happen quickly and will require heartfelt communication, enhanced by the emotional intimacy and the supports you have built.

Marriages that experience a traumatic event, like the death of a child, a debilitating illness, bankruptcy, a marital affair, substance issues, or a natural disaster, cannot only survive but can deepen the love and determination that strengthens a marriage. Sometimes stressful events last for brief periods, where you can see an end in sight. Others create more chronic stress. Survival will require stamina that represents a true triumph of the human spirit.

This was the case with friends of ours following an automobile accident. Jim a healthy, athletic, forty-year-old husband and father became a quadriplegic. This confined him to a wheelchair and required 24 hour, complex, home nursing care. Over time, Jim and Meg each carved out a life with new pursuits. Jim, having wide interests and computer access, developed some beautiful collections about the history of the city, sports memorabilia, and coin collections. Meg pursued singing with a choral group, a membership in an outing club, and physical activities with friends. Aided by nursing care, they have been able to enjoy an occasional outing to the theatre and gatherings with friends at their home. This couple's ability to establish collateral circulation early in their marriage allowed them to remain married many years following this unfathomable event. Meg would say that this horrific experience has not been without its collateral damage as well. Yet, the relationships and activities they enjoyed with family and friends in their early marriage are the support systems they have utilized to sustain them.

Given such a scenario, many of us might say: "If that ever happened to me, I would not be able to go on" or "I could never handle that." None of us know how we will react to challenging circumstances until we are faced with them. But in fact, couples do go on, often even reacting in a way totally opposite from how they would have predicted. Why? Where does such strength come from?

Author Victor Frankl describes a person's ability to survive unthinkable circumstances, like those found in Nazi death camps, including Auschwitz and Dachau, during World War II. Dr. Frankl, a psychiatrist, documented his personal experiences, and those of fellow prisoners, in his book, *Man's Search for Meaning*. Prisoners endured isolation, frigid temperatures, and twelve-hour days of manual labor with only a daily ration of watery soup and a piece of bread, all while living under the constant fear of being sent to the gas chamber.

Dr. Frankl defined the attributes that helped him, and other prisoners, survive. He described *humor* as "one of the soul's weapons in the fight for self -preservation." *Gratitude* for "the smallest of mercies" was an attribute that sustained them in the most trying moments. *Social connection* with other prisoners and an increasingly deep *spiritual life* offered solace. *Love* he noted "is the ultimate and highest goal to which man can aspire." Focusing on his wife and their marriage and the love they shared helped him endure inhuman circumstances for three years. He did not learn until after his release that his wife had also been in a concentration camp. She, however, did not survive. Frankl concluded that "to survive is to *find meaning in the suffering* and use *the freedom to choose one's attitude* in a given set of circumstances [emphasis added]." To find meaning amidst pain is often discovered in retrospect, but it can have a powerful influence on your attitude and ability to cope with difficulties. I have italicized the qualities to highlight those attributes that make a difference to all humans, whether facing serious challenges or even trying to get through a tough day.

If we had known that during our marriage we, along with our extended families, would face debilitating injury, cancer, mental health issues, substance abuse, severe financial stresses, divorces, and the loss of our four parents and a sibling, it would have seemed too much to handle. When speaking with the engaged couples, Patrick shares that if our lives were laid out in front of him before we were married, he would not have had the courage to step out on the dance floor. I understand completely. What made the difference? These events did not occur at the same time, and over our years together, we have learned the importance of building these support systems into our life. Partnership and emotional intimacy are built one experience on another.

In my younger years, I could have been devastated by a cancer diagnosis. By the time I was 59, Patrick and I had dealt with many life events that had tested our reserve. Those experiences changed my perspective from what it would have been earlier in our marriage. Because I always sought routine care, my early breast cancer diagnosis meant that I did not require radiation or chemotherapy. Our youngest was 20 and our other three children were on already their own. That is a very different set of circumstances from that of a young mother with toddlers who must undergo extensive treatment with debilitating side effects. Following my mastectomy, my kids counted 164 get well cards taped to the kitchen doors and seven weeks' worth of meals in the freezer. That type of collateral circulation certainly contributed to our healing. We have found that with a strong partnership and a support system, the joy is doubled, and the sorrow is halved.

The faith, health, and friendships fostered during our early years became an integral part of our life before we knew they would be so vital. These supports provided us with the needed courage and strength to move ahead. A faith in God sustained us during the troubling times. The support of family and friends helped us maintain a positive outlook and see beyond the obstacles. Many long-married couples say their greatest challenges resulted in unforeseen benefits. Future joy is often intensified by the sorrow that is endured.

Steps:

- Look to your faith to help you during trying times.

- Recognize and appreciate your own strengths and those of your spouse.

- Employ humor when you can, to lighten the tension.

- Express gratitude and love to each other for the blessings you have.

- Assist others in need.

- Ask for help when you need it. People want to be useful.

- Try to identify some meaning from the challenges you are experiencing.

WORK CITED

Frankl, Victor E. *Man's Search for Meaning;* Boston: Beacon Press, 1959, 2006

CHAPTER 8

Affirming Positive Thoughts About Your Marriage

"The world as we have created it is a process of our thinking. It cannot be changed without changing our thinking."

ALBERT EINSTEIN

After you have built in reserves and established support systems, you may find that even those are not enough to help you through the rough patches. This is when each of you want to look at self-defeating habits that may be sabotaging your relationship.

When you think about your marriage, what is the picture that you hold for your future? When you were falling in love, and later engaged, you undoubtedly saw your relationship as happy and love filled. Now that you have moved beyond the tango stage and life is busier, is the reality different than you hoped? Your attitudes, words, self-talk, affirmations, and visualizations about your spouse have a profound influence on the intimacy and future of your marriage.

In his *Psychology Today* article, "How to Manage Your Thoughts, Feelings, and Behaviors," Dr. Gleb Tsipursky explains the two thinking systems, autopilot and intentional. He based his theory on the work of Nobel Prize-winning Daniel Kahneman. As Dr. Tsipursky defines it, the autopilot system "requires no conscious effort to function" but responds to our emotions and intuitions from primarily the amygdala part of the brain. It "guides our daily habits, helps us make snap decisions and reacts instantly" to situations that threaten us. The intentional system "reflects our rational thinking and centers around the prefrontal cortex," which is a part of the brain not fully developed until the mid- to late twenties. This system helps us manage "individual and group relationships, logical reasoning, probabilistic thinking and learning new information and patterns of thinking and behavior." Dr. Tsipursky writes that the "intentional system takes deliberate effort to turn on," but with training, "you can use the intentional system to change your automatic thinking, feeling and behavioral patterns."

When we were married for ten years, Patrick and I had the opportunity to attend a workshop titled "Achieving Your Potential." It was offered by the Pacific Institute, based in Seattle, Washington. The seminar was about affirming what you want to happen in your life and in your relationships and using affirmations and visualization to achieve your goals. At the beginning of the presentation, co-founder Lou Tice stated, "our present thoughts determine our future." Our thoughts are often reflected in our self-talk. He went on to say, "if you don't control your self-talk, your self-talk controls you."

The goal of the program was to discover concepts and skills that allow for the development of an individual's potential. The seminar turned out to be life-changing for us in our personal and professional lives and, most importantly, for our marriage. Learning how to express ourselves, without accusing each other, allowed for calmer discussions. An example: "I would like the house to be neater, and I am feeling stressed that it is taking up most of the weekend. I would like to have more time for us to have some fun. How do you think we could organize things better?" Dr. Gottman calls this a "soft start-up." It works a whole lot better than saying, "You need to help out more around the house. I am tired of doing all the work." Such a statement invites a defensive response with the likelihood of an argument.

We also learned the value of expressing fondness and admiration for each other, rather than criticism. "Since I enjoy you a whole lot more than housework, how can we be more efficient getting things done?" This kind of dialogue prevents negativity from escalating and requires thinking about the desired outcome instead of criticizing each other.

Tice also explained how "all meaningful and lasting change starts first on the inside and works its way out into the world." This advice suggests that when we want change, we should look to the only person we can change—ourselves—rather than our partner. On the way home from the seminar, Patrick and I talked about what we had heard and continued our discussion during our daily teatime. We looked at what habits we could work on to help us change our response to situations that caused stress: household chores, parenting, and organization were among the top. Rest assured this was not a quick process! A two-day seminar did not do it, but we had the basics to get us launched. Then, we had to practice. Several months later, we attended the seminar again and brought along some colleagues. This was an opportunity to reinforce what was working and to hear things we missed the first time. What you think and say to yourself, your spouse, and others about your marriage matters. We learned the following steps at the seminar and began putting them into practice.

Self-Talk:

Most of us do not talk to ourselves out loud, but we all talk to ourselves in our head.

Many of us carry on quite a negative monologue! You might think "I can't believe I lost my keys again. I am so stupid." Or you might berate yourself with "Why am I always late? I am such an idiot for not planning on traffic." Try paying attention to your self-talk for a week. Jot down the number of times you criticize yourself at work and at home. Does it surprise you? Are you more encouraging or more demeaning? Most of us would not hang around with someone who spoke to us the way we speak to ourselves, and we would certainly be upset with a spouse who did.

Do you realize you are reinforcing the very behaviors that you do not like by berating yourself? Know that you are capable of learning to rephrase your dialogue. Healthier self-talk will reinforce the positive behaviors you want for yourself. Maybe it is time to pay attention and be kinder to you and see what happens.

Start by learning to replace negative statements with positive ones. Think to yourself "I wonder where my keys are. It is not like me to misplace them. I usually hang them up when I come home," even if the latter has not been the case. If you chronically run late, think "I can't believe I am late today. I usually allow myself extra time to get ready." Even if your history has been one of chronic tardiness, remember this is all about habit change! Yes, you are frustrated, but you are not going to beat yourself further with negative self-talk. You are working toward improvement.

Affirmations:

Affirmations are the opposite of negative self-talk. They are statements about those habits you would like to own. Consciously reprogramming the tape that is already running in your head does not mean you are denying the issue or pretending there is not a problem. Rather, you are setting yourself up for a change of habit. When you do this consistently, you are altering the picture you hold of that habit.

We tend to work toward the mental picture we hold in our brain. This has been proven time and time again with athletes who are training to improve their performance. They need to visualize what they want to happen, not reinforce the mistakes they have been making. The coach who says, "stop with the outside pitch," is creating the picture of an outside pitch, which is what he does *not* want to happen. Research shows he should be stating the desired outcome and say, "aim the ball right over the plate." The brain works toward what is pictured, and the behavior that is visualized is the most likely result.

An affirmation should be one sentence, first person, present tense, and contain a positive emotion. To work toward a new behavior, write down affirmations like "I am more relaxed now that I hang up my keys in the same place every day and know where to find them" and "Leaving 15 minutes earlier makes me feel so much more relaxed." When reading these affirmations, take a deep breath and feel the positive sensations that result from these changes—own them.

If you are not a morning person and you feel like your mood gets the day off to a bad start, you might want to affirm a different attitude. Write "I am so proud of myself putting a smile on my face in the morning and feeling happier when I greet my spouse." If coming home stressed from work has set a negative tone, you may want to affirm for a different start to your evening. Write "I am happy and relaxed to be home and greet my spouse with a hug" or "Having a quiet dinner together without technology is a great time to talk about our day and enjoy the evening."

Visualization:

Another component of habit change is visualization. Visualizing is picturing what it looks and feels like to own those behaviors as you are reading your affirmations. Start seeing yourself already possessing the very habits you would like to adopt. As you are reading your affirmation, allow yourself to feel the emotion associated with owning the habit. Let this last for at least 20 seconds. The power of this activity was vividly brought home to me when a woman at our seminar talked about her desire to have nice fingernails. Noreen bit her nails and hated the way her hands looked. She made an affirmation about how happy she felt having lovely nails. I saw her weeks after the workshop, and she was thrilled to show me her hands. Noreen said she worked daily at her self-talk, written affirmations, and visualization. The power of intentional habit change was made real with this personal example. The same technique can be employed for your behaviors and relationships.

In the article "Here's How Long It Really Takes to Break a Habit According to Science," Signe Dean refers to a 2009 study where researchers from University College London "found that the average time it takes for a new habit to stick is actually 66 days," sometimes even longer. The current belief is that you should count on two months of effort if you are actively working to embrace a new habit. It may take longer to break an old habit than it takes to assimilate a new one.

How can self-talk, written positive affirmations, and visualization affect your marriage? Profoundly! If you want to improve communication in your relationship, affirm for it both in your self-talk and written affirmations. Think and write statements like: "I am proud that I ask for what I need and compliment my spouse when there is an effort to meet my request" and "It really makes a positive difference when I get home from work and power down my cell phone, so I can talk with my spouse without interruption."

Patrick and I had not realized how our self-talk and our habits were influencing important aspects of our life. We reflected that much of what we had experienced was what we talked about, both positive and negative. During the early decades of our life, we owned secondhand cars. Despite good maintenance, we had frequent car trouble. After that seminar, we realized that we started every vacation anticipating car problems and it happened a lot! We changed those negative thoughts and at least started our vacations with less stress. We had more fun and dealt with issues when they arose instead of affirming that they *would* happen. Even though affirmations do not mean events will always go your way, you will be less stressed when you think and talk positively. Anticipating bad things sucks the joy from the present.

While learning about the power of self-talk, affirmations, and visualization, I recalled a time during my sophomore year in college when many of my fellow students and I were challenged by the rigors of the nursing curriculum. Several classmates talked about other plans if they did not pass. I remember feeling shocked that they did not see themselves graduating. I could only picture myself earning my degree from our college. I was not aware at the time that I was affirming and visualizing. Yet, thinking back, all my classmates who expressed alternate plans did not graduate.

For some people, mental exercises involving affirmations, meditation, or visualization are too "out of the box" and they may not believe in these concepts. It was very advantageous for Patrick and me to have attended this seminar together, as it put us on the same page. For many of us, this information is very different from what we have witnessed and been taught about how events in our life would unfold. I remember hearing someone say, "you don't have to believe in gravity, but when you throw a rock into the air, it will *still* hit you in the head." Not believing something does not mean it is not true. What we affirm, how we talk, and how we visualize events often becomes our reality. Be careful what you think about because often that is exactly what happens.

Once you tune into the importance of self-talk and affirmations, you cannot help but notice the self-defeating dialogue of others. I was at a meeting when a couple arrived late. When it was time for them to introduce themselves, they said, "We are the Smiths and we are always late." They gave themselves the perfect affirmation for continuing their tardiness! Many times, I have heard people say, "I always get a bad cold or the flu this time of year." Although there were no symptoms at the time, within the week, they were sick. I am not at all suggesting that we can control all of life's occurrences. We do, however, control our thoughts and our internal monologue, and the expectations we project often affect the outcome of what we experience.

Some couples emphasize the qualities they find distressing about their mate, and they wish they would change. With statements like "You *always* expect me to make dinner, even though I am also working full time" or "You *never* think ahead about what we could do on the weekend that would be fun," you are not only criticizing your spouse, you are thwarting the possibility of a new habit. These statements focus on and reinforce the very behaviors you would like to alter. The words *never* and *always* do not bode well for a positive outcome. Avoiding them could allow for a different result.

Talk about what you want to happen, not the behavior you want to stop. A better conversation could start with "I would really appreciate it if we could share the responsibility for making dinner. We could make up a meal plan on the weekend. That would give each of us a break during the week. Sound good?" Or "If you get the groceries and banking done early on Saturday, we could have the afternoon free for something fun. What would you like to do?" If your spouse is hesitant, you might want to add, "I'll help with the planning to get us started." You are setting a tone of optimism and support, rather than accusation and anger. Your tone of voice and body language make a difference. Statements like these offer positive alternatives, rather than triggering a defensive reaction.

In addition to these examples, think about the major areas of conflict in marriage: money, sex, careers, religion, in-laws, children, and household chores. Take inventory of those areas that you would like to work on. Initiating change can create a domino effect; holding a positive picture of your marriage in your mind results in improving expectations, which in turn changes the dynamics of your relationship, and ultimately the atmosphere in your home. Invest time and energy into habit changes by utilizing self-talk, written affirmations, and visualization and enrich the emotional intimacy of your marriage.

It is important to know that we cannot affirm, or habit change, for anyone else. Too bad, huh? When you make changes within yourself, however, others are forced to respond differently because your behavior is different. The old rules no longer apply because you are changing your dance steps.

Steps:

- Track your self-talk for a week.

- Rephrase your negative self-talk with positive statements.

- Each of you pick one positive habit you would like to adopt for yourself.

- Write an affirmation for the habit you would like to change or improve.

- Read the affirmation at least twice a day until change occurs.

- Visualize and feel the result you want for 20 seconds while affirming.

- Acknowledge each other's *efforts* as well as the successes.

- Persist. Remember that it often takes two months or more to change a habit.

- Hold the picture you *want* for your marriage, not one you fear.

WORKS CITED

Dean, Signe. "Here's How Long It Really Takes to Break a Habit According to Science." *ScienceAlert.* June 9, 2018. https://www.sciencealert.com/how-long-it-takes-to-break-a-habit-according-to-science.

Lally, Phillippa, Cornelia H.M. Van Jaarsveld, Henry W.W. Potts and Jane Wardle. European Journal of Social Psychology, "How are habits formed: Modelling habit formation in the real world." Published online 16 July 2009 in Wiley Online Library. University College London, London, UK

Tice, Lou. *Smart Talk for Achieving Your Potential.* Pacific Institute Publishing, 2005.

Tsipursky, Gleb Ph.D. "How to Manage Your Thoughts, Feelings, and Behaviors." *Psychology Today.* April 13, 2016. https://www.psychologytoday.com/us/blog/intentional-insights/201604/how-manage-your-thoughts-feelings-and-behaviors.

CHAPTER 9

Taking on Technology

"If we are to remain a free and viable society, we need to spend less time looking at screens and more time looking into each other's eyes."

GLENN CLOSE

When Patrick and I first began our work with engaged couples, there were no cell phones, and computers were only used by large corporations. Recently, in a room with 45 couples, everyone owned a cell phone and a laptop, and many had watches that served multiple applications.

There are convenient, time-saving benefits to technology: online banking, travel planning, educational seminars, convenience of shopping, etc. It can also pose one of the biggest challenges to your marriage. Because technology is insidious, it is easy not think about the impact. Since it is not going away, you want to determine what role technology will play in your personal life.

According to an article on the blog *Black and Married with Kids*, there are several red flags to watch out for when it comes to technology and your marriage. Some of these indicators include "you text your spouse more than you talk," you "fall asleep with a smart phone, tablet or laptop on the bed," "you keep [your] smart phone in the kitchen during meal times," and "you check your phone whenever an alert goes off—even if your spouse is in the middle of talking." I would also ask, "When your spouse enters the room, do you quickly close the site you were on for fear of what they would think?"

Will you respect time alone with your spouse, or will you allow the outside world to interrupt? Because interrupt it will. Allowing yourselves

30 minutes for a meal together at the end of the day, with no tech interference, can solidify your emotional connection. The ubiquitous presence of electronics requires a deliberate commitment from both of you. Blocking out all other interruptions during this time makes for a sacred space at the end of the workday that you both can anticipate. If you decide what you want for your marriage, and later for your family, you can build this habit into your life together.

There will be new decisions when children are added to the picture. You might be interested in Bill Gate's advice. As the founder of Microsoft and the guru of technology, he advises waiting until your kids are in eighth grade. You may worry that your child needs a phone in case of an emergency, but at that age, it would be unusual that they are not with someone who could reach you from school or a friend's house. The easy access to harmful sites and the bullying that occurs often pose more of a risk to your child than an unlikely emergency. Talk together and weigh the options.

When you are having date night, can you resist the urge to check the incessant buzzing? There it is, demanding to be addressed, as if you have nothing to say about its presence. You do, however, have a say in the role your devices play, not in the work environment maybe, but certainly in your home and with each other. And that is the good news. Setting up your parameters will force others to adjust to you. And they will.

Technology can be a major intrusion into your communication and intimacy. You are wise to discuss where these devices fall on your priority list, the role you want them to play in your life, and the limits you want to establish in your home. If you are annoyed that your spouse is always checking their phone, taking calls during your time together, or texting friends when you are trying to converse, address it. If you find it rude, say so. By not coming to an understanding and defining some limits, you allow a formidable intruder into your life. You both are the head and the heart of your family and can determine the climate in your home. When boundaries are not set, tech devices can cause you to zone out and destroy intimacy.

What about the impact of the first major device to enter the American household—the television? More families in America have five televisions in their homes, than families that have only one. A twentysomething I spoke with said her dad just installed two TVs into the bathrooms, which now makes seven in their house. She said that he did not want to miss the news or sports. What does that mean for communication in a relationship? Maybe nothing. Maybe a lot.

Often, couples do not think twice about having a TV in their bedroom. They just decorate around it. Media will be pervasive in your life, both at work and at home. Leaving it out of your bedroom will permit you to have one place of solitude and intimacy. Create a place for lovemaking and sleep. Use this private space as a haven from the world, a place where you can have your most intimate communication, and where you can discover things about each other that only you two know. Play relaxing music with soft lighting. Yes, there will be some nights you will not be happy with each other, and the room will scream with silence. So be it. It is easy to fill the void with the late-night talking heads, but don't. Deal with the quiet. Keeping a TV out of the bedroom is a hard sell for many couples. Chances are, after a few weeks of adjusting, you will not be sorry. Give it a try. Your marriage will thank you.

When it comes to your relationship and Facebook, blogs, Twitter, YouTube, and Instagram, do not engage in discussing your spouse with others. If something is problematic, you should be addressing it with each other or a counselor. Remember there is no privacy with technology. What might get you worked up one day, can blow over the next, but it will forever remain for the world to see or read. Value your privacy and respect that of your spouse.

Talk about technology now. To stay plugged into your marriage, you may need to unplug some electronics and invest more time in each other. It is so much easier to determine technology's role in your marriage ahead of time, than it is to change the rules after habits have developed. Remember, you control IT or IT controls you. The pun is intended as a reminder that you are in charge.

Steps:

- Talk about the role you want technology to play in your life.

- Turn off your cell phone on arriving home.

- Create an electronic-free dinner time.

- Consider Bill Gate's advice for your kid's cell phone: wait until eighth grade.

- Turn off the phone for date nights and when your spouse needs to talk.

- Establish a tech-free bedroom.

- Take charge of IT, so IT is not in charge of you.

WORKS CITED

Foreman, Martine. "7 Indicators that Technology is Killing Your Marriage?" *Black and Married with Kids.* https://blackandmarriedwithkids.com/7-indicators-that-technology-is-killing-your-marriage/

Shannon, Brooke. "Wait Until 8th Smartphone Pledge Signed in 14 States and 40 Schools in First Month." https://www.waituntil8th.org/blog/2017/4/30/wait-until-8th-smartphone-pledge-signed-in-14-states-and-40-schools-in-first-month.

CHAPTER 10

Maintaining Your Marriages

"A marriage may be made in heaven, but the maintenance must be done on earth."

UNKNOWN

When you hear the word marriage, you are apt to think only of your relationship. There are other entities, however, within your marriage which should be recognized. Your career, your children, your home, your body, and your health are among the competing demands on your time and energy.

For those of you who own a home, can you recall signing the mortgage papers? It was an exciting day: the freedom from a landlord, the knowledge your money was now going into equity instead of rent, and the pride of owning your own home. After celebrating your accomplishment, you went to work the next morning, as you would for the next 30 years, in order to pay the mortgage. When you are not working or sleeping, is all your free time spent watching TV, playing golf, or shopping? Unlikely.

Now, home maintenance required attention: landscaping, sprucing up the outside, and cleaning gutters. Then you focused on the inside with painting, wallpapering, maybe tiling a floor, or knocking down a wall. You paint your house before it chips and replace the roof before it leaks. You do this because your home is an expensive investment. You want to enjoy it, and you want it to be pleasant for your family and friends to visit. When the day comes to move, you would like to sell it at a profit and leave with happy memories. Is any of this going to happen if your attitude is "I bought a house, now I'm done"? Hardly! All homeowners know that the care and upkeep never end.

Buying a home heralds new responsibility and so does marriage. Author and therapist, Daphne de Marneffe compares a couple's union to creating a new entity: the marriage. Some couples confuse a great wedding as a culmination rather than a commencement. They think "We did it! We had a great day. Done. We're married." Your marriage, however, is the house that can fall into disrepair if it does not receive regular attention and maintenance. If you can afford to pay someone to do all the household tasks for you, you may be able to avoid home maintenance yourself, but you will not be able to pay anyone to keep your marriage together.

When couples treat their relationship with the time, energy, and respect they give to their jobs, there is a whole paradigm shift. When the marriage is respected at this level, the relationship is regarded with attention, one that will ensure that it receives the energy needed to keep it vibrant.

Patrick and I were at a nutritional seminar where the presenter posed the question "If I told you that I would buy you any car you wanted but the hitch was that it would be the only car you would ever own, how would you take care of it?" It prompted the audience to respond with the expected answers: regular oil change, a tune-up as needed, replacing the tires before the treads are worn, and routine washing and waxing. His point, of course, was that you have been given only one body. How are you caring for it? It is a question that can be similarly applied to married couples. How are you maintaining the relationship you want to last a lifetime?

A few years ago, I read an article which suggested that 20 minutes a day spent on your relationship would yield three times the health benefit of the treadmill. Given all the attention to aerobic exercise, heart disease, and diabetes that seemed an interesting finding. Now, I do not believe the article was recommending giving up aerobic exercise, but rather emphasizing the importance of giving equal time to your marriage.

We Americans are great consumers and spend a lot of time and money to look good. Why? Maybe because it makes us happy, but it is also about attracting attention in hopes of pursuing a meaningful relationship. Why is that so important, even for those very capable, independent souls among us? An online article from *Imprific*, titled "The Hedonic Treadmill—If Only Happiness Were as Easy as Marriage, a Big House, and Kids," provides an apropos quote from the previously mentioned Dr. Kahneman regarding the material things we may value too highly: "People are exposed to many messages that encourage them to believe that a change of weight, scent, hair color (or coverage), car, clothes, or many other aspects will produce a marked improvement in their happiness. Our research suggests a moral, and a warning: Nothing that you focus on will make as much difference as you think."

The effort placed on appearance may not yield nearly as much benefit as attention given to your most important relationship. The value of investing 20 minutes a day in connecting with your spouse coincides with research from sociology professor and relationship expert Terri Orbuch. In her book, *5 Simple Steps to Take Your Marriage From Good to Great,* she describes the benefits of a "daily briefing in which you and your spouse make time to talk about anything under the sun—except kids, work, and household tasks or responsibilities." Orbuch developed this "rule" after learning that most of the happy couples she studied knew their spouse "intimately"—outside the bedroom — and often make time to exchange special knowledge. According to Orbuch, learning new information about your partner makes things feel fresh and new again and "mimics the emotional and physical state you were in during the first few years of your marriage."

For those of you who took Psychology 101, you may remember Abraham Maslow's hierarchy of needs. If not, the diagram below will introduce you to the famed American psychologist and the theory he proposed in his 1943 paper, "A Theory of Human Motivation." Maslow was one of the earliest psychologists to focus attention on happiness and self-fulfillment. At the lowest level are the physical, basic human needs. The more complex needs are at the top of the pyramid. Lower level needs must be satisfied before achieving one's full potential. The message is that, given everything we may *want* in life, there are few material things that we *need*.

Maslow's Hierarchy of Needs

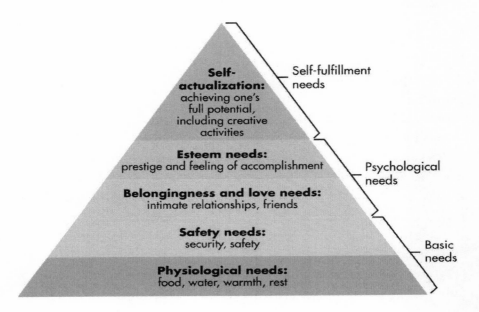

I thought a lot about this hierarchy while working with my pe-diatric patients, and the necessity of meeting their basic needs to achieve fulfillment as an adult. Most of the children lived in the inner city and came from low-income families, where meeting their basic needs was a challenge. Medical care was aligned with social services to ensure that food, clothing, and housing needs were being addressed. Childhood safety was discussed as well as discipline, promoting a positive, loving parent/child relationship, and setting age-appropriate boundaries. These assets provide the child a sense of belonging to better ensure a healthy, productive, and satisfying adult life. If a couple is expected to provide all these needs for their child, it is important that their own needs are also met. The marriage relationship is essential in forming a solid foundation.

Maslow's model and the building block concept made sense to me; a strong foundation increases the chance for the best outcome. When I started working with engaged couples, and later writing about healthy marriages, I reflected on this and shared my Marriage Hierarchy of Needs.

The Marriage Hierarchy of Needs.

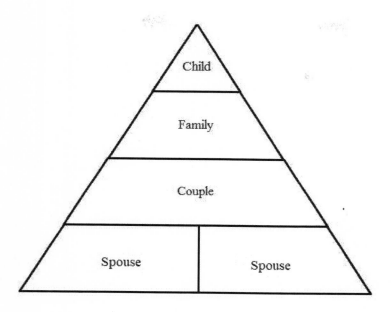

I developed this model as a reminder that the two of you are the foundation for your marriage and the children and family you may create. I split the base of the triangle, *Spouse/Spouse* to represent you as individuals. You each come to this partnership as separate people, each with your own physical, emotional, financial, social, and spiritual experiences as well as your own medical history, temperament, personality, education, career, hobbies, family, and friends.

Respect for your partner's personhood is something that is essential to a healthy relationship. This person that you fell in love with had experiences, interests, and activities unique to them. These are all part of their package. To deny them the opportunity to engage in activities and the company of other people is to smother the essence of your spouse.

Your marital status will alter your life, but alter does not mean extinguish. If he plays pickup basketball five nights a week, that may cause problems and probably should be curtailed to a weekly game. But for a spouse to demand the cessation of that outlet would be a big mistake. Likewise, if she enjoys her book club and the associated reading time, it is the wise spouse who encourages her continued participation. A controlling spouse can initiate a slow-burning resentment, apt to explode later over an unrelated issue.

After college graduation, Patrick and I took summer jobs on Cape Cod. Although we were in a committed relationship, we did not live together and had our own schedules. With different days off, we made our own plans, some alone and some with friends, with evenings usually together. The following summer, after we were married, we returned to the Cape. It took us a few weeks to adjust to our schedules, which were not completely our own now as someone was waiting for us at home. Yes, things were different now that we were married. We realized that our new roles required altering our dance steps, and daily communication was needed if we were to avoid worry, hurt feelings, and repeated arguments. We also needed to allow each other space. Without cell phones, we were required to talk about our plans before leaving for the day.

The bottom row of my Marriage Hierarchy of Needs should serve as a reminder to encourage your spouse to grow as an individual, to pursue things that are important to them, and even take on new ventures. Work to foster each other's growth throughout your lifetime together. Two good questions to ask periodically during your marriage are "Do I know my spouse's dreams?" and "Am I supporting and encouraging those ambitions?" That knowledge reflects the intimacy of a relationship.

I recently had coffee with Anita, an older friend, who is anything but elderly. She is highly accomplished in several arenas of her life. When she married at 19, Anita had not had the opportunity to attend college. When her husband finished his stint in the armed service, he developed a successful career, while she raised their two children. My friend is a bright woman, an avid reader, and a very talented artist. She and her husband had a happy marriage, with extensive travel, but she yearned for higher education. When their younger child left for college, Anita told her husband she wanted to pursue a degree. He listened but was concerned that it would interfere with their travel and their time together. She told me, "It was something I just had to do, and I said to him, 'If you say no, I will leave you.' And I would have." He acquiesced.

Every evening, he would fall asleep watching television, and she would go into the study, work until 2 a.m., and then go wake him up to go to bed. "He didn't feel my studying interfered with anything," she said proudly. She earned her bachelor's degree and two master's degrees as well! Some people would assert that he did not contribute to her achieving her goals. I contend that she took responsibility for herself and her aspirations and figured out the dance that worked for their marriage. I find it a great example of not expecting or waiting for someone else to make things happen for you. Know what you want, share that with your partner, and figure out how to make it work. To do otherwise predicts that one spouse gives up their dreams, allowing resentment to eventually consume a marriage.

The second tier of the hierarchy is the *Couple*. This may seem easy at first. In the early years, you saw each other frequently, and there was likely no one else's company you preferred. Over time, life complicates your couple-hood. Other areas demand your attention: career, children, friends, extended family, health issues, community boards, church activities, and home maintenance, to name a few. Addressing these needs requires a discussion about your priorities. Other people will quickly ask for your time, be it some worthwhile community project or errands to help someone. These things are not unimportant, they just need to be balanced with responsibilities to you, your spouse, and your marriage.

Date night is one way to prioritize your relationship and preferably happens out of the house. This does not have to be an expensive event. It just needs to be a new venue where you are not distracted by children or household demands. When was the last time you went out alone, no children? When I would ask my patient's parents this question, they often look puzzled trying to remember. The worst answer I had was "Well, I guess it has been eight years, before we had the kids." Not good! This time spent together without children keeps the focus on your relationship and is critical to a healthy marriage. Look at the Marriage Hierarchy pyramid periodically to keep your priorities in check. As a nurse practitioner, I wrote more prescriptions for a date than I did for antibiotics!

The third tier of the marriage pyramid is *Family*. For those couples who do not have children, this tier may include extended family or friends. Carving out time for this tier can be a challenge. There was a time when Sunday was a sacred day, not only for religious services, but also when businesses were closed. People had fewer distractions. This is no longer the case. Businesses are open to accommodate the working world, some 18 to

24 hours a day. With both spouses working full-time, one day of the weekend is often designated as chore day and the other day for getting ready for the workweek ahead. This routine can devour family time and connecting with each other.

Recognizing the importance of family time early in your marriage makes it easier to make it a natural part of your life. Otherwise, time can be gobbled up by household chores, community involvement, and work demands. While certain obligations must be respected, routine duties should not take precedence over quality time with family. A quote by the late Senator Paul Tsongas is a good reminder: "No one on their deathbed ever said, 'I wish I had spent more time at the office.'"

When value is placed on your time together, everyone benefits. There is a billboard on the highway near where we live promoting recreation in the mountains stating, "The family who plays together stays together." There is something to be said for creating fun memories through different activities that connects children and parents and deepens the connection between spouses.

The Search Institute, a research firm out of Minneapolis, Minnesota, reports that time spent with family has more long-term impact on your child's development than the personal, social, school, and community connections your child experiences. In the article, "Why Spending Time with the Family is More Important Than Ever," *Telegraph* columnist Tim Cummings posed the question: "Are digital diversions robbing us of the vital lessons of play and connection when it comes to raising families?" asserts that "we seem to be glued to our digital devices more than ever, ending up in a kind of voluntary solitary confinement" and "we risk becoming ever more remote from real-life experiences as families, whether that be playing games, sharing outdoors adventures, reading together, or simply sitting down to eat at the same time." These latter activities are what enriches children's lives and will be the ones they remember. When you witness your children thriving, your marriage is also enriched.

When they are young, kids are eager to be involved, and they enjoy activities and outings. In his article, Cumming references Dr. Amanda Gummer, author of *Play: Fun Ways to Help Your Child Develop in The First Five Years*. Dr. Gummer writes, "parents know intuitively what a real moment of connection feels like with their child or teenager, and they also know that awful flat empty feeling when, for hours, their child or teenager is connecting with technical devices and not with them." She does not want to demonize technology, but rather wants to see free time balanced with family activities. She notes that "quality family time—sharing experiences and creating memories—gives children that sense of belonging." With your time together, you can talk about a range of topics where your children get to know you as a person. Some of these moments also allow you to witness your spouse through a different lens.

Dr. Margot Sunderland, a child psychologist and author of *The Science of Parenting: How Today's Brain Research Can Help You Raise Happy, Emotionally Balanced Children*, writes that activities "release the brain's bonding and attachment chemicals, namely opioids and oxytocin, which are also anti-anxiety and anti-aggression molecules." She notes these pursuits can include physical play, creative projects, storytelling, cooking, and exploring nature, even watching a good film together and talking about it afterwards. Talking to each family member about what activities they would enjoy is a one way to involve everyone. Some families pick a weeknight to connect. This may involve a church function or a board game at home. This connection serves as a strong protective factor for children, who gain a sense of belonging as a contributing member of the family.

Organizing these family activities requires planning and creativity. There will be times you may not be sure the effort is worth it, but as Dr. Sunderland points out, "research shows that repeated daily good connections between parent and child leads to better functioning, a stronger immune system, better physiology, higher academic marks, a sense of well-being and contentment, and it prevents mental and physical ill-health later in life." The benefits for your children will be a boost to your marriage as well.

Dr. Sunderland, like Dr. Gummer, does not believe in a digital ban, but rather suggests moderation. It is not the devices that are the problem, but rather what activities are *not* happening because of them. Both experts focus on play and the importance of imagination. Dr. Gummer asserts that "with imagination, there's a definite use it or lose it thing." Both experts encourage parents to focus on the active world of play and personal connection rather than technology. Doing activities together gives your child a sense of importance. There is an emotional bonding that happens when children realize you prefer and enjoy interacting with them.

Long after childhood ends, kids often develop adult interests and careers from the activities you exposed them to as children. When my friend Lu was in grad school as a young, single mother with little money, she brought her six-year-old son Michael to a free outdoor summer symphony every Thursday. He later became a music teacher and now has three children of his own, with the two older ones playing musical instruments. Lu had long forgotten their summer outings until Michael reminded her that his love of music came from those concerts. What a compelling testimony about the impact your activities can have on your child's later life.

The top of my pyramid, *Child*, signifies the importance of individual time. Families with more than one child can find great benefit on taking some time to focus on each child as a person. For those couples without children, this level may be a special cause where you want to invest your energy: a community project, a church fund raiser, or helping an elderly neighbor.

When there is a health or behavioral concern, the child will be the priority. The purpose of the pyramid is to serve as a reminder that the child should not be, as a rule, the focal point of the family. This model helped us raise four teenagers. Even amid the sometime chaotic activities, we made sure we had date night and fun with friends. The schedule may have needed adjustment, but our time was not dismissed.

In working with families, I often found that the pyramid was inverted, with the child(ren) as the foundation and all attention revolving around them and their activities. The child had regular physical exams, immunizations, and screenings. She never missed a music lesson. He was on a sports team. No one missed a birthday party or sleep over. Then I would ask Mom and Dad about their own care, which got a vastly different response. Often, there had been no medical exam, no outing with a friend, or no date night due to "lack of time." Using the pyramid, I would encourage them to refocus with themselves as the foundation.

This adapted model can be a win-win. The Marriage Hierarchy model is one you can write down on the little card you have in your wallet. This can serve to remind you that your individual personhoods are important, and the two of you are the foundation for your marriage, your family, and your children. As your marriage benefits from keeping your priorities in order, your children are the beneficiaries of Maslow's hierarchy as well. They too are enjoying the sense of security, love, and belonging needed to experience their own self-actualization.

According to a study by the Creighton Center for Marriage and Family, time is one of three problematic issues for couples in the first five years of marriage (the others are sex and money). It may be wise for you to check your priorities monthly about what areas of your lives are getting the most time, money, and energy. Is your marriage receiving at least as much attention as your career, your house, your appearance, and your health? Are outside community activities or children's sporting events consuming all your energy? If so, a refocus on you and your marriage is probably in order. Shut out the world long enough to connect with your spouse and let them know how much you value their presence in your life. Taking that time enriches your marriage and your health. Now there is a win-win!

Steps:

- Value your marriage as your most important investment.

- Take time for each of you to engage in an activity you enjoy.

- Talk every day about the routine goings-on.

- Set time aside for an evening alone at least monthly.

- Connect with friends, alone and as a couple.

- Schedule regular health care for you and your children.

- Have a family calendar and make digital-free family time a priority.

- Watch media together and talk about the issues and values that you are viewing.

WORKS CITED

Amin, Amit. "The Hedonic Treadmill—If Only Happiness Were as Easy as Marriage, a Big House, and Kids." *Imprific.com*. July 1, 2016. https://imprific.com/maintain/hedonic-treadmill.

Cumming, Tim. "Why spending time with the family is more important than ever." *The Telegraph*. June 29, 2018. https://www.telegraph.co.uk/lifestyle/family-time/why-we-need-more-family-time/.

de Marneffe, Daphne. *The Rough Patch*. New York: Scribner, 2018.

"Developmental Assets." *Search Institute*. https://www.search-institute.org/our research/development-assets/.

Orbuch, Terri. *5 Simple Steps to Take Your Marriage From Good to Great*. Austin: River Grove Books, 2009

Sunderland, Margot. *The Science of Parenting: How Today's Brain Research Can Help You Raise Happy, Emotionally Balanced Children*. New York: D.K., July 2016.

CHAPTER 11

Communicating Through Personality and Temperament Differences

"A great marriage is not when the 'perfect couple' comes together. It is when an imperfect couple learns to enjoy their differences."

DAVE MEURER

D o you ever wonder why your spouse reacts a certain way, when your inclination is entirely the opposite? You may jump at a dinner invitation from friends, when your spouse was hoping for a quiet night at home. Often, the reactions are due to differences in personalities and temperaments. To expect any real change in your personalities is unrealistic, and no spouse should count on it. Acknowledging and accepting your partner's basic nature can avoid a lot of friction in an otherwise good marriage.

Personality types were first described by the Greek physician Hippocrates over 2,400 years ago. Over the ensuing years, social scientists have described the various combinations of temperamental traits. In her *Personality Plus for Couples*, lecturer and author Florence Littauer describes the characteristics and the needs of each personality type. The information encourages each of you to seek what you need for yourself—e.g., stimulation, time to think, socialization, activity with a sense of accomplishment—as well as better understanding your spouse's needs.

Most writers on the subject describe four main personality types. Although we all possess some qualities from each category, there is a personality that is dominant for each of us. The names assigned to the four basic types may vary depending on the source. I based my description off Littauer's writing and the Australian Institute of Applied Mindfulness.

- The Sanguine(the Expressive): This temperament is fundamentally an extrovert, impulsive, and fun loving. They are very social, make new friends easily, and tend to be boisterous, while also being sensitive, thoughtful, and compassionate. They can be chronically late, forgetful, and don't always follow through on tasks. This personality type will often be the one who finishes your sentences or gives your punch line! They do not lack confidence.

- The Choleric (the Driver): This temperament is ambitious and displays leadership qualities. They have a take-charge kind of personality which can be intimidating to others. Political and military leaders tend to fall into this category. Interestingly, they can be either very organized or very disorganized, and those extremes can result in mood swings.

- The Phlegmatic (the Amiable): This temperament tends to be relaxed, quiet, and more of a watcher than a doer. They tend to be kind and content with themselves and may seem lazy at times. They often resist change and prefer family stability. Because they are calm, rational, and observant, they tend to be good administrators. They are often passive-aggressive, a characteristic that can make them challenging at times. This can be the easiest personality type to be around because they tend to agree with the prevailing opinions, yet frustrating when they seem to not take a stand.

- The Melancholic (the Analytical): This temperament is more introverted and thoughtful. They are considerate and can be highly creative. They tend to worry about being late and may expand that worry to include the chaos in the world. While self-reliant, they are often perfectionists. Because they focus on a task, they can forget to consider others. They are thinkers, organized, and they like to be right.

Two amiable types, who both choose to avoid conflict, may appear harmonious, but they do not always fare well. The appearance of harmony is often masking a failure to address an issue. Burying emotions can suppress anger that emerges later over an unrelated topic or gets repressed entirely.

With couples who both like to jump into the ring, words can shoot out like venom from a snake startled in the underbrush. They can spout critical insults in the heat of the moment that would better be left unsaid. Making up after a heated argument may seem like fun, but there are things to consider before engaging in such an exercise. Are you someone who will apologize if need be? It is essential in a healthy relationship to admit when you have overstepped your bounds. A contrite apology is needed if you have any hope of making up. If you are a person who tends to run amok with profane words that demean your spouse, you may be inflicting permanent scars that no apology will ever erase.

There are strengths and weaknesses with every type, and one is not better than another. Awareness of the characteristics will allow you to play to each other's strengths. When taken to an extreme, the dominant trait can cause problems for the individual and their relationships. When the Sanguine/Expressive type is excited about trying out the new restaurant in town, the Melancholy/Analytical spouse may respond with, "What, tonight? I haven't read the reviews yet." While spontaneity is not his strong suit, and she is ready to jump at any offering, such a response may frustrate both spouses. Perhaps next time, the expressive could show respect for their differences by giving a day's notice, and the analytic could occasionally acquiesce and be spontaneous. When you are willing to take turns, you might even have a good time! And if you do not know which personality type you are, just ask your spouse. Chances are, they have a pretty good idea!

Many couples make the initial mistake of responding to an invitation before consulting with the other. Hopefully, this happens only once before you realize the better policy would be to say, "Thank you, that sounds lovely. I am not sure if we have plans, so let me check and I will call you back." This type of response can avoid conflict by considering your spouse's feelings.

In her book, *Quiet: The Power of Introverts in a World That Can't Stop Talking*, author Susan Cain offers an insightful look, with extensive research, into the strengths of the introvert. This is the person who sits quietly at a gathering, contributes little to the conversation, but is having a perfectly fine time. This temperament style is often overshadowed by the extrovert who may present as very vocal and confident. Extroverts are no more intelligent than introverts, but they can often sway others to their way of thinking. In a marriage, the extrovert's more dominant style may leave an introverted spouse feeling sidelined. Both partners need to acknowledge the right to have equal say. Learning to respect these differences will be critical to a couple's marital dance.

Patrick and I are both extroverts, which has generally worked well for us but can be exhausting to introverts. We need to be conscious not to dominate conversations with others who are quieter. A gentle nudge under the table is often the loving reminder to reign it in! When telling stories, we need to cue each other with a glance to share the stage and remember to not interrupt the other. This is an ongoing dance for us!

In addition to personality and temperament, disagreements can occur over cultural attitudes, religious beliefs, political views, and different perspectives that are fraught with emotions. The wise couple will learn how to dance gingerly over sensitive ground. The goal is to use differences to enrich your union, not destroy it, by improving your communication skills.

Dr. Gottman, the famed researcher on marital conflict, writes about the communication blockers that he refers to as "The Four Horsemen of the Apocalypse:" criticism (blaming the person rather than the behavior), contempt (psychological abuse with words and tone of voice), defensiveness (playing the victim to protect yourself, not listening), and stonewalling (removing yourself with stony silence).

These are behaviors that you want to avoid when addressing inevitable disagreements. They are unhealthy and will result in resentment, the slow growing virus destructive to a marriage. As Nelson Mandela aptly described, "Resentment is like drinking poison and then hoping it will kill your enemies."

Dr. Gottman's research confirms that there will be some differences that will never be resolved. He writes: "All marriages experience a certain number of perpetual conflicts—differences that don't go away, no matter what . . . The goal is to live with them in ways that allow understanding, dialogue, and compromise." Couples in strong marriages know that one party cannot always dominate, and compromise is a key factor. Discussions when emotions are at their peak usually do not end well. If you ignore talking later, you can pretty much guarantee it will come up during the next argument, even when the conflict is over a different subject. Mastering this skill is an ongoing exercise for us.

Patrick and I have a lot of similarities that we can take no credit for. They just are. This has minimized disagreements in the major areas of marital friction. Our arguments usually revolve around the frustrations of daily life: my being late, his not helping enough in the house etc. When arguing over one of these issues, I want to stick with it until it is resolved or until I have said everything I want to say, even when emotions are escalating. When Patrick, on the other hand, is angry, he prefers to walk away and then forget it. Neither of these is a healthy approach. I need to allow time to cool off and get some perspective. Patrick needs to be willing to talk about it later. While the issue may not have a resolution, the *feelings* around it deserve attention to avoid future resentment. The critical issue is that we each feel respected about how things were handled.

The basic principles for dealing with conflict are easier to learn than they are to apply. Practicing healthy communication is a good place to start. In her article, "How to Improve Your Relationships with Effective Communication Skills," Elizabeth Scott, author and wellness coach, writes about the importance of focusing on the issue at hand and "own what's yours." Admitting when you are wrong can open communication and the opportunity for compromise. When you have calmed down, set aside a time to talk that is agreeable to both of you, and shut off technology (that includes cell phones, computers, iPads, television, video games, and radio!). Avoid finger-pointing and "you" messages. Rather, try for direct statements:

- "I was upset last night because I thought or expected…."

- "I felt (disrespected, angry, hurt, etc.) because…."

- "Next time, could we try to…"

Keeping the dialogue in the first person ("I" not "You") prevents your spouse from becoming defensive. Defensiveness tends to interfere with listening and escalates arguments. Many discussions focus on facts, not feelings. Frame your conversation in the context of how you feel. Feelings are not right or wrong. They are not good or bad. They are personal, and they are real. You may not understand why your mate feels the way they do, but that really is irrelevant. Your spouse feels how they feel. Listen, respect those feelings, and try to see the issue from your partner's perspective. Respect will always trump understanding.

The phrase "next time." is hopeful as it indicates things can be different in the future. If you find yourself arguing about the same matter repeatedly, you are not getting at the heart of the issue. Talking about possible solutions means that the next time the topic comes up you will have some alternate ways of handling it.

With communication, it is important to remember the role body language and tone of voice play in the message you are delivering. While words are important, they account for only seven percent of your message. Tone of voice (e.g., angry, condescending) is responsible for 38 percent, and 55 percent is conveyed by your body language (e.g., posture, eye contact, facial expression). These are factors to remember when verbally communicating. Even though words are considered a small percentage of communication, I also learned how effective they are in certain situations.

I had the opportunity to interview a woman who shared how she and her husband addressed difficult topics using only words. Alicia was introduced to her husband Hanzel 67 years ago by his aunt, who on meeting her, thought they would be a good match. However, it was impossible for them to meet in person as Alicia was living in Jamaica and Hanzel was in New York City. Back then, a long-distance call was very expensive, so their introduction and communication had to happen via letters. Alicia shared with me what an advantage that correspondence was in strengthening their relationship.

For 18 months, they continuously wrote back and forth to get to know each other. Alicia related that when a difficult topic needed to be addressed, she found it helpful to write what she wanted to say. She would then reread her letter and scratch out, erase, and rewrite her words to say what she wanted without sounding angry or critical, knowing such words would interfere with her message. After that year and a half of constant correspondence Hanzel, 34, flew to meet Alicia, 24, in Jamaica. They married six days later! Hanzel is now 99, and Alicia is 89. They raised their five children, all college graduates, and they still live independently in their home. Alicia's experience about written communication may have happened serendipitously, but the wisdom is one that could be incorporated into any couple's toolbox.

Learning to address conflict will be one of the more critical steps you master. You want differences to enhance your union, not destroy it. As you learn to appreciate each other's personality traits, you can go to your spouse's strengths, allowing for a smoother dance. Learning these skills is not easy, but like any habit, it becomes easier with practice. The results are a lot less stepping on toes.

Steps:

- Know the strengths and weaknesses of your own personality.

- Focus on your spouse's strengths.

- Avoid the extremes of each type: being too domineering, too talkative, etc.

- Discuss plans with your partner before making a commitment.

- Compromise on your different preferences.

- Allow for space when emotions are high; talk when emotions calm down.

- Consider writing to organize your thoughts and feelings.

- Shut off ALL electronics while you are talking and maintain eye contact.

- Speak in the first person, state your feelings, and say what you need.

- Be willing to listen without forming a rebuttal.

- Try to see things from your spouse's perspective.

- Clarify what you think your spouse is saying until it is clear.

- Make sure you each feel listened to and respected on how the issue was handled.

WORKS CITED

Cain, Susan. *Quiet: The Power of Introverts in a World That Can't Stop Talking.* Clive, Iowa: Turtleback Books, January 2013.

Gottman, John M., Julie Schwartz Gottman, and Joan DeClaire. *10 Lessons to Transform Your Marriage: America's Love Lab Experts Share Their Strategies for Strengthening Your Relationship.* Crown Publishers, New York, 2006.

Gottman, John, and Nan Silver. *Why Marriages Succeed or Fail: And How You Can Make Yours Last.* Simon and Schuster, New York, NY, 1994.

"Hippocrates 4 Temperaments." *Australian Institute of Applied Mindfulness.* http://www.theaiam.com.au/wp-content/uploads/2016/09/Hippocrates-4-Temperaments-Digital-Copy.pdf

Littauer, Florence. *Personality Plus for Couples.* Grand Rapids: Revell, 1983, 2001.

Scott, Elizabeth. "How to Improve Your Relationship with Effective Communication Skills." *Verywell Mind.* May 4, 2019. https://www.verywellmind.com/managing-conflict-in-relationships-communication-tips-3144967.

CHAPTER 12

Handling Parents and In-Laws with Care

"It is only complicated when you make it complicated."

UNKNOWN

Among the top stressors in a marriage are in-laws. Unlike other contentious areas of your relationship, this one involves third and fourth parties (sometimes more depending on parental remarriages). These are the ones who, for better or worse, have had the most impact on you and your spouse's lives. Conflict over in-laws has contributed to many unions ending in divorce. Despite the legendary jokes about husbands and mothers-in-law, it is the wife/mother-in-law dyad that is known for the most tension. Prevention calls for some ground rules.

In an article in the *Telegraph*, Tarinth Carey reports that "six out of 10 married women find their relationship with their mothers-in-laws a strain, according to Cambridge University research." Carey also notes "After all, it's a bond that brings women with different values and upbringings together with the expectation they should agree on what it means to be a wife and mother."

The time spent with both of your families during your dating days should have provided you with some insight of possible problem areas. Some couples minimize concerns thinking that, after marriage, things will get better. Later, many couples admit this was foolish thinking. Even if you do not live geographically close to your in-laws, their influence will be felt by you and your spouse and can affect your marriage. Living at a distance can minimize the drop-in factor, but it does not prevent the sometimes longer-than-wanted visits, telephone calls with unsolicited advice and opinions, or guilt-ridden demands. Without straightforward discussions and setting boundaries early, you are creating a fertile ground for fireworks.

When we first began speaking with engaged couples, they were in their early 20s, often leaving their parents' home to marry. Today's couples are in their late 20s or early 30s, having lived on their own for several years before marrying. This is a good thing. You are more likely to have defined your independence, and you now have the freedom to decide what you want for your married life. The sooner you establish boundaries as a couple, the less conflict will occur between the two of you and your parents and in-laws. This is especially important if one or both of you were living with parents prior to marriage. Breaking the ties may be emotional for your parents but this should be done with respect and without ambivalence.

Fortunately for me, Patrick was supportive and assertive when it came to issues that arose with his mother. We were married for 31 years before we lost my mother-in-law, when she was 88. During those years, there were several occasions that had the potential to result in major confrontations. Among the reasons that she and I did not experience more conflicts could be attributed to the fact that we lived 135 miles apart. Not having regular contact meant that visits were less frequent and more special. There is no doubt, however, that Patrick gets the major credit for smooth sailing in the in-law department. He always stepped in.

I did not doubt my mother-in-law's love and appreciation for me, but her way of addressing situations when they did not match her standards was startlingly direct, softened only by her disarming brogue. Sometimes her comments were so cleverly phrased they could slide over my head, before slamming me on the backside! Like the time she and my father-in-law were on a road trip with friends and called to ask if they could stop by. She wanted to see the grandchildren and show her friends our home. I never hesitated to welcome them and assured her that it was fine to come by. We did the usual quick pick up, but with short notice, three little ones running around, plus a nursing baby, the house was not ready for a white-glove inspection like her house would have been.

My mother-in-law epitomized the spotless homemaker. On my best day, I am a casual. I even had a poem on my fridge titled "Babies Don't Keep" by Ruth Hulburt Hamilton where the last two lines read,

"I'm rocking my baby. Babies don't keep." I loved that poem because it was my philosophy for priorities right out there for all the world to see. As she toured her friend around the house, my mother-in-law stopped at the fridge, smiled at her friend, and pointed at the poem. She quietly commented, "That's why," as if justifying the state of the house. Patrick caught it and responded with, "Yes, it is, and that is just fine with us."

Patrick would call his mother to task when she made any comment that might be construed as insulting to me, us, or the household. Whenever she made a remark that could be viewed as demeaning, he respectfully, but firmly, challenged her on the spot. I felt so supported that I could move past her criticism and enjoy her many redeeming and loving qualities. After all, I only needed to remind myself that she did raise a son who is a good and loving husband, and I thanked her for that on many occasions. What better accolade can a mother receive?

Patrick provides an important lesson for married couples. Your first responsibility is to your spouse. While it is important to be loving and respectful to one's parents, it is essential to be loyal to each other first. When issues arise, or comments are made, that are critical or undermining of your mate, you must lovingly, but firmly, intervene. Doing this early on can prevent hurt and discord and set a supportive tone for your marriage. Otherwise, you risk having a relationship that is constantly under barrage.

It is easy to get caught off guard by well-meaning in-laws if you are not prepared. Patrick, for example, was familiar with his mother's positive, assuming statements! One tactic that has worked for many couples is to not commit to any plans before you consult with one another. If your mother should catch you as you leave her house in October and say, "So we will see you for Thanksgiving, right?" best not say, "Sure Mom," or it will be an eventful ride home! A better response would be, "Oh, thanks for the invite, Mom. We haven't had a chance to talk about the holidays yet, but we'll get back to you next week." She will likely be taken aback, perhaps a bit hurt, but she will get the message that you have other considerations now that you are married, and you will have set a healthy boundary.

Your spouse is the person you are sharing your life with now and with whom you are building a family. In the natural course of life, you and your spouse will probably outlive your in-laws. If you allow cracks that leave your partner feeling hurt and inadequate, you, in the end, will be the victim of your mate's destroyed self-esteem. Stick up for each other. Your loyalty will reap huge benefits and keep your dance much smoother.

Steps:

- Do not allow a parent to criticize or demean your spouse.

- Politely, but firmly correct your parent.

- Do not commit to any plans without first discussing with each other.

- Compliment your spouse in front of your parents.

- Talk openly if you felt unsupported and how to improve things next time.

WORKS CITED

Carey, Tarinth. "The relationship between women and their mothers-in-law is often fraught, but it needn't be impossible." *The Telegraph*. January 27, 2018 https://www.telegraph.co.uk/family/relationships/relationship-women-theirmothers-in-law-often-fraught-itneednt/.

"Song for a Fifth Child (Babies Don't Keep) by Ruth Hulburt Hamilton" http://www.lullaby-link.com/song-for-a-fifth-child.html.

CHAPTER 13

Examining the Role of Religion and Spirituality in Your Marriage

"We are not human beings having a spiritual experience. We are spiritual beings having a human experience."

PIERRE TEILHARD DE CHARDIN

When Patrick and I were first asked to speak with engaged couples about spirituality in marriage, I gave a lot of thought to making this important subject meaningful and relevant to their day-to-day relationships. I figured they were expecting us to tell them how critical it is to go to weekly services and become involved with their church. As a Catholic, my religion has always been part of my life, as it has been for Patrick also. My faith is a deeply held belief in God that continues to sustain me through difficult times. Spirituality for me, however, is a broader belief that encompasses day-to-day interactions and is often more challenging. While I feel both religion and faith are important and do strengthen a marriage, I wanted to draw a distinction between the practice of religion and the practice of spirituality in their daily lives. Spirituality is not that simple. In fact, I tell them that when I am finished speaking, they would realize that going to church is the easy part! Yes, we do go to weekly Mass, and we have found it beneficial to our marriage and raising a family, but that is only the religious aspect. Incorporating true spirituality into a marriage is far more difficult.

Let's start with the role of religion. The participation in a weekly service represents the institutional facet of your spiritual life. If you chose to be married in a church service, you have already infused a religious aspect into your relationship. In the past, differences in religion have been among the top reasons for divorce. Some religions strongly discourage, if not forbid, marrying outside one's own faith. This practice has lessened over the past generation as interfaith marriages are more common. As society has grown more accepting of diversity, religion is less apt to derail a marriage when the spouse's beliefs and means of worship are respected and supported.

Using research from the Pew Research Center and other studies, Jennifer Betts reports that divorce rates vary by religion and can even vary within the same religion. According to the Pew Research Center, Catholics had one of the lowest divorce rates compared to other faiths. However, according to a study by the Gospel Coalition, there is a difference between those who are practicing Catholics (31 percent less likely to divorce) and nominal Catholics (5 percent less likely to divorce).

Patrick tells the engaged couples that those statistics do not surprise him. He relates his feelings about some Sundays, when we were in the throes of kids, careers, and trying to keep love alive where getting four children looking presentable and on time for church wore thin on his patience. He tells the couples it was like herding kittens, and I was often the one running late (likely finding the lost shoe or wiping a dirty face!) By the time we settled in the pew, he was not speaking to me. He goes on to describe how he managed to use two of the kids as a buffer. When the time came for the "Our Father," we are supposed to hold hands. That is followed by the "dreaded kiss of peace," as he called it. Patrick admits feeling obligated to do something, since everyone is looking. He asks the couples "Do you know you can brush someone's cheek so lightly that they don't even know they've been kissed?" He continues, "Then she squeezes my hand and I smile. I am so mad that I smiled because I just wanted to stay angry. Sometimes, it's the reading or the homily that seems directed at me, 'Hey, you in the blue jacket, you have been behaving like a jerk. Shape up.' And it's over. If I hadn't gone to church, I would have carried on all day."

Of course, Patrick is not the only one who feels grace. That very grace is likely what has me squeeze his hand when I am not inclined. But it lets the healing begin. After you have communicated your feelings, and feel you have been heard and respected, forgiveness allows you to move on. If you find yourselves repeatedly dealing with the same issues, it means that you are holding onto resentment rather than forgiveness. Patience and forgiveness are the essence of spirituality for which all married couples should strive. When there are disagreements, can you admit when you are wrong? Do you have the courage to say you are sorry with a sincere apology, not followed by a "but"? Will you grant your spouse forgiveness when you have been wronged? These are true demonstrations of spirituality in your daily life.

One of the hallmarks of a strong marriage is that you take God on as a partner. On the back of the card where I had the couples list their qualities describing a good marriage, I have them draw two triangles: one for the Marriage Hierarchy and the other for their spiritual growth. I ask them to label themselves on the corner bases and then write God on the top.

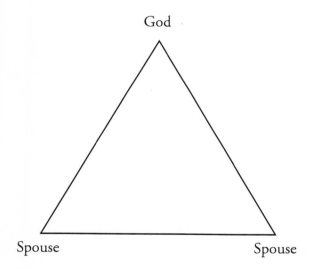

This Spiritual Triangle serves to support your personal relationship with God. This relationship is described in the article "Sex in Marriage: Ecstasy or Agony?" Let this model serve as a reminder that, as you each strive for a closer connection to God, you will be drawn closer together as a couple. As you each experience spiritual growth, you will discover a different intimacy in your union. In 2013, the *Journal of Family Issues* included a study based on data from 342 married couples and "results indicate that one's individual relationship with God is important to marital quality indirectly as it appears to manifest itself in religious communication between partners, which in turn is directly linked to marital quality." The study also stated that "joint religious communication is more strongly associated with marital satisfaction among mixed-faith couples than same-faith couples."

On the Institute for Family Studies' website, Tyler J. VanderWeele summarizes a study he conducted, which "links religious service attendance to a number of better health outcomes, including longer life, lower incidence of depression, and less suicide." The study "also indicates that religious service attendance is associated with greater marital stability—or more specifically, with a lower likelihood of divorce." It goes on to say, "those who attended religious services were 47 percent less likely to subsequently divorce." If not able to guarantee marital happiness, attending a religious service can at least provide the opportunity to work at improving your relationship. Why have a mediocre marriage when you could strengthen it with more spiritual and emotional intimacy?

For couples who practice different religions, sharing services occasionally can enrich their union and allow their children to appreciate different practices and traditions. Friends of ours have integrated their Judeo-Christian practices into their 40-year marriage by celebrating Hanukkah along with Christmas festivities.

In contrast to religion, spirituality is more than a perfunctory attendance at a weekly service or joining a Bible study group. It is what comprises the other 166 hours in a week. Spirituality is more concerned with the human spirit or soul. It is the life, energy, and enthusiasm you infuse into all your relationships. You can experience spirituality when caring for each other and when communing with God's gifts in nature. Patrick feels skiing through fresh powder is a spiritual experience for him. Mine is found kayaking on Squam Lake. Such spiritual events can make your marriage come alive.

Enthusiasm comes from the Greek word *enthous*, meaning "possessed by a god, inspired." Are you demonstrating that in your marriage? Does your spouse feel better when they are in your company? Is your glass half full or half empty? Someone who saps energy is difficult to be around. High maintenance people are always looking for others to pump them up. Being married to someone like this gets old very fast.

Do you take responsibility for your disposition and attitude? To expect your spouse to compensate for your moods is placing an undue stress on your marriage. Integrating spirituality into your life is likely to pose more of a challenge than religion. How do you incorporate a spiritual quality into your marriage? The way you care for yourself and how you allow your spouse to care for their self is the spiritual essence of your marriage.

Controlling behavior, jealousy, criticism of your spouse, and discouraging their personal growth is in direct opposition to spirituality. When Richard Chartres, the Bishop of London at the time, performed the marriage for Prince William and Kate Middleton in 2011, he gave a homily in which he stated that "It is possible to transform so long as we do not harbor ambitions to reform our partners. There must be no coercion if the Spirit is to flow, each must give the other space and freedom." This beautifully describes the growth that can occur in your marriage when you take responsibility for your own spiritual growth and support your spouse to do the same. *Spirituality is not something you do. It is something you are,* to each other and the world with which you connect.

I am reminded of a brief exchange I witnessed when we had friends over for dinner. As they were getting ready to leave, my friend said, "Oh, Susan, I have something for you in the car." She turned to her husband and said "Tommy, would you please go out to the car?" She had barely finished her request when he responded, "Sure" and headed out the door. Now there is a four-letter word that can make a marriage! How do you respond to a spousal request? Is it after a deep sigh, a "Just a minute," or "Yeah, when I am done with this?" These responses are all communicated with a less than an enthusiastic tone which erases any goodwill about the action you are likely to do anyway. And let's be honest, you lose all hope of scoring any points for a nice gesture!

At times of frustration with your partner, try to focus on why you married them. Give your spouse something to live up to with positive expectations and encouragement. Expressing gratitude in your life has an amazing effect on a person. Counting your blessings and minimizing your frustrations are daily expressions of spirituality. Showing respect for your spouse and their feelings, even when you do not understand them, is the essence of love.

Remember, in my opening comments I said that going to church would be simple. While attending a religious service can add an important dimension to your marriage, it is the situations that you encounter every day where the true spirituality of your life is found: how you greet each other in the morning, or doing a chore without being asked. The opportunities are not be found in grandiose moments. They are found in the mundane. Seek them out.

Steps:

- Be forthright about your religious beliefs and practices.

- Listen and respect your spouse's beliefs and how they choose to practice.

- Strive for a personal connection to God.

- Practice kindness, patience, and forgiveness.

- Address any destructive issues of control, jealousy, and criticism.

- Show appreciation and gratitude to your spouse every day.

WORKS CITED

Betts, Jennifer. "Divorce Statistics by Religion," *lovetoknow.com*. https://divorce.lovetoknow.com/Divorce_Statistics_by_Religion.

Chartres, Richard. "Bishop of London's Amazing Speech to William and Kate." April 30, 2011. Video, 7:25. https://www.youtube.com/watch?v=11vh-zWt9h8&feature=youtube.

Christian Family Life. "Sex in Marriage: Ecstasy or Agony?" *Christian Family Life*. July 18, 2018. https://www.christianfamilylife.com/sex-in-marriage-ecstasy-or-agony.

"Enthusiasm." https://www.vocabulary.com/dictionary/enthusiasm.

Praha, David, Laura Stafford. "A Relational Approach to Religion and Spirituality in Marriage." *Journal of Family Issues*. April 24, 2013. https://doi.org/10.1177/0192513X13485922.

Sharon, Jeremy. "Divorce rates continue to rise." *The Jerusalem Post.* June 20, 2017. https://www.jpost.com/Israel-News/Divorce-rates-continue-slow-rise-say-Rabbinical-Courts statistics-497352.

VanderWeele, Tyler J. "Religious Service Attendance, Marriage, and Health." *Institute for Family Studies.* November 29, 2016. https://ifstudies.org/blog/religious-service-attendance-marriage-and-health.

CHAPTER 14

Preventing Contamination

"You can't always control your circumstances, but you can control how you react to them"

UNKNOWN

I arrived home from work one afternoon irritated with a co-worker. Not only did I feel crabby, but my face reflected my mood. Patrick picked up my vibes, but without asking what happened, he assumed that he was responsible for my bad mood. Even though it was not true, I was irritated at his reaction. Instead of telling him what was on my mind, I stewed in silence. Because of an incident that had nothing to do with him, and which I chose not to share, I lost the benefit of a supportive spouse. My lack of self-reflection and Patrick's assumption he was the cause resulted in both of us missing out on what should have been a pleasant evening.

In psychology, this behavior is an example of "misplaced anger." I call it "contaminating" and define it as allowing one dirty area to mess up another that could have, and should have, remained clean. It can happen in a marriage when you expect your partner to absorb your frustrations without taking responsibility for your own emotions. Such behavior is unfair, results in hurt feelings, and deprives your relationship of joy. It is *not the circumstances, but rather how you react* that will determine the atmosphere in your marriage.

When working with engaged couples, I encourage them to try this experiment to avoid the scene I just described. It will likely upset a night of your life, but if it saves a thousand others, it will be worth it. The next time you come home from work, greet your spouse with a grunt, no smile, no hello, just a "humph." Do not ask about your partner's day, just drop down behind the newspaper or grab the remote control and cocoon yourself. See how the rest of your evening goes.

A few nights later, regardless of the kind of day you have had, walk in from work with a smile (it changes the tone of your voice) and greet your spouse by name and a gentle hug. Offer to fix a cup of tea or pour a glass of wine. Turn on some relaxing music. Ask your spouse about their day, listen with interest, and have eye contact. Offer to set the table or start dinner. See how your evening goes. What made the difference? You did!

Realizing how your actions and attitude set the tone for your marriage every day will have a profound effect over your years together. One tool that can be useful in preventing contamination is compartmentalization. In his *Psychology Today* article, "Putting Your Feelings Where They Belong," Dr. Barton Goldsmith writes, "Compartmentalization is not about being in denial; it's about putting things where they belong and not letting them get in the way of the rest of your life. You can't just ignore your issues and expect them to go away but obsessing on them won't help either." Learning to compartmentalize and set priorities can help you manage your reactions to situations. This skill may come more naturally to some, but it can also be learned.

In her book, *Becoming*, Michelle Obama writes that her husband "who's always been good at compartmentalizing, managed to be admirably present when he was with us . . . Fences needed to go up; boundaries required protecting. Bin Laden was not invited to dinner." Now, there is a dramatic example of compartmentalizing. Talk about having the weight of the world on your shoulders!

In her article, "How to Compartmentalize Emotional Problems for Peace of Mind," Dr. Audrey Sherman discusses the advantages of compartmentalizing our emotional issues to make them easier to work with. She writes: "Think of the paperwork you deal with routinely. It is a lot easier to deal with when it is organized and filed properly than when it is all over the place." She goes on to describe how you can categorize the issues in your life into compartments and go in there to deal with them and then re-file them until you need to address them again. Some compartments may have a quick resolution, others may be more chronic, like financial concerns or raising children, and require repeated visits. You can decide, however, to take some action and then retreat from that compartment until it again requires your attention.

Have you ever seen mailroom letter boxes? They are rows of slots where the postmaster places letters to be picked up by the addressee. This sorting system is how my brain works at compartmentalizing the various aspects of my life. The many different boxes are mentally labeled: faith, health, marriage, children, grandchildren, parents, siblings, finances, education, job, colleagues, friends, neighbors, community, home, etc. There are separate boxes for each of the people and issues in my life. How I react and manage each of these compartments will affect my marriage. I try to be deliberate in not letting a troublesome area contaminate an otherwise good one.

Prior to writing this chapter, I was not aware that compartmentalizing was the subject of research. I had found it to be a helpful tool in dealing with stressful issues, and all along I thought I adopted it from my mother! She possessed a remarkable ability to prioritize what situations were worth getting upset over. One Christmas afternoon, when her house was filled with her five adult children, their spouses, and nine young grandchildren, my mother noticed water dripping through the kitchen light fixture. This had happened before, requiring a ceiling repair, so she was familiar with the cause. When she noticed the drops falling on the kitchen table as she was preparing dinner, she calmly commented, "Oh, would someone go upstairs and check on the kids? They must have overrun the sink again." She then instructed my brother to get the wet/dry vac from the basement and clean it up. Sure enough, two little cousins were found bathing their new dolls. Everything was cleaned up and dinner proceeded as planned, my mother unrattled. How did she carry on in such a matter-of-fact way? What she shared with me became a useful tool.

Since she lost her father at a young age, my mother went to work after high school. By her early 30s, she was working full time and living at home with her mother and sister. On an otherwise typical morning, she went to say goodbye before leaving for work and found her 58-year-old mother dead in bed from a stroke. My mother would often say, "That was something worth being upset about," adding, "It was then I realized most other things in life are not." That traumatic event seemed to be the measuring stick she used to decide if something was serious. The way she related that experience had a profound impact on me. Perspective, a healthy attribute for marriage and parenting, is one that can help compartmentalize issues and prevent relatively minor frustrations (a leaky ceiling) from contaminating an event that should be enjoyed (a family Christmas gathering.)

As a woman, I have multiple roles, wearing numerous hats in many areas of my life, as do most adults. There are issues in all these areas at various times. Fortunately, they usually do not all demand attention simultaneously. I have noticed, however, there is the danger of one compartment contaminating another one if I am not aware of boundaries.

When someone asks me how I am, I usually reply, "Terrific," which is fortunately how I feel most of the time. To people with whom I have an intimate friendship, I may respond, "Which compartment are you asking about?" Blessings though they may be, some compartments are challenging and require more attention and energy. The degree of personal investment will vary; a daughter who needs my help recovering from surgery or a broken refrigerator in July. I can choose to give the refrigerator only the time needed to replace it and focus my resources on my daughter. They both require attention, but the investment of my energy will be different. Awareness, setting priorities, and action are key to prevent contaminating the blessings in life.

The ability to go into the individual compartments can allow you to look at the situation in an objective way. In order not to contaminate the good areas of your life with chronic discussion and worry, you need to practice compartmentalization. Decide what steps are needed, seek the appropriate expertise, pray on it, do what needs to be done, and then put it away until other action is needed.

When Patrick and I leave to go out for the evening or an overnight getaway, we join hands in the car and state those compartments we are worried about and then say a prayer. Knowing there is nothing else we can do about it at that time, we free ourselves up to enjoy the respite. We talk about hopeful things, events to look forward to, with the anticipation of better days. This allows us time to breathe. It does not mean that we were in denial or not concerned, but this strategy lets us put the issue to bed, at least for a while. We will address tough issues during the week at teatime or as needed.

Within the compartments of your life, there are external forces and dynamics that can disrupt and raise conflict in your marriage. When you are aware of these influences, you can control the degree to which you allow them to negatively affect your relationship. Sadly, these may be individuals whom you love and are strongly connected to, like family members or old friends. Now, as a married couple, you may notice they are not an asset to your relationship. Perhaps they are high-maintenance people who always seem to bring drama, and nothing is ever quite right with them. Maybe it is a couple that bickers or often criticizes each other. When you are alone with them, they talk about the flaws in their mate. Over time, you may find yourself focusing on your mate's shortcomings. This negativity is as much a virus as the flu. The vaccine is avoidance. Protecting your marriage will require curtailing the time and intimate conversations you have with them. Because you may feel obligated to see certain people occasionally, like old friends or family members, set up activities like going to a play, concert, or movie. This shows an effort on your part to stay connected, but it minimizes the negative effects on your evening and on your marriage.

Tiya Cunningham-Sumter, certified life and relationship coach, warns about the people to avoid if you want to strengthen your relationship in her article, "BEWARE: 5 Bad Influences on Your Marriage." Cunningham-Sumter writes: "Negativity can be contagious. Couples must strategically surround themselves with those ready, willing and able to encourage us in our marriage." Patrick and I have found this to be true and have heeded this advice in our own marriage.

Frustrations with your spouse are inevitable but watch with whom you talk. Discussing personal issues about your partner with friends and co-workers is what I refer to as "emotional infidelity." Complaining about your spouse to others is destructive to the intimacy of a marriage. Doing the opposite, saying nice things about your spouse and complimenting them in front of others, goes a long way to foster loving feelings.

I have been taken aback when a relative stranger, like a bank teller or a store clerk whose business we frequent, will say, "Oh, your husband always talks so nicely about you. You are so lucky. Most husbands don't do that." That gesture has encouraged me to overlook petty aggravations and be grateful for the kindness Patrick has expressed about me to others. It has also served as a reminder to me to do the same. Simple? Yes, but some things seem so simple, we forget their importance.

On Valentine's Day several years ago, we were having a quiet dinner at home when Patrick commented on how blessed we were to know so many happily married couples. Then, he proposed the idea of kicking spring off with a dinner party at our home with other couples to celebrate our marriages. Seven couples happily responded. That first year, each person talked about when they met their spouse and how they knew this person was the one. The next year, the topic was their most special meal. Subsequent gatherings included the most memorable getaway and what qualities about their spouse helped them survive difficult periods in their marriage. Couples were encouraged not to talk to each other about their answers before the evening, so it became an added surprise for each of us to learn what most impressed our spouse. There were lots of laughs and surprises, kind of like "The Newlywed Game" but with a positive twist! The eight years we hosted these dinners were empowering to all our marriages. The gatherings have now evolved into retirement and special birthday parties, events that continue to enrich our lives.

Celebrating the blessings in your life is a deliberate way of compartmentalizing. There will be difficult circumstances during your marriage that will tax both your physical and emotional reserves. You, however, do not have to *live* in those compartments *all* the time. Doing what needs to be done about challenging issues, then focusing on your blessings, can bring respite and renewed energy. The Serenity Prayer serves as a useful reminder to act on what you can control and to take solace on what you cannot: "*God grant me the serenity to accept the things I cannot change, courage to change the things I can, and wisdom to know the difference.*"

You each have the power to establish the atmosphere in your home and improve even the mundane days of your life. As a result, ordinary days can become extraordinary.

Steps:

- Debrief together about the highs and lows of your day.

- Practice compartmentalizing so as not to contaminate your many blessings.

- Let your time alone revitalize you both by having positive, forward-looking talk.

- Socialize with couples who respect marriage and its commitment.

- Avoid unhappy couples and those who seem jealous of your happiness.

- Do not talk with others about your spouse's shortcomings or aggravations

- Say something nice about your spouse in front of others. Nothing says "I love you" like a public compliment!

WORKS CITED

Cunningham, Ty. "BEWARE: 5 Bad Influences on Your Marriage." *Black and Married with Kids.* May 28, 2014. https://blackandmarriedwithkids.com/beware-5-bad-influences-on-your-marriage/.

Goldsmith, Barton. "Putting Your Feelings Where They Belong." *Psychology Today.* Sept. 8, 2015. https://www.psychologytoday.com/us/blog/emotional-fitness/201509/putting-your-feelings-where-they-belong.

Obama, Michelle. *Becoming.* New York: Crown Publishing, 2018

Sherman, Audrey. "How to Compartmentalize Emotional Problems for Peace of Mind." April 17, 2017. *Dysfunction Interrupted.* https://blogs.psychcentral.com/dysfunction/2017/04/how-to-compartmentalize-emotional-problems-for-peace-of-mind

CHAPTER 15

Attending to Finances

"The most powerful advantage of money: The ability to think of things besides money."

TARA WESTOVER

There are many issues that result in marital stress, but conflict over finances ranks as the number one. Financial issues can drain the life out of an otherwise healthy marriage. When the other areas of your life are in good order, it is unfortunate to have your relationship negatively impacted by money.

How a couple views and manages money is the cause of much marital discord. Even couples with high incomes report significant disagreements about how money is handled. If one of you is a spender and the other is a saver, there can be continuous conflicts. Coming to some compromise is essential. Early in your marriage, you will likely determine that one of you is better at finances and managing the budget. The other, however, should always be aware of household finances and know how to pay the bills. This approach is a practical one. Should the primary money manager have to be away, become ill, or die, the spouse's financial ignorance will compound the stress.

If one of you is paying the bills and the other is disregarding the budget, there will be financial friction. You both need to decide how best to prevent this conflict. Should your money go into one joint account? Or do you want a joint account for household expenses and your larger goals and have separate accounts for your own purchases and hobbies? These decisions are important and can lessen financial disagreements.

Housing expenses, credit card debt, educational loans, and the cost of raising a family need to be balanced against household income. Trust is important in all areas of marriage and is critical when it comes to money. Withholding information, especially regarding debt, will affect not only your financial plans but the trust that is essential to your partnership.

At least monthly, you need to discuss finances so you both know where the accounts stand: how much debt you have, how the repayment of education loans and credit cards is coming along, what is being saved, what charities you are supporting, and how the plans for your next major goal are evolving. Are the expected big bills planned for, and are routine bills being paid on time? The latter will determine your credit rating. A low score will affect the interest you are paying on your credit cards and will determine if you are able to secure a personal loan, a home mortgage, and may even be the deciding factor for a job. If one of you has a high credit score and the other a low one, do not combine your accounts as your score will drop to the lower rating.

Scheduling a 15–30-minute financial chat each month, can help you stay on top of your financial plans. In an article titled "Financial Ties That Bind: A Money Checklist for Newlyweds," Sam Schultz, co-founder of the Honeyfi app, advises "'If you're having trouble starting the conversation about money, try talking about three-to-five financial goals for the next few years.'" In another article, Schutz explains: "'Whether you like it or not, money will affect your relationship a lot . . . 'It's a leading cause of divorce, and it's one of the biggest stressors on a relationship.'"

A paradigm shift has occurred with two working parents or with dads at home raising the children because the wife has a stronger earning potential. These are common situations, yet they often leave a couple in a quandary over what is the best financial plan for their marriage and family. Money is often as much an emotional issue as it is a financial one, and the feelings of each partner are an important aspect of the discussion. Early and ongoing dialogue about earning potential, individual salaries, and household income is critical.

Data from a study at the University of Bath, which included over 6,000 American heterosexual couples, indicated that "husbands are least stressed when their wives earn up to 40 percent of household income . . . and are most stressed when they are entirely economically dependent on their partner." Study author Dr. Joanna Syrda noted "that husbands did not suffer psychological distress about their wives' income if their wife was the higher earner before marriage and the existing and potential income gap was clear to them."

This discrepancy in earning can result in a husband feeling a sense of inadequacy that can lead to resentment, if not acknowledged and discussed. If the higher earner has a *generous* attitude, literally and figuratively, and the lower earner feels confident about the role that they play in the household, this issue need not be contentious. Open, frequent communication about roles, decision-making, and emotions about money need to be front and center.

The single biggest stress we faced in our marriage involved finances. Although we faced challenges with personal health and raising four adolescents, financial problems were different. Other stresses seemed easier to accept because they felt out of our control. Money, however, was something we felt we should have in order. Hence, if finances were not in good shape, it felt like a personal failure.

Patrick and I did not live extravagantly, and neither of us were big spenders. We were married for four years before having children. That gave us time to establish our financial goals and work toward them. We went to grad school, traveled, and had no debt. We were proud of our financial life. We basically lived on one salary and saved for a house. Four months after having a daughter, we purchased our first home. I had planned to stay home for three months before returning to work full-time but found I liked being with the baby. I also wanted to stay active with my profession. How could I do both?

Patrick and I agreed that my role at home was important. His income as a teacher presented a challenge. Patrick contemplated other work, but we both knew education was his passion, and he was excellent with his special-needs students. To have a partner who is happy in their career is an important factor in a satisfying partnership. Work consumes too many hours to spend them at a job that makes you miserable. Once we determined that he would continue in his teaching career, we needed to consider other options.

Things became especially critical when the teachers went on strike. Ironically, that same week we were speaking at the Engaged Couples Program. Another leader couple brought up the topic of the strike and asked if we were interested in additional income. They invited us to see a business presentation the following night. That decision proved to be a pivotal one in our marriage.

We were intrigued by the business plan we saw presented and the possibilities that the opportunity might offer. I knew nothing about the Amway Corporation, but I recently had heard two pediatricians I was working with recommend the laundry detergent to mothers whose infants had a rash due to sensitive skin. That perked my interests enough to want to try some of the products. Selling and recruiting were not skills in our wheelhouse or even ones we were looking to develop. The emphasis was to expand the business with others who were interested in additional income or wanted to diversify. Those who chose not to pursue the business aspect could become customers. The fact that the products had a satisfaction guarantee and were consumable gave the benefit of built-in, repeat business.

Patrick and I had made the policy early in our marriage to not make decisions without sleeping on it. We found this would give us time to talk and think things over and be more planful. We have sorely regretted when we strayed from that strategy, like buying a $900 vacuum cleaner that we ended up hating! We took several weeks discussing the potential of this new endeavor and trying the merchandise. They were the type of products that we were routinely purchasing anyway, and we liked the way they performed. We read through all the material, after which Patrick stated matter-of-factly, "Well, if this shit does half of what it says, we'll be in Bermuda in no time." We had been there on our honeymoon and could not see how we could ever go back. With that proclamation, we made the monumental decision to spend the $39 on a starter kit and give it a try! No one else was offering to pay our bills, and no one else cared if I stayed home with our baby. We figured we had nothing to lose.

That decision proved life changing for us in many ways. Our initial purpose was to replace my salary. We knew that would take time and effort. We worked on our business in the evening, after the children were in bed. This made for long days, but we were committed. Although there were many serendipities, building the business was not always easy. There were times early on when the babysitter was making more than we were. The upside was that we were doing it together. The hardest part was presenting the business to people already making a much higher income than we were. It was a real boost when they were interested, but a disappointment when they were not.

On one occasion, I vividly remember pulling into the driveway to show the business in our second-hand car with some rust on the side and parking it next to three shiny new cars. They were a group of airline pilots and their wives, one of whom had just arrived home from Germany, where he had purchased his new Mercedes. A pleasant evening but no takers for the business. I knew that was a tough night for Patrick. Yet, he recognized that he was no less capable than these men who earned much more money. The episode strengthened his resolve and I loved him for that. He did not quit and neither did I.

My tough experience came a few months later when I contacted a childhood neighbor. She and her husband were friends with my sister and were quite successful. We drove the three hours to show them and their friends the business, and it did not go as we hoped. Afterward, I had the same pit in the stomach as when a high school boyfriend broke up with me. Patrick understood my feelings of rejection. During that long ride home, the gnawing in my stomach turned into conviction; we would indeed do well in this enterprise. Fortunately, we were seldom discouraged at the same time, and action helped conquer fear.

We kept at the business and had many more good times than bad. The tough times were the ones that strengthened our resolve and our marriage. Our little $39 purchase was the vehicle that allowed Patrick to remain teaching and for me to work part-time and be home with our children. The income more than replaced my salary. We also learned the importance of goal setting, communication, and positive attitude. These are skills we came to rely on over the course of our marriage. And we not only returned to Bermuda, we took our parents with us!

With the expenses incurred raising children, there were continuous financial decisions that required staying focused on priorities. Patrick and I agreed on our financial goals, but we made a decision that proved to be a risky one; we decided to buy a new home when we were expecting our third child before we sold the one where we were living. We had outgrown our two-bedroom ranch house and could afford a larger mortgage. We knew, having looked at several properties, that the house we liked was priced to sell, and our offer was accepted. Although both properties were solid investments, we were in no financial position to own two homes.

The economy was in a recession and the exorbitant interest rates made mortgages prohibitive for buyers who were interested. Our new home had a mortgage rate of 15¼ percent, and the bridge loan the bank issued us, pending the sale of our first house, was at 19½ percent. We paid $1600, in interest only, every 90 days waiting for the house to sell. We ended up carrying both homes for nine months before the first one sold, leaving us with a $25,000 debt over and above our new mortgage. That was in 1981! The anxiety and strain during that period affected me by a noticeable weight loss, as I had no appetite. Patrick's *modus operandi* was yelling. He was uncharacteristically irritable, with a short fuse for routine annoyances. The experience confirmed for us the impact financial stress can have on one's health, quality of life, and marriage. It was a tough lesson, yet the perspective it provided us for future decisions was priceless.

When we were advised to continue putting money into savings each month after we had children, we did not think we could manage that with the added expenses. We did take the advice, however, and had a small amount direct deposited. Now, many years later, we see the benefits of compound interest. If your company offers a 401(k) match, take full advantage of it. You will never receive a higher interest rate. It is painless when automatically withdrawn from your paycheck. You will not miss what you do not see. It is the easiest money you will ever make.

While debit cards are like dealing in cash and can prevent overspending, there are reasons to consider using a credit card instead. We heard Frank Abagnale, con man turned security consultant, speak in Boston. Abagnale, portrayed by Leonardo DiCaprio in the 2002 movie *Catch Me if You Can*, recommended the use of a credit card over a debit card for several reasons: the insurance coverage provided by the company if your purchase was broken, the quick reimbursement of your money if there was fraudulent use of your card, and the benefit of having a card that offers cash back or points for airlines or hotels. His reasons made sense, but we were reluctant to be faced with a large bill at the end of the month. We fixed that problem by deciding to pay off the balance every Thursday. We have never had a late fee or paid interest, and the points have provided us with terrific benefits on airlines and hotels.

One of the financial stresses facing young people today is the interest charged on student loans. This is an issue facing most of the couples we speak with regarding finances. They report a rate between 7–10 percent on their education loans, when the interest being offered on savings is currently less than two percent. That is usury and one we urge them to protest with their representatives in Congress. Student debt is a serious financial burden for young families while they try to save for *their* children's education and their own retirement. We encourage them to try to refinance with lower rates.

Because financial issues remain the number one cause for divorce, if the topic becomes too hot to handle, you are wise to seek professional help from both a marriage counselor and a finance professional. Many financial institutions have a certified financial planner available to members with advice on investments, tax benefits, and retirement planning. If you lack expertise in these areas, using this resource can help you stay on track with your goals.

There are many excellent resources regarding money and financial management. The magazine *Kiplinger's Personal Finance* and the Kiplinger website give good, basic financial information. The *Consumer Reports* magazine and website can educate you about making wise purchases based on research. Financial expert and author Suze Orman and author and radio host Dave Ramsey both offer a broad range of financial advice. They focus on the importance of being debt-free with solid information on dealing with debt and investing.

International presenter Rob Parsons' presentation titled "21*st* Century Marriage" can be found on YouTube. He addresses the impact that debt can have on your relationship, and a plan for achieving a debt-free life. The plan he presents is recommended by other experts in the field and the one we used to survive our house fiasco.

You do not have to start a business to gain the financial benefits to enhance your marriage. Listen and support each other in discussing and setting your financial goals. Surround yourself with supportive friends and learn from financial blogs, podcasts, and books on how to make wise economic decisions. A strong financial partnership is invaluable to your marriage, your parenting, your job, and your personal relationships. To remain ignorant about financial matters can be very costly to your pocket-book, your physical and emotional health, and your marriage. Staying out of debt, other than your mortgage and a reasonable car payment, should be your number one priority. Financial experts also talk about setting aside 10 percent of your net income for charities of your choice. That figure sounded exorbitant to us, but we set that goal and discovered a strange law of the universe: what you give comes back to you. Try it!

There is a lot of emotion around money and addressing the role that money plays for each of you is important to maintaining your emotional intimacy. Financial obligations increase during these heavy expense years, but they need not overwhelm if you set your marriage as the priority. Taking some financial dance lessons can help you stay in sync and keep moving forward.

Steps:

- Know each other's credit score.

- Set up a plan to attack your debt, one bill at a time. If your employer offers and matches a 401(k), put in the maximum amount allowed.

- Put 10 percent of your take-home pay into debt repayment. Cut expenses, if needed

- Save 10 percent of your paycheck

- Share 10 percent of your paycheck with the charities of your choice.

- Live on 70 percent of your take home pay until you are debt free.

- When you are debt free (excluding mortgage), put 10 percent into investment.

- Pay bills on time to avoid late fees and an increase in credit card interest rate.

- Use a credit card (not a debit card) with benefits and pay it off fully and promptly.

- Discuss and share the responsibility for your financial decisions

- Educate yourselves with financial magazines and online websites

- Seek financial counseling with an advisor through your bank.

WORKS CITED

"Husbands' stress increases if wives earn more than 40% of household income." *ScienceDailey.* https://www.sciencedaily.com/releases/2019/11/191119105549.htm.

O'Connell, Brian. "Financial Ties That Bind: A Money Checklist for Newlyweds." *Experian.* July 24, 2018. https://www.experian.com/blogs/ask-experian/financial-ties-that-bind-a-money-checklist-for-newlyweds/.

Wisniewski, Mary. "3 money-management apps built for couples." *Bankrate.* April 29, 2019. https://www.bankrate.com/banking/money-management-apps-for-couples/

CHAPTER 16

Implementing the Language of Love

"Never love anybody that treats you like you're ordinary."

OSCAR WILDE

If you can remember back to your first high school exposure to Spanish or French, you may recall that understanding the teacher was easier than attempting to speak aloud. Just as children learn by listening before they talk, "receptive language" always comes before "expressive language". Meaning, they can understand what words mean before they can express the message themselves.

In his book, *The Five Love Languages*, Gary Chapman writes about knowing your own love language and that of your partner so you can better meet each other's needs. He compares learning the "language of quality conversations" to learning a foreign language. Understanding each other's love language provides an incredible advantage to your marriage. Becoming proficient requires insight and new skills and, like any new skill, it will entail practice.

Chapman refers to the Minimal Daily Requirements (MDR) for "quality conversation." He suggests talking about three events that happened that day, being careful not to talk about what you did or said, but rather how you *felt* about what occurred. This often does not come naturally because most couples talk about facts: the secretary who did not finish the report you needed or the boss who delayed the discussion about a raise. When you recognize this, you can focus on your feelings about what occurred. With a few weeks of concentrated practice, conversation can flow more easily. You will notice that your dialogue increases the emotional intimacy within your relationship, a critical ingredient for a healthy marriage.

In addition to your personality differences, you were raised in a family with a unique culture of communication. Perhaps your family was loud and boisterous; no topic was off limits. Dinnertime was rambunctious. Or, you may have grown up in a household where difficulties were not acknowledged; displays of emotions were not encouraged. You may have learned to keep any sadness to yourself or were punished when you showed unhappiness or anger. This environment teaches you to keep your feelings under wrap; deal with them on your own or not at all. Then, once you are married, you are expected to be the great communicator. How does that work? Pretty poorly unless you are open to learning new skills.

Chapman recognizes five love languages: words of affirmation, quality time, giving gifts, acts of service, and physical touch. Knowing how to fill your "love tank," and your spouse's too, can make a critical difference in your marriage. What your spouse craves may not be a personal need for you at all, requiring you to think differently. Knowing your needs and understanding your spouse's is the difference between a marriage that is thriving and one that is merely surviving.

Words of Affirmation:

Affirming each other is a way of letting your spouse know they are appreciated. In our marriage, appreciation has been an important love language. This is probably true for most couples and why Chapman lists it first. No one wants to be taken for granted. Historically, men's work was outside the home, not witnessed by their wives and often underappreciated. Likewise, multitasking women were left with mundane chores at home for generations and often taken for granted too. Nowhere is this scenario more painfully described than in Richard Yates' novel *Revolutionary Road* where the reader witnesses the tragic implosion of a 1955 marriage due to boredom, unmet needs, and lack of appreciation.

Money, sex, careers, religion, and in-laws have been the top issues for divorce, and now household chores and raising children rank right alongside them. Husbands have more demands on them at home now, and working wives often feel underappreciated for the domestic tasks still expected of them. Both situations can make a couple more vulnerable to a depleted appreciation tank. When there is an unmet need and an opportunity arises to get that space filled somewhere else, or by someone else, a marriage can be at high risk.

Quality Time:

Patrick has let me know that time spent together is one of his greatest joys. If I do not allow time to watch an occasional movie at home or I am out too many evenings in a row, I know he is missing that time together by the pout that forms on his face. His body language forces me to state the obvious when he does not want to appear demanding. I really enjoy playing an occasional game, with cribbage being one of my favorites. Early in our marriage, we used to play with good friends. Then, with the kids, we got away from playing, and Patrick's enjoyment apparently had faded too. One year, he agreed to a New Year's Day cribbage game. On winning, he declared himself "champ for the year." That title turned into "champ for the decade," as he did not play for the next 10 years! You can imagine my surprise when, on the first night of vacation after his retirement, he pulled out the cribbage board he had packed for our road trip. That kind of surprise adds some pizzazz to a marriage!

Giving Gifts:

Early in our marriage, I won a silly $5 bet about a song title. Later, when Patrick came home from errands, he hiked up to our third floor, three-room apartment holding a small bouquet of flowers with a five-dollar bill stapled around the stems. How classy was that?! My heart melted. Over time, the occasional flowers were accompanied by a note. I came to treasure the note more than the flowers. With the addition of children and a bigger house, he could fill my love tank by doing chores. Now, anytime a back scratch is offered, it is a trip to Shangri-La! When you know what you need, ask for it. It will stop your love tank from hitting empty. That is prevention in action!

Acts of Service:

Over the course of your marriage, more serious needs will arise when a loving response will make the difference. When your spouse has a health issue that interferes with your plans, do you change course and offer the help needed? One woman I know was having a bout with kidney stones and her husband responded with, "Does this mean I can't go bowling?" Not surprisingly, the marriage had been out of sync for years, and they divorced several months later.

One mistake I am guilty of is not acknowledging chores that I view as routine and expected: mowing the lawn, shoveling snow, washing the dishes, and sweeping the floor. I try to remind myself that, just like "please" and "thank you" should be part of my regular vocabulary, so, too, should appreciation for the acts of service that keeps our home afloat. Cooking nightly dinner was the daily routine that fell to me. Every evening, I would slap the food on six plates with such monotony that you could not tell which one was for Patrick and which one was for the three-year-old! The gesture that probably prevented me from hanging the sign "Kitchen Closed" was that Patrick rarely missed saying "thank you" after dinner. Although I was less than enthusiastic, I appreciated his recognizing my act of service.

Physical Touch:

From the newborn emerging from the birth canal to the dying person whose hand is held by a loved one, humans rely on touch as the most intimate form of communication. By utilizing the positive role that touch can have, you will add a level of intimacy that anneals your bond. Remember your first kiss? How innocent. How sensual.

Early in marriage, touch seems natural as you explore and enjoy the physical aspects of your relationship. In addition to the sexual aspects of touch, there are many other benefits to this sense. In his *Psychology Today* article "Touch Hunger," Dr. Neel Burton writes that "in adults, the benefits of gentle touch include: reducing stress and protecting against future stress, lifting mood and self-esteem, strengthening interpersonal bonds, improving cognitive function, and boosting the immune system." He mentions how people today are more physically "isolated than in any other time in human history . . . [and how] we crave touch when we are lonely."

A quick kiss when leaving in the morning, a guiding hand in the small of the back when heading out together, a hand on the knee when riding in the car, an arm over the shoulder watching a movie, and a spontaneous hug while cooking dinner or doing the dishes can keep you connected when there is little time or energy for anything else. The wise couple incorporates touch as a regular part of their dance sequence.

Steps:

- Remember the basic manners of "please" and "thank you."

- Use touch to connect during your daily routine.

- Never miss an opportunity to express appreciation.

- Track yourself this week and see how you are doing keeping love alive.

- Show affection to your mate: a hug, a note, a chore, a compliment, or a fun outing.

WORKS CITED

Burton, Neel. "Touch Hunger." *Psychology Today.* June 20, 2017. https://www.psychologytoday.com/us/blog/hide-and-seek/201706/touch-hunger.

Chapman, Gary D. *The Five Love Languages.* Chicago: Northfield Publishing, 2015.

CHAPTER 17

Worrying Can Affect Your Health and Your Marriage

"Worry is like a rocking chair; it gives you something to do but never gets you anywhere."

ERMA BOMBECK

Worrying is part of being human. Some people are natural worriers. My dad was like that. For others, worry is a temporary occurrence that arises when a situation needs attention and then abates when the issue is resolved. My mother was like that. Perhaps she left all the worrying to my father. The concern for worry is, if left unchecked, it could evolve into chronic anxiety and have detrimental effects on your health and the happiness of your marriage.

It is a true gift of marriage to have a spouse to share concerns. There is a balance, however, between a loving ear and habitually discussing your worry. The latter may negatively affect your relationship. Worries are real, but they differ in their severity. *Situational* worry is a temporary condition, like worrying about an impending exam or preparing for a presentation. *Serious* worry can occur around health or financial concerns. *Chronic* worry can result from prolonged financial stress, a serious chronic illness, or working a job you despise.

Weather is an example of situational worry because fretting about it is not going to change anything. If you are holding a function that will be affected by weather, prepare a plan B. My dear Patrick is a *wannabe* weatherman. When our daughter was planning her outside wedding in our cul-de-sac, the Weather Channel took up residence in our home for a full week before the event. From my perspective, since the reception was indoors, plans were not going to change for the outdoor ceremony. Everyone could bring an umbrella if need be. While Patrick listened to the forecast, I turned my worry over to God, saying if the weather cooperated, I would never, ever, again ask for any weather favors. We both won out with 85 degrees and sunshine. I have never filed a weather request again!

A diagnosis of an illness poses a serious worry. When I was diagnosed with breast cancer, there was an initial shock as no one on either side of my family had cancer of any type. Seeking good medical care, learning the options, and understanding the needed treatment provided a plan to follow. Due to my own worry, I could not comprehend all the information during the visit. Patrick's presence with notetaking at every exam lessened my stress. We both felt more confident when he was able to clarify his notes with the medical team. Trusting the health providers and understanding the care plan prevented my worry from becoming chronic anxiety.

The declining health of a parent or sibling may require extended care. Ideally, it would be shared with other siblings, but this is not always the case. Many of our friends had parents who lived into their 90s and required much time and energy dealing with their housing, medical care, and finances. Understanding and support from a spouse is critical at a time when your own reserves are tested to the max.

The loss of a job often causes emotional and financial havoc to a marriage. The decision to go on strike, whatever the worthwhile reason may be, places tremendous stress on a relationship. Being laid off can be emotionally devastating. The longest government shutdown in 2019 caused 800,000 people to lose their pay through no fault of their own and wrecked many families who were not prepared to go without a paycheck. These situations do not have an end in sight and therefore require a couple to pull together all their resources. The legs of support you have built into your marriage will be called on during these times to survive the unexpected.

A long commute or a job you abhor can cause chronic worry. To ignore these circumstances only serves to convert your worry into chronic anxiety, never a good thing for your relationship. Talk about possible options and decide on a plan for the good of your marriage. Keep in mind the saying, "Not to decide is to decide." If you are not happy with a situation, do something about it.

Patrick and I are optimistic people, with a generally positive outlook on life. But we have our breaking point like everyone else. When we unintentionally owned two homes as described in a previous chapter, the financial worry was overwhelming. We could not control the recession or the rising interest rates. Unlike other loans that have a time frame, our debt was increasing every month the house did not sell, and there was no known end date. This caused a daily worry that taxed our physical, mental, and financial reserves. When people inquired if I was losing weight, I said, "Yes, it's called 'The House Diet,' and I don't recommend it." We would fall asleep at night only to wake a few hours later imagining how much debt we would have to deal with when this fiasco was over. We came within weeks of putting our new home on the market to see which house would sell first. Before making that drastic decision, we went to our legs of support: spiritual, physical, social, emotional, and financial.

I did not read the Bible growing up, but during that stressful time, I would open to a random page and receive some solace. Daily prayer is part of our life, but we went into overdrive. We stayed active doing no-cost activities: walking, swimming, sledding, and free community events like outdoor concerts and open exhibits at the museum. We kept up with physical exams and screenings with the goal of staying healthy. In our fear of bankruptcy, it was next to impossible to focus on the many blessings we had.

To prevent being swallowed up with negativity, we chose our entertainment thoughtfully. An antidote to worry is humor. While we may not have felt like laughing, humor was very therapeutic. We binged on funny reruns and watched comedy movies. Humor helped get the endorphins flowing and balanced out the downers that we could not control. Recognize when you need a laugh and be proactive in finding humor.

We also watched upbeat and educational shows and read books that focused on having a positive attitude. We listened to tapes in our car that supported optimism. Having friends over for simple dinners was relaxing and got our minds off the problem for a few hours. Two close friends collaborated on a getaway, with one taking our kids and the other giving us their lake home for a weekend. Their kindness was mind soothing. Another friend gave us tickets to a fundraiser that was a delightful diversion. Our friends' kind acts saw us through a painful period. Their support provided emotional respite that eased our worry and helped sustain us. These are gestures we try to remember when we see others going through stressful times. Patrick and I recall that period as the most self-centered time in our marriage. We had no energy to be other-oriented with volunteerism or random acts of kindness. We hated that feeling and vowed to never again let self-induced financial decisions overtake our lives.

We found taking some action made us feel less helpless. We set up time to meet with a banker and different real estate agents who gave us information. The actions resulted in the sale of our house, allowing us to begin to tackle the debt we had incurred, as shared in the chapter "Attending to Finance." Action does help deal with worry.

Talking with each other about the problem, using your support systems, seeking professional advice, prayer, counseling, and following a plan can provide you with new dance steps. Partnership lessens the worry load on each of you and helps sustain your marriage during difficult times. Without a plan of action, your marriage can be swallowed up by chronic worry.

Several years ago, I read an insightful short story titled, "The Worry Tree." Each night, when a carpenter came home from a long day's work, he paused and touched a branch outside his front door. He referred to it as the Worry Tree, where he left all the day's frustrations before walking in to greet his wife and children. He recognized that his family played no role in the stresses he had from his job. The next morning, he would symbolically pluck his problems off the tree when leaving for work, and he was always amazed how few there were. Was it because he was able to play with his children? Did talking alone with his wife lessen his worry? Did some issues not seem so troublesome after a good night's sleep? Had some things resolved themselves? Or was it a conscious choice? Likely, all these factors played a role and may be worth considering when faced with worry.

Many issues that cause worry never materialize. The nightly news may report negative economic projections or present national data on crime that does not directly affect you and that you cannot change. To worry about things that you cannot control is a waste of mental and emotional energy. It can also drain the life out of you and your marriage. If you are a natural worrier, you would do well to limit the amount of negative news you listen to daily. But even with conscious effort, it is impossible to escape all of life's difficult events.

In the article "Anxiety Problems, Part II: 3 Habits That Help," Dr. Susan Heitler describes anxiety as a "blinking yellow light that signals a potential problem ahead." Sometimes, I will notice some subtle tension in my stomach for no obvious reason. This makes me curious about what is behind the feeling. With some thought and introspection, I can usually relate a sensation—a smell, a sound, a vision—to a negative memory that has nothing to do with the current situation, but nonetheless makes me feel anxious.

When our son was trying to sell his house without success, we started reliving our stress of 35 years earlier, and I lost five pounds. When I understood what was happening, I was able to put my thoughts in proper perspective. And, unfortunately, I gained the weight back! This process can be helpful to those who have experienced trauma and find that anxiety crops up in situations that, by themselves, should not cause worry but rather bring up memories of a past and painful time. Lacking this insight can allow unrelated, past stress affect your current, otherwise good, situation.

In a different article, titled "3 Mistakes That Invite Anxiety to Undermine Your Performance," Dr. Heitler writes about three factors that create anxiety. The first factor is viewing events as "*big* or *new*," She recommends keeping issues equal in our thinking and not seeing something as more important than it really is. The second factor is "jumping ahead." Too often, we think about how bad a situation is going to be beforehand, but it usually turns out fine. The third factor is worrying about "what others think." In truth, everyone else is so wrapped up in their own lives that they do not have the time to worry about you.

Prioritizing where to put your energy can help you focus on what is most important. If stress originates at work, address it at work. If you are having problems with a friend, talk to them. When an issue warrants attention, planning with your spouse can help lessen anxiety. You can affect change by deciding to be proactive and develop a plan of action. The alternative is to wait until circumstances demand your response and then react, often with little time to think through the best strategy. This creates the worry of unpredictability and has a greater chance of creating more chaos. No marriage should be treated like a roulette wheel. You do not need to face problems alone. Seek expert advice. Regular and ongoing communication can allow you to engage in constructive problem solving.

Worry that progresses to chronic anxiety can cause physical symptoms that affect your health. An article in *Harvard Women's Health Watch* states: "Anxiety has been implicated in several chronic physical illnesses, including heart disease, chronic respiratory disorders, and gastrointestinal conditions. When people with these disorders have untreated anxiety, the disease itself is more difficult to treat, and their physical symptoms often become worse."

Worrying may be related to personality type and life experiences. The important thing is to know that about yourself, so you can begin to address ways to manage it and not allow it to interfere with your everyday life and relationships. Anxiety can undermine your marriage if it prevents you from talking together about issues that cause you stress. Your spouse should be your first sounding board. The better your skills for communicating as a couple, the less likely that anxiety will overwhelm your relationship.

The suggestion of utilizing a tool like "The Worry Tree" may seem nearly impossible for some people at first. Be willing to recognize the effect of worry on your health and marriage by confronting your concerns. Prevent worry from draining your emotional reserves and progressing to chronic anxiety and eroding the joy from your marriage. Dealing with your worry can help you stay in sync.

Steps:

- Recognize and acknowledge your own tendency to worry.

- Be aware of your self-talk

- Admit what you can control and what you cannot.

- Determine if the issue is situational, serious, or chronic.

- Brainstorm with your spouse about possible solutions

- Take action to minimize worry and consider counseling.

- Enlist humor and limit exposure to negative input.

WORKS CITED

"Anxiety and Physical Illness." *Harvard Health Publishing.* Published July 2008, Updated May 9, 2018. https://www.health.harvard.edu/staying-healthy/anxiety_and_physical_illness.

Heitler, Susan. "3 Mistakes that Invite Anxiety to Undermine Your Performance." *Psychology Today.* March 21, 2012. https://www.psychologytoday.com/us/blog/resolution-not-conflict/201203/3-mistakes-invite-anxiety-undermine-your-performance.

Heitler, Susan. "Anxiety Problems, Part II: 3 Habits That Help." *Psychology Today.* https://www.psychologytoday.com/us/blog/resolution-not-conflict/201205/anxiety-problems-part-ii-3-habits-help.

Hansch, Henry. "The Worry Tree" — A quick story we can all learn from…" https://henryhansch.com/the-worry-tree-a-quick-story-we-can-all-learn-from/.

CHAPTER 18

Solving Life's Smaller Problems

"When things go wrong don't go wrong with them."

ELVIS PRESLEY

Problems, big and small, are part of life. The problem-solving habits you adopt in your marriage can provide the foundation for facing the more serious challenges you will encounter during your life together. Be aware of your differing reaction styles when an unwanted event happens. One of you may need to work out your frustrations before addressing the issue. The other may tend to jump right in with a plan. Respect the space your partner needs before coming together to work on a solution.

Consider this: you are trying to save for a house, and the car needs brakes. One of you may question, "*Why us*? Just when we are trying to get ahead, something goes wrong." This reaction is like questioning the inevitable. This is often followed by the *blaming game*, which is when you seek to pin blame on the other. You might say, "If you didn't drive with your foot on the brake all the time, this wouldn't have happened." Watch out for this game because it will come back to bite you. Everyone makes mistakes sometimes: you lock the keys in the car, get into a fender bender, or leave the stove on when you leave the house. The next time you will likely be the guilty one. Remember, support rather than criticism will be appreciated when it's your turn. There is also the *repetitive scenario*. This is when you keep talking about the problem over and over, stuck in a loop, with no plan on how to move forward.

There are some problems where you can come to a ready solution. Other problems are not going to have a quick fix, but you usually can come up with a plan. Years ago, Patrick and I heard a couple speak about one way they addressed life's annoyances: car breakdowns, weather problems, minor health issues, missing a plane. These situations happen to everyone, and they are not fun. Putting a good spin on a bad event is not easy, but it sometimes saves the day and makes for a good story later. This couple found that *stating the problem once and then talking about solutions* was a technique that helped them handle these inevitable aggravations. They learned to avoid the nonproductive, repetitive dance. Instead of cycling in and out of the "Why us?" and blaming game, they found that considering options prevented regurgitating the problem. For them, open, constructive communication and formulating a plan was the beginning of moving ahead.

Tackling a problem together starts with recognizing how you feel and having the freedom to express your emotions without being judged. Do not be surprised if you and your spouse have completely opposite reactions about the same event. The important part is that you listen to how your partner is feeling, even if you may not fully understand their perspective. Events may involve emotions and experiences you have never had to face. Listening to each other will help you to formulate a plan.

Life provided Patrick and me several opportunities to practice problem solving during our stint in VISTA, when we had no disposable income and a lot of car problems. After one episode, we were at the end of our funds. Having enough money to finish out our volunteer year was in question. Patrick expressed his initial frustration by yelling. I prayed. Together we turned it over to God, saying, "We are willing to work hard, so if you want us to complete this year, please help us handle this situation." A mechanic solved the problem with an inexpensive fix. We were then able to start saving for the next incident. Financial challenges can sometimes be addressed with a plan and implemented with discipline and focused work.

Those events, however, did not prepare me for when, after being back home, Patrick called me from the grocery store saying that our car had been stolen. After much planning and thoughtful car shopping, we had bought a secondhand, one-owner, big boat of an old Oldsmobile (not cool, but practical!) with the little savings we had. We needed a second car for our jobs. When Patrick explained that the car was gone, I was apoplectic. By the time I arrived at the store to pick him up, I was a wild woman. How could anyone take our car? We worked hard for that car! We needed that car! I knew then, and I believe to this day, if I had met up with the car thieves with the adrenaline I had, I would have handled them all by myself.

When we reached the police department, Patrick locked me in the car with the threat of arrest if I entered the station. In those moments, I became a person I never met before and hope to never meet again. Patrick did a notable job of calming me down that night as we formulated a plan. When the police called the next morning to say they found the car, sans the contents of the trunk (all our camping and camera equipment), they told us we were the lucky ones to be getting it back. I tried to feel joy.

With luck, you may find that you and your spouse will not experience intense emotions at the same time. One of you having a level head can make a positive difference. Another attribute that can be helpful is when one spouse has more knowledge in an area than the other, be it financial, medical, or psychosocial. The ability to acquiesce to your partner's expertise can prove invaluable when facing a serious problem.

The inconveniences you will face may be dealt with first by having a pity party. This can be a healthy way for you both to wail the "woe is us" song. Then, define the problem. This allows you to become solution oriented and begin to set up a plan of remedial action. Brainstorm on how you can address the issue. Throw all the ideas on the table, and then sort them based on which are the most realistic and doable for your situation. When Patrick and I were feeling overwhelmed by owning two homes, we came up with some wacky ideas in our brainstorming activity. In sorting them out, we discarded the idea of raffling off one of the houses and decided instead to meet with a banker to learn who was selling homes in the tight market. That meeting put us on a path that resulted in a sale.

This approach ties right into a question I heard years ago. It was an "Aha!" moment and became our mantra: "If this is the reality, what's the plan?" Answering this question has proven invaluable in dealing with the little frustrations in life, like locking the keys in the car, to the more major ones of family health issues or financial stress. That probing question prompted us to face the realities of a situation, some frustrating and some painful, and move forward.

One of my writing colleagues talked about the importance of recognizing the difference between emotional and rational decision-making when working through a situation. She stated that her decisions as a younger person were often based on fear, wanting to avoid what *might* happen, rather than choosing what she really wanted. Weigh the possible outcomes: some anxiety versus too risky a decision. Taking the time to process the situation and not rush to a decision may bode well for a better conclusion.

Planning and taking action can give a sense of control in situations that can otherwise seem overwhelming. Some couples can do this on their own. Other couples require professional help. To seek support is not a sign of weakness but rather a display of wisdom and courage in recognizing when you need another set of ears and eyes about what will be most helpful. Figure out what works best for you as a couple.

Learning to problem solve can empower your marriage and cement your partnership. Practice on the small issues, and it will give you the skills to deal with the bigger ones later. The ability to deal with life's unavoidable difficulties and move forward will be one of your more complex dance routines.

Steps:

- Define the problem

- Do not cast blame.

- Ask yourselves, "If this is reality, what is our plan?"

- Brainstorm possible solutions—every idea should be considered.

- Focus on those ideas that are doable.

- Acquiesce to your spouse's expertise.

- Engage professional support if needed to move ahead.

CHAPTER 19

Surviving Life's Unexpected Events

*"Together we can face any challenges as deep as the ocean and
as high as the sky."*

SONIA GANDHI

While it may be a rare day to not have any worries, it is important to recognize the difference between life's minor setbacks and other more serious issues. There are unexpected, major incidents that can have a life-changing impact on your marriage, from health events to natural disasters. Responding to an unpredictable, catastrophic event will require faith, fortitude, and support. You will be tested on your communication skills, partnership, faith, and endurance, as you navigate the aftermath of circumstances over which you have no control.

I spoke separately with three mothers who gave birth to infants with severe disabilities, all of whom have thriving, long-term marriages. What helped them survive the unexpected and kept their relationships intact? They all acknowledged the initial shock. Grief settles in as they realize what they never could have imagined will now be lifelong. Their days will be consumed by medical appointments, negotiating with insurance companies, and dealing with agencies to help them navigate systems that feel like traveling in a foreign country where they do not speak the language.

Sandy was unknowingly exposed to a virus during her second pregnancy, resulting in her baby having a seizure disorder and severe disabilities. She and her husband, Brian, continue to care for their 37-year-old son, Matthew, at home. Many years later, in reflecting about the impact on her marriage, Sandy states that the commitment to her marriage was foremost. For them, divorce was never an option. Knowing they were facing this together provided the strength to deal with that unexpected event, which they knew would have long-term implications. Their church family has been a source of spiritual, social, and respite support for them as a couple and for their family. Brian carried on with his profession as a pilot while Sandy had to put aside her flying career to care for their son. When Matthew began school, Sandy was able to work as a teacher. She is now flying again and working toward regaining her certification as a flight instructor. Sandy admits this is a challenge given her ongoing responsibilities. She and her husband have been a source of faith and encouragement to many others who face similar life-changing situations.

Kathy's first child, James, experienced birth trauma that resulted in multiple disabilities, requiring 24-hour care until he died at 20 years old. Kathy acknowledged that she and her husband, Rich, were older, so she felt that their maturity, their strong four-year marriage, education, careers, stable income, and good health insurance were definite assets that helped them cope with the long-term impact of James's disabilities. Kathy recalls the support they received from friends and neighbors. She and James were offered the gift of normalcy, as they were included in the day-to-day activities of play groups, swimming lessons, and routine outings with other mothers. As a couple, Kathy and Rich were embraced into the social circle of adults in their town. Kathy joined a local Junior Women's Club with other mothers her age. She had the privilege of taking a break from her nursing career and pursue volunteer projects related to James's care, while Rich continued with his career in higher education.

In the early months, while sitting in stark waiting rooms during James's long evaluations, the couple recognized gaps in the system for families with children with multiple needs. Kathy was invited to sit on the New Hampshire Disabilities Council, and this exposure confirmed her belief that families needed better support and information. She went on to edit a parent's guidebook for navigating the system and finding resources. Parents benefited from the educational materials made available and the peer support they received from others dealing with special needs children.

"Managing the impact of such a catastrophic event is a process," Kathy said. She notes that "it took about three years for the shoes to stop dropping." She was referring to other issues that arose around James's changing educational and physical needs. This points to the endurance needed when coping with issues that are not going to be cured.

When Kathy and Rich were able to have their first getaway alone, it made them realize how exhausted they were. She remarked, "All our energies had gone into paying the bills and taking care of James and not much else." Kathy also mentioned that the physical care and ever-present needs "created an incredible amount of frustration, anger, guilt, depression, and sense of powerlessness during those early years." On returning home, they felt renewed. She explained, "To have someone care for James so we could get away was very important. Respite care became the single most important support to our family in the next several years."

Their experiences motivated them, individually and together, to channel their energies into working with several groups developing respite care, starting a newsletter, and testifying before state and federal committees for changes in public policy for families raising a child with severe disabilities. Kathy and Rich accomplished these changes through volunteerism and their careers. Their activism benefitted other families and allowed them to maintain their professions. Kathy did not know the metaphor that I use in my writing, but ironically, she concluded our visit by saying, "We did not become a disabled family. We kept on dancing." They continued their dance raising two daughters.

In many marriages, one spouse may have more knowledge in an area than the other, be it financial, medical, or psychosocial expertise. Kathy's background as a maternal/child-care nurse certainly helped her network and advocate on James's behalf. One spouse's willingness to acquiesce to their partner's expertise can prove invaluable when facing a serious problem. This was the situation that occurred with the third friend I spoke with. Their experience demonstrates how a couple's respect for each other's strengths helped address a serious challenge without derailing their marriage.

Ellen and Frank lost their first child at three months old due to congenital complications. She later gave birth to Kristin, who presented with similar, serious birth problems. Ellen, who was highly educated in the medical field, knew the outcome for Kristin was likely going to be the same. After her previous loss, Ellen knew her own strengths in dealing with another such bereavement. She expressed what to others may seem unthinkable: having her baby adopted by a couple who cared for special-needs children. Frank, equally distraught, respected his wife's expertise and pain, and together they made the decision. The emotional ambivalence they undoubtedly experienced was softened only by the fact that Ellen's worst fear did indeed happen. Kristin also died at three months old under the loving care of the adoptive parents. Few people would understand the anguish they endured. This is an example of implementing some intricate dance steps in a very personal, complicated situation and making decisions with open and skilled communication based in love and respect.

When asked how a couple survives such catastrophic losses, Ellen noted that she and Frank were together for 10 years prior to having children. Before their marriage was faced with the unexpected, they had established several legs of support. They knew each other well, enjoyed the same activities, and encouraged each other in their careers. Today, Ellen and Frank have two adult children and a solid marriage of over forty years.

Ellen shared with me four points that someone told her upon her engagement that were the ingredients to a happy marriage. She feels they have been important elements in sustaining their marriage through the unimaginable. She said she thinks of these often as she sees young couples and wishes the same for them as they face an unknown future. These four points are noteworthy as preventive ingredients to support a couple when a marriage faces the unexpected:

- Be best friends.
- Make each other's heart sing.
- Make your partner the best they can be.
- Dream the same dreams.

Few things are more challenging to a marriage than reorienting the life you had planned. These three couples faced unexpected, life-impacting events. They were able to continue even when life presented a different scenario than they expected. Their commitment, friendship, faith, giving space to grieve in their own way, encouraging each other in their careers, and advocating all played a role in their ability to move on in their lives and marriage.

Couples who have given birth to healthy children may encounter difficulties later when a child faces severe learning problems, autism, cancer, mental health diagnoses, or substance issues. Having a child with these or a myriad of other unforeseen conditions can result in physical, emotional, and financial stresses on a marriage. Dealing with these will require commitment, energy, and strong communication skills.

Many years ago, our own child suffered depression following a concussion. We also experienced substance use issues during their adolescence. Dealing with these events required working with the medical community, insurance companies, and advocating for expanding behavioral health services. As we wrestled with how best to cope with these isolating conditions, we relied heavily on support systems: faith, friends, staying active, maintaining our health, being sensible with finances, and having regular time alone. I sought out counseling for ourselves and our children, along with involvement in mental health and substance use organizations. Being proactive helped us cope with issues we could not control.

For our date nights, Patrick asked that our talk be problem-free; that was a healthy request. We built in individual time for exercise and breakfast with a friend. Patrick found attending Trivial Pursuit nights a mentally stimulating change, as I did with book club. Creating these times for self-care can be the brain cleansing needed during stressful times.

Losses are an integral part of all chronic illnesses and disabilities. Autism, cerebral palsy, cancer, mental illness, and substance use disorder (SUD), as well as other physical, mental, and cognitive conditions often result in a couple experiencing chronic sorrow. In an article in the *Los Angeles Times*, columnist Judith Daubenmier describes the effects chronic sorrow can have on parents. Although this an older article, the term is still used to describe the feelings many parents experience having a child with chronic illness or serious handicaps.

A pediatrician relates his experience as a father of a son with severe developmental disabilities: "It's the grieving of a loss—not the loss of a person, but the loss of expectations. There's just a level of sadness that never goes away completely." While parents of children with impairments certainly still laugh, love their children, and enjoy good times, grief creeps over them unannounced. "This response of chronic sorrow surfaces throughout the child's lifetime," said Kathleen Delp, a genetics counselor at Michigan State University. She adds, "They grieve the child because their whole life was oftentimes wrapped around that child, but they are still grieving on the other level. They are still grieving the child that was never born." This loss of expectations may be more responsible for a parent's grief than the disability itself.

We have seen similar grief play out in our support group with parents dealing with children suffering from a SUD or serious mental illness (SMI). Often, they miss witnessing their children experience events that are part of a typical adolescence and young adulthood: attending the prom, graduating high school, attending college, and living an independent adult life. If their child has SUD, many lose out on the simpler joys of grandparenthood, when they are responsible for raising their grandchildren. These losses need to be acknowledged, even when the child is still alive, because life has turned out differently than they expected.

For 41 years, Patrick worked as special needs teacher and witnessed chronic sorrow as he dealt with parents of children with cognitive disorders. The emotional impact occurs when a parent realizes the impairment is not going to be cured. Knowledge, information, resources, and support are needed to help a couple navigate such an unplanned trip. The family and marriage they envisioned is different from the reality they have. In addition to supportive family and friends, a couple can benefit from emotional reinforcement from other couples who have faced similar issues.

Divorce is higher among couples who have a child with chronic disability or have lost a child. Every individual grieves in their own way and within their own time frame. One challenge is allowing each other the space to grieve while staying close. Couples often find themselves unable to support each other due to the depth of their own pain. It is critical to recognize your need for help and not expect your spouse to be your only support system.

Couples who, after the death of their child from SUD, have attended support groups specifically for this loss have done well in sustaining their marriage. Peer groups allow them to connect with others who understand their pain and learn about helpful resources. Group wisdom and the sharing of experiences can be invaluable in navigating this new mine field and lessen their sense of isolation. Couple counseling can help spouses gain insight into each other's pain and understand how best to support each other.

Those couples with chronically ill children who can leave behind their expectations have been able to re-channel their grief for positive outcomes. When the intensity of the loss becomes less acute, parents and family members can participate in advocacy. This can happen through town forums, public hearings, or health seminars. Couples have found this a positive and reinforcing strategy to move beyond grief.

"Show-Up, Speak-Up and Cheerlead!" is the mantra that has worked for us. There was great power in meeting with other activists and speaking up on issues. I involved myself with a statewide organization addressing substance abuse. In the first six months, we witnessed the legislature pass five bills related to substance use prevention. Speaking up made a difference.

When you work with others who share your passion, you will witness increased public awareness, funding, and public policy changes. Fear of what you are facing can initially seem overwhelming, but taking action has an incredible way of overriding fear, isolation, and fatigue. Educating yourselves, showing up, and speaking to legislators can make a difference in your ability as a couple to live with what you cannot change. Your actions may enhance the care and support that your child and other families receive in the future. Involvement can be a source of healing. Remember Margaret Mead's quote: "Never doubt that a small group of thoughtful, committed citizens can change the world. Indeed, it is the only thing that ever has." When you, as a couple, experience positive results from your efforts, it reinforces your emotional intimacy, the bedrock of a strong, satisfying marriage.

As I write this book, the world is living with the pandemic of 2020. In an article in *Psychology Today*, Dr. George S. Everly writes: "It's a virtual truism that you really don't know another person until you see them under stress." The article refers to the research of Dr. John Gottman and Dr. Robert Levenson, which found "the difference between the successful couples and the unsuccessful couples turned out to be the balance between positive and negative interactions during conflict." Specifically, "'the magic ratio' is five-to-one" for successful marriages, so for every negative interaction, there were five or more positive ones.

Every relationship goes through times of disruption, and some challenges carry a life-long impact. Couples who face serious, unexpected events will find that their commitment to their marriage and the habits they establish make a critical difference. Having a loving, trusting, and respectful partnership gives you a definite advantage as you enter these unforeseen, chaotic dance arenas. If you want a positive outcome, do not pretend things are fine. Recruit the support of family and friends. Seek help in your community by connecting with peers who know firsthand the challenges you are facing. Rely on your faith as a leg of support. Dances of endurance deserve all the help available. Remember the healthy habits you established early in your relationship? If you have allowed them to slide, this is a good time to shore them up.

Steps:

- When faced with a crisis, give each other space to grieve.

- Think about what this life-changing event means to you.

- Join a peer group to connect with others who share similar experiences.

- Utilize your legs of support: physical, emotional, social, spiritual, and financial.

- Attend public gatherings that address the topics you are concerned about.

- Speak and write to legislators who are voting on bills that affect your issue.

WORKS CITED

Daubenmier, Judith, "Chronic Sorrow, Heartache Afflict Parents of the Mentally Disabled," *Los Angeles Times.* March 29, 1992. https://www.latimes.com/archives/la-xpm-1992-03-29-mn-307-story.html.

Everly, George S. Jr. "Relationships Under Stress-Does adversity strengthen, heal, or destroy relationships?" *Psychology Today*, April 12, 2018. https://www.psychologytoday.com/us/blog/when-disaster-strikes-inside-disaster-psychology/201804/relationships-under-stress

CHAPTER 20

Investing in Your Health for the Sake of Your Marriage

"Happily-ever-after is not a fairy tale. It's a choice."

FAWN WEAVER

There is emphasis today on the importance of eating well, daily exercise, and reducing stress. Years ago, the YMCA and the local high school were the only gyms available. Now, the ubiquitous advertisements for work-out clubs can make you feel very uncool if you do not have a gym membership. You are bombarded about the risk of health complications if you do not achieve your 10,000 steps every day. You read about the prevalence of obesity and the high rates of diabetes. The warning signs for heart attack and stroke can be found posted on the sides of buses, as heart disease remains the number one killer. Checking food labels has become a part-time job as you try to avoid trans fats, partially hydrogenated oils, and limit your salt and sugar intake. You have long been made aware of the dangers of smoking. Now, the recent message that "sitting is the new smoking" has resulted in some sedentary workers requesting standing desks.

The sensory input can become overwhelming when your mind gets inundated with so many messages. The danger is that you tune out vital information and ignore facts that could benefit your health. If you are serious about wanting to stay healthy and live a long life, it does require holding yourself accountable and becoming proactive. Do not expect your spouse to take responsibility for your well-being. That is your job. To ignore your health is putting an unfair burden on your mate as you are expecting them to care for you when your health fails from preventable illnesses.

Choose a primary care provider (PCP) wisely. Make sure it is some-one you trust and with whom you feel comfortable. Plan on at least a yearly exam to stay up to date on your weight, blood pressure, labs, recom-mended screenings, and vaccines. This professional knows you, your med-ical and family history, and can see you when concerns arise. Sometimes, you may be referred to a specialist, like a dermatologist or cardiologist. Be aware that they may not be in touch with your PCP regularly. Take charge of connecting the dots on your medical records and make sure all providers know what is going on. One important area of health care that tends to be minimized, if not out rightly ignored, is dental care. There are adults who have a phobia about dentists and avoid regular cleanings, resulting in seri-ous systemic disease. Prevention in dental care goes a long way to ensuring good health. As I am known to frequently say, "Do you know who your PCP is? It is you." Do not depend on your spouse to nag you about health issues. Take responsibility for your own well-being.

Several years ago, I was reminded of the importance of prevention and being proactive about my health. I had seen my PCP for my annual visit, and we were discussing my cholesterol level in relation to my family history. I had been trying to keep it in check with diet and exercise, but I finally agreed to medication. The doctor was so pleased that he forgot to or-der my annual mammogram. Some women might gladly have waited until the following year, but not me. There is no history of any type of cancer in my family, but I like keeping up with my health screenings, so I called the radiology department and scheduled the mammogram that evening. Twelve hours later they called to say I needed a biopsy! Two months later, after two failed lumpectomies, I had a mastectomy with reconstruction. The upside? Since the mass was detected so early, I did not require radiation or chemo-therapy. After several weeks of recuperation, I was back to my normal life. If I had ever doubted the value of prevention, that sealed it for me.

In a *Men's Journal* article, Michael Pollard, a sociologist with the RAND Corporation, explains: "Research shows that healthier people are more likely to get married in [the] first place and less likely to divorce. However, while this is part of the equation, most of these studies suggest that marriage also causes good health and improves overall well-being—es-pecially for men." There is a tendency to delay sometimes minor issues un-til they become major health concerns. Procrastination or denial in dealing with health issues can complicate a medical condition and have long term effects on the quality of your life and your marriage.

One of my friends tried, without success, to get her husband to make an appointment about a skin condition. He procrastinated so long it resulted in the amputation of his lower arm to limit the spread of cancer. Indeed, the fact that married men do better with their overall health than single men is shown in research. That same article suggests that "men, more so than women, rely on their spouses for emotional support and companionship, which leads to improved mental health." Susan Brown, co-director of the National Center for Family and Marriage Research notes, "When a woman is down in the dumps, she might call a girlfriend, but a man will rely on his wife much more than his friends."

If you value your marriage, your health should command a top priority. If the engaged couples my husband and I speak with are any indication, they all want to live until they are 85 and some hope for 90 plus. This may be because they see many people living long lives, and they are hoping that for themselves. According to data from the National Center for Health Statistics (NCHS), if you made it to 65 in 2018, you have a high chance of living 84.6 years. But let's look at the definition of "living." If you have visited a nursing home, you have witnessed people who are technically "living." Many residents there, however, would argue they are "surviving." Given the choice, many would prefer being more active, engaged in a higher quality of life, or to die.

Many people who are hoping for longevity, picture vitality, and enjoying the activities in which they are currently engaged or hope to participate in when they have more time and money. They are not thinking about the physical trials of aging: a sore back, achy joints, or knee and hip replacements. But you want to think about these challenges of aging when you have time on your side. The key to quality longevity is prevention. The natural aging process cannot be stopped, but there are things that you can do to delay some of the health issues that interfere with an enjoyable life now and later.

One of the major diseases affecting health in our country is diabetes. In 2018, according to the American Diabetes Association, over 30 million people had diabetes and over seven million of those were undiagnosed. Chances are increasing that you will develop diabetes as you age, since nearly half of all adults age 65 and older currently have prediabetes.

There can be a hereditary factor associated with type 2 diabetes, but it is largely influenced by poor diet and lack of exercise leading to excess body weight. Body mass index (BMI), which relates body weight to height, is one screening tool used. A BMI of more than 25 is considered overweight and a BMI over 30 is considered obese. Weight issues seldom start in adulthood. The fat cells are laid down in childhood, increase in adolescence, and worsen in adulthood. There is a definite advantage in having a healthy lifestyle modeled for you when you are young, but it is never too late to start eating healthy. Eat more vegetables, fruits, legumes, nuts, whole grains and dairy, and eat less processed foods, red meats, and sweets, including sweetened beverages.

In 2015–2016, data from NCHC revealed that "the prevalence of obesity was 39.8 percent in adults and 18.5 percent in youth." The study also revealed that "the prevalence of obesity was higher among middle-aged adults (42.8 percent) than among younger adults (35.7 percent)." What is evident with these statistics is that the issue of obesity starts early and increases with aging. The key is prevention, and making healthy choices benefits your overall fitness. But how do you adopt behaviors compatible with your busy lifestyle? You do that by making the decision to set your health as a priority and taking the time to attend to your well-being, physically and mentally. Notice I wrote "take" the time, not "make" the time, because you cannot "make" time. You have 168 hours in your week. You need to decide how you are going to spend them. When you subtract hours for work (including commuting), eating, and sleeping, there is precious little time left. Between time spent on technology (television, movies, and social media) and exercise, making the conscious decision to choose the latter might make the difference in a healthier outcome.

While you do not have control over all of life's challenges or your family's medical history, there are areas over which you do have influence. Think about the quality of life you want in the decades to come. Are there activities you would like to do in the future when you have more time and money? What could prevent you from being able to participate? What could you do now to increase the odds that your life will include those fun activities? Staying active now will be the difference in determining what you will be able to participate in as you age. When you make healthy, deliberate choices, the outcome is apt to be a positive one.

Patrick and I have enjoyed generally good health. We were not obese as children, so maintaining an okay BMI has not been a major challenge. I was never athletic, and Patrick's serious athletic pursuits ended in college after he developed osteomyelitis following a construction accident. Numerous joint issues have plagued him, but most have been fixable. When we were raising the children, we could not afford to join a gym, nor did we have the time to play sports. So, we cannot take credit for having a masterful plan. When we entered our 70s, we realized that the small, doable choices we made along the way have made a big difference in our quality of life. We always walked and took stairs whenever possible. After the girls left home for college and the Peace Corps, at the boys' request, we got a dog. We know all children want a dog; they just do not want to care for it. Lucky for me, I walked the dog. After nine years of daily walks, I continued the habit after losing our dear Duke. We learned, in retrospect, staying active makes for a healthy outcome.

Before children, we took up cross country skiing and, later, snowshoeing. At 50, we started to accumulate secondhand ski equipment and started downhill skiing at inexpensive, small, local ski areas. We loved it, and now we enjoy season passes at bigger areas. Patrick purchased new ski boots at 72 and called it "the height of optimism!" We have never trained for a marathon, but we have managed to stay active, enjoying biking along flat trails and kayaking on quiet lakes. I swim whenever I can, enjoy water aerobics, and a daily walk, sometimes alone, sometimes with a friend. Patrick walks three miles at least five days a week with "the boys," which includes a coffee break too.

Taking the onus for your health relieves your spouse from worrying about issues they cannot control. When you care for your own well-being, your body, your health, and your marriage will all benefit. It is also another way of expressing love. Investing in your health now is sure to keep you dancing well into the future.

Steps:

- Find an exercise you *like* and do it three to five times a week.

- Stay active with a *variety* of activities you enjoy and mix them up!

- If you drink, limit alcohol intake at one a day for women and two a day for men.

- Walk and use stairs whenever you have the option.

- Know your family's medical history and pay attention to it.

- See your PCP for a yearly checkup and as needed.

- Stay current with the recommended screenings and vaccines.

- Know your weight and BMI and keep it under 25.

- Monitor your blood values (cholesterol and lipids) and blood pressure.

WORKS CITED

Juntti, Melaina. "Does Marriage Help You Live Longer?" *Men's Health Journal.* https://www.mensjournal.com/health-fitness/does-marriage-helps-you-live-longer-20140610/.

Pesce, Nicole Lyn. "U.S. life expectancy rises for the first time in four years — here's how much longer Americans are living." *MarketWatch.* https://www.marketwatch.com/story/americans-are-living-a-month-longer-as-us-life-expectancy-rises-for-the-first-time-in-four-years-2020-01-30.

"Statistics About Diabetes." *American Diabetes Association.* https://www.diabetes.org/resources/statistics/statistics-about-diabetes.

CHAPTER 21

Acknowledging the Challenge of Dual Working Spouses

"Unity is strength. When there is teamwork and collaboration, wonderful things can be achieved."

MATTIE STEPANEK

Whether you are a dual career, upwardly mobile couple or a husband and wife who are working full-time jobs, you are dealing with issues that many couples in previous generations did not have. The dual working model is a paradigm shift for marriage. Roles are no longer easy to define. This dance requires your partnership to have insight, communication, and respect. You cannot ask your parents how they dealt with these marital and family issues. More than likely, they did not have them.

In 1952, when my father-in-law, Jack, said to his wife, "Molly, I think we should move to America," she just packed up their household in Ireland, left family behind, and moved with their three young sons. She joined millions of other European women immigrating to the United States for a better life. It remained the expectation for decades that American wives follow their husbands wherever they were transferred, as he was the provider.

Career demands, excessive travel, time away from home and family, and long commutes put stress on a marriage. Those in the medical and legal professions, or those working two jobs or double shifts, have long hours and job pressures that cause marital strain. The economic benefits do not eliminate the burden. In years past, the wives I observed who managed this journey successfully were the ones who went into their marriage understanding the reality of these challenges. These women learned to balance the at-home and maternal duties with their spousal role. Many women also volunteered in their church and community, gaining a sense of purpose outside the home.

Our dear friends Claire and Bob are a great example of a couple who worked to balance their marriage during that time. Claire was a model corporate wife. She understood and accepted the pros and cons of her husband's job. They discussed Bob's career pursuits and business obligations in the context of their combined family commitments. They both had a clear understanding of what to expect, so their roles were not an ongoing source of aggravation or conflict. Claire appreciated the economic benefits and accepted the downside of Bob's frequent business travels. He respected their partnership and did his best to prioritize his roles of husband and father. She managed the home and children in his absence and relocated without complaints. When the children started school, they settled in one place. Later, Claire earned a master's degree and pursued a career in teaching with Bob's full support.

Another friend, Ann, had a husband whose medical specialty meant long, often unpredictable hours. Nightly dinner was made for the family, and when Jay could make it home, he ate with them. This often necessitated returning to the hospital after dinner to finish seeing patients. If Jay did not make it home, his dinner was put aside, and she moved ahead with the children's bedtimes. Ann planned social engagements that did not conflict with Jay's on-call schedule. These are both examples of spouses who understood the demands of the partner working outside the home. They learned the dance steps that worked for them and how to meet their own needs, thus avoiding continuous marital friction.

In the 1960s and '70s, the culture began to shift. With the introduction of the birth control pill and the chaos of the Vietnam War, it was a turbulent and changing time in our country that witnessed the beginning of the feminist movement. In her book, *Marriage, a History*, historian and educator Stephanie Coontz wrote, "The relations between men and women have changed more in the last 30 years than they did the previous three thousand." In the book *Wife, Inc.: The Business of Marriage in the Twenty-First Century*, author Suzanne Leonard quotes Coontz, who writes "[i]n less than 20 years, the whole legal, political, and economic context of marriage was transformed . . . [and] during the 1980s and 1990s, all these changes came together to irrevocably transform the role of marriage in society at large and in people's personal lives."

Women accessed higher education, affording them more career opportunities. The economics in America changed with the recession and higher interest rates. A woman's income was often needed to keep the household afloat. Some women had invested so much in their education that they needed to work to pay their student loans. Others wanted to put their education to work and experience professional fulfillment and advancement. The feminist movement that started in the 1960s was in full swing, and many would agree it was long overdue. But everything comes with a price.

As a pediatric nurse practitioner, I noticed that price with new mothers distressed at *having* to return to work. Every week there would be mothers in tears as they contemplated leaving their infant. Whether working for minimum wage or in well-paying, professional careers, their reactions were remarkably similar. The common denominator was the lack of choice they felt about returning to work. As a professional person, and a new mother myself, I empathized with them. I was challenged with childcare issues and juggling schedules working only one or two days a week, so I respected them working full time.

Today, the traditional roles are often reversed. Now, it may well be the wife who is the physician or corporate executive and primary breadwinner, with a husband who may be the full-time caregiver for the children or working in a lower-paying job. Look at these headlines, for example: "Women Are Now the Majority of Those Students Entering Medical School Nationwide," "Veterinary Medicine Is a Women's World," and "There Are Now More Women in Law School Than Ever Before." And the same holds true for dental schools. More women are now ascending the corporate ladder than ever before, with more fathers at home raising children. What does this mean to a marriage? It does not have to be a cause for ongoing friction or divorce, but regular communication and respect for each other will be critical to finding your own dance.

When the upwardly mobile, aspiring wife excitedly arrives home one evening announcing that she received the big promotion to the corporate office in Fargo, will it be met with a supportive response? With 38 percent of women making more than their husbands, this scenario is a reality for many couples. Current sitcoms and ads on television portray these role reversals. One of our friends shakes his head, both in amazement and admiration, when talking about his attorney son staying home raising the children while his physician-wife is the working professional.

What is the reaction in your marriage to such a paradigm shift? What effects will these situations have on your family? The discussion will require putting egos aside and listening to each other's feelings and perspective. Can you talk openly about the economic reality, the impact on family dynamics, and what it means to each of you while respecting the other's needs? It is critical that the higher earning spouse values the contribution that the lower or no-wage earner makes to the household. Emotional and financial generosity and appreciation are the keys to marital satisfaction in this age of shifting roles.

An article about the struggles of professional working mothers in *The Atlantic* titled, "Why Women Still Can't Have It All," by Anne-Marie Slaughter gives one perspective on this issue. Ms. Slaughter is highly educated and married to an equally well-educated and supportive husband. She landed her dream job in the State Department in Washington D.C., while her family stayed in New Jersey. That meant she was only able to be home on weekends. The fact that her boys were 12- and 14-years-old weighed heavily on her, even though she knew they were well cared for and supervised. Ms. Slaughter concluded that women can "'have it all at the same time.' but not today, not with the way America's economy and society are currently structured." She was criticized by several high-profile female colleagues who felt she was giving "a terrible signal to younger generations of women." Ms. Slaughter felt she was just being honest. I think her concluding statement is the point that should be noted: women may not be able to have it all *at once*. She also acknowledged that having it all was not possible in many types of jobs.

Yes, there are some superhuman women who seem to pull off the mother/professional career role, but they are in the minority. Others can do it because they have the financial resources for household help and childcare. Many mothers, however, do not have the means and family help to make it happen. They are working to keep their husband, children, and boss happy, usually at their own expense, and all too often, no one is happy.

Maternal attachment is a healthy and desired outcome, but there are important financial implications if a mother does not work. If she does, the cost of childcare along with the emotional separation are often issues that cause personal and marital stress. One mother I saw was torn about leaving her infant and wondered if the financial renumeration was worth it. She and her husband figured out the cost of working (childcare, commuting, clothing, lunches) and subtracted that from her take-home pay. They decided the hourly wage was not worth the financial cost and the emotional stress. She ended up working a couple of evenings a week and found they could cover their expenses. Parents may find working opposite shifts, or part-time, provides enough resources to make finances work.

One couple I met had a situation when the wife was finishing her medical training. Julie and Jim had always planned to return home to the west coast when Julie completed med school. This became a dilemma when she was offered the Chief Resident position, necessitating remaining in New England. While Julie agreed to honor their original plans, Jim sensed her desire to accept the position, and he recognized what it would mean to her résumé. He agreed to stay, and they made a new plan, pushing out the date to return home. In tough situations, instituting a time frame can provide a solution; a decision does not have to mean forever.

There are many variables to consider around career priorities and the impact they have on your marriage and family. To weigh out the pros and cons of a problem and arrive at a thoughtful decision, using the T-chart developed by Benjamin Franklin may prove helpful. It involves making a list of the pros and cons of one decision and the pros and cons of the alternate decision. This exercise can help you see the advantages and disadvantages of a situation. You can more objectively arrive at a decision that more closely aligns with your needs.

Using this tool may help you decide what makes the best sense. There may be a car that one of you is hot to buy, but it may not be a practical financial choice. Rather than feeling that one wins and the other loses, writing out the pros and cons of buying the car as well as the pros and cons of not buying the car can help lessen the emotional impact of the outcome. Even though one of you may not get the car you want, the process can take the bite out of the final decision. There is always next time!

Gainful occupation will take up well over one third of your life. If you hate your job, it is likely to become a serious, mental drain. Over time, these feelings will affect your physical and mental health and your relationships, primarily your marriage. Something needs to change to prevent this fallout. This is when your priorities and basic values will come into play. When your core values are similarly aligned, you will make the best choice for your marriage.

One of the issues that arises for many couples is commute time. Amy Morin, psychotherapist and author, addresses this in a *Forbes* article. She cites many studies that address the toll that a long commute has on your physical and mental health. High blood pressure and weight gain are among the physical effects resulting from more time spent in the car. This often results in less time to exercise. Along with often missing out on the children's' activities and socializing with friends, a long commute results in "decreased energy, increased stress, and higher illness-related work absences." When a commute is 90 minutes or longer, there is less time for social events, which contributes to "decreased life satisfaction."

Some commutes, however, can serve to allow time to wind down after a stressful day before walking into the house and dealing with family issues. Morin refers to a 2008 study that found that "Engaging in pleasurable activities, such as listening to music, enjoying the scenery, or simply being alone with your thoughts may help you view the commute as leisure time." If you can take a walk or go to the gym, you are likely to experience fewer negative effects. Morin recognizes that not everyone has a choice, so her advice is a change of attitude. Instead of contaminating your home life with a grumpy mood every day, look at the benefits your job is contributing to your life. If you find that misery is outweighing the benefits, then maybe it is time to look for a new job.

Professional women still face wage disparity with their male colleagues. In the '60s and the '70s, this inequality resulted in some radical views on marriage. In her book, *Wife, Inc.*, Leonard recounts how "the writings of activist feminists who claimed that the abolition of marriage was necessary because women's free labor in the home sabotaged their demands for equal pay outside of it." My approach is less radical. I advocate *for* marriage, not abolishing it, and I encourage couples to tackle the challenges, shore up their partnership, and define positive ways to strengthen their marriage while continuing to fight for equality in and outside the workplace.

Situations that demand decisions and compromise exist in every marriage. Spouses need to support each other, because such backing does not always come from the outside world. My friend, Kate, recalled how her two sisters bickered over their personal working/mothering decision; one chose to stay home and raise her children, while the other wanted to return to work. Each mother defended her position but was also critical of the other. Every situation is unique. What is right for one woman, her family, and her marriage may not be right for another. The important factor is that they, not outsiders, decide on what is best for them, their family, and their marriage.

As a couple, talking with each other about your aspirations, dreams, and career goals will be an important and ongoing discussion throughout your marriage. Balancing careers today is a marital challenge that previous generations did not have to deal with in the same way. These issues represent emotional topics for both spouses. Addressing them with attention and respect will keep you on the dance floor, together!

Steps:

- Listen to each other about what is important regarding work/home priorities. Write down both sets of hopes.

- Talk about the desired time frames for your goals.

- What are the priorities based on your values as a couple?

- Discuss financial implication and your feelings about different options.

- Employ Ben Franklin's T-Chart to weigh important decisions.

WORKS CITED

Chandler, Michael Alison. "Women Are Now a Majority of Entering Medical Students Nationwide." *Washington Post.* January 22, 2018. https://www. washingtonpost.com/local/social-issues/women-are-now-a-majority-of-entering-medical-students-nationwide/2018/01/22/b2eb00e8-f22e-11e7-b3bf-ab90a706e175_story.html.

Coontz, Stephanie. *Marriage, a History*. New York: Viking, 2005

Kelly, Greg. "Veterinary Medicine Is a Woman's World." *Veterinarian's Money Digest*. May 7,2017. https://www.vmdtoday.com/news/veterinary-medicine-is-a-womans-world.

Leonard, Suzanne. *Wife, Inc.: The Business of Marriage in the Twenty-First Century*. New York University Press. New York, 2018.

Morin, Amy. "Want to Be Happier? Change Your Career or Change Your Attitude." *Forbes*. December 7, 2014. https://www.forbes.com/sites/amymorin/2014/12/07/want-to-be-happier-change-your-commute-or-change-your-attitude/#7c0927077417.

Oliver, Mark. "More Women Are Outearning Their Husbands Than Ever – But We Aren't Willing to Talk About It." *KSLNewsRadio*. https://kslnewsradio.com/1905294/more-women-are-outearning-their-husbands-than-ever-but-we-arent-willing-to-talk-about-it/?.

Slaughter, Anne-Marie. "Why Women Still Can't Have It All," *The Atlantic*. April 2012. https://www.theatlantic.com/magazine/archive/2012/07/why-women-still-cant-have-it-all/309020/.

Stok, Glenn. "How Ben Franklin Analyzed Pros and Cons to Make Decisions." Updated on May 20, 2020. https://owlcation.com/humanities/Benjamin-Franklin-Pros-and-Cons.

Zaretsky, Staci. "There Are Now More Women in Law School Than Ever Before." *Above the Law*. https://abovethelaw.com/2018/03/there-are-now-more-women-in-law-school-than-ever-before/.

CHAPTER 22

Understanding Sexual Compatibility

"If sexuality is one dimension of our ability to live passionately in the world then in cutting off our sexual feelings we diminish our overall power to feel, know, and value deeply."

JUDITH PLASKOW

Stress around sexual issues follows financial concerns as one of the top reasons cited for divorce. The term "sexual incompatibility" sounds like a dire, permanent condition. It certainly need not be. The experts who deal with couples around sexual issues describe differences in libido as a common issue for many couples. The inability to acknowledge and the unwillingness to address sexual issues is more the crux of the problem than so-called incompatibility.

How does a couple deal with differences in their libido? Communication, caring, and compromise seem to show up consistently with the experts. Talk openly with each other about your likes and dislikes, hopes and desires. Some couples find writing them down and comparing the commonalities is a good starting point for understanding and compromise. Having respect and caring for your partner's feelings provides a strong foundation for success in dealing with sexual issues.

Transitions in life often precipitate changes in libido. Getting married is the first transition most couples face. Even couples who have lived together find that being married brings a different meaning to their love-making. There is no longer the unspoken belief that, "I can just leave if things don't work out." The very commitment of marriage is often the blessing that gives couples the gifts of time and security to grow together.

The vow of fidelity can transform sex from a selfish desire focused on physical satisfaction without an emotional connection, to lovemaking, involving transparency, emotional investment, and caring more about your spouse than yourself.

Marriage provides the stability to explore the frequency and the variety of how you choose to express yourselves to each other physically. Discovering your sexual selves can be one of the greatest joys and rewards of your marriage. Intimacy expert and author Laura Brotherton writes: "Sexual compatibility is a learned behavior; it's something that comes with time, effort, and lots of practice within the unique relationship of marriage." Assuming you will be perfectly compatible in this arena during your early life together is like sitting down for your first piano lesson and expecting to play a concerto. Unrealistic? Yes, but that does not mean that you both cannot enjoy learning different pieces while mastering the classics!

The willingness to bridge the gap of variances in libido and recognize "spontaneous" versus "responsive" desire can make a positive difference, according to marriage and family therapist Dr. Ian Kerner. Spontaneous desire is experienced early in relationships and readily portrayed in the media. By contrast, responsive desire arises with "physical touch . . . and emotional connection" and ignites desire, which are the ingredients necessary for long-term sexual satisfaction.

Other transitions, like health challenges and pregnancy, may put your lovemaking on hold, as it was for us with Patrick's back injury. Having a baby requires time for healing. Absences for business travel or military deployment, sometimes for long periods, place significant stress on couples. Starting anew to re-establish your sexual connection will be enhanced when you are willing to talk openly about your needs and listen to those of your spouse. If one of you is more tentative, the other can successfully shift the dynamics by a willingness to consider your partner's needs above your own, showing patience and gentleness. Demeaning a spouse with a lower libido can result in conveying a feeling of inadequacy and shame, with negative personal and marital consequences.

Compromise around the frequency of sex can help avoid frustration, resentment, guilt, and contempt. Experts have helped clients reduce stress by scheduling lovemaking. While making an appointment may initially sound very business-like, couples report that knowing when to expect intimacy lessens stress for the one with a lower libido and calms the spouse with the higher sex drive. The anticipation can help both partners and avoids feelings of rejection. Antonieta Contreras, a Licensed Clinical Social Worker (LCSW), talks about creating compatibility by learning about each other's needs and "working together on discovering what's missing." Learning to connect physically in non-sexual ways can greatly enhance your relationship. A spontaneous hug, holding hands, cuddling, and spooning can "redefine what is physical, sensual, and sexual." These acts can serve to reduce tension and have sex be more relaxing and intimate.

Some couples ask the experts "what is the normal frequency for sex?" The consensus is there is no norm. Factors such as a couple's relationship, what is going on in their lives, and their individual needs prevent there from being a "normal." The belief is that how a couple handles their circumstances is what makes the difference. In a *Healthline* article, Dr. Ian Kerner notes how "sex seems to be rapidly falling to the bottom of America's to-do list." He suggests that "when couples stop having sex their relationships become vulnerable to anger, detachment, infidelity and, ultimately, divorce" That seems to confirm the saying, "use it or lose it."

Sexual satisfaction is influenced by physical, psychological, emotional, and interpersonal factors. When there are concerns around libido, you are wise to have a medical exam to rule out or treat any physical condition or medications that may be responsible. It is also important to understand if there has been any history of trauma for either partner. This would hopefully have been discussed earlier, but if not, realize that traumatic life experiences can significantly interfere with sexual satisfaction. Try to get to the root of the problem. If this is not addressed, sex can become perfunctory, passive aggressive, or even hostile.

While communication is important to all areas of your marriage, your sexual life will be greatly influenced by your ability to be open, honest, and respectful. If your spouse finds watching porn or engaging in certain acts distasteful, insistence will inhibit physical intimacy. Such resolve can drive a wedge, making your spouse feel more like an object than a lover. When one of you has a stronger libido, the willingness to temper your drive with kindness can help bring your spouse to share greater physical intimacy over time. Remember the piano example? Every classic pianist started with scales.

Patrick and I have found that lovemaking can mean different things at different times. One memory that we still laugh about happened when we had been married for six months. As mentioned in a previous chapter, when we were starting our stint as VISTA Volunteers in rural Texas, we spent our first three weeks in a flop house. While we never went to the bathroom in the place, we did have some great sex!

Lovemaking can fill many needs, depending on circumstances. During times of stress, it can be soothing. After a sexy movie, it can be exciting. Sex can be comforting during times of sadness. Allowing your love for each other to direct your lovemaking can prevent sexual incompatibility from becoming a barrier in your marriage and turn lovemaking into the asset it is meant to be. Working on how you communicate in all areas of your marriage can positively impact your sexual life. The love, commitment, and caring you share can serve to make any disruption a temporary condition. If obstacles persist, seeking counseling with a licensed sex therapist can help you move ahead in this important aspect of your marriage. Do not ignore it. There is too much to lose.

Steps:

- Address any physical or emotional issues that may be affecting your sex life.

- Talk to your spouse about what making love means to you.

- Talk about what you like and do not like. Do not be passive or vague.

- Listen to your partner's expectations and needs.

- Find your commonalities regarding your desires.

- Compromise on your differences.

- Enjoy non-sexual physical connections.

- Focus on what is working, not incompatibility.

- Be patient during times of transition.

- Avoid blame and be willing to make things better.

- Acknowledge stresses before they become chronic.

- Engage a licensed sex therapist if problems persist.

WORKS CITED

Brotherson, Laura M. *And They Were Not Ashamed: Strengthening Marriage through Sexual Fulfillment.* San Diego: Inspire Book, March 2004.

Pace, Rachael. "22 Experts Reveal: How to Deal with Sexual Incompatibility." *Marriage.com.* Updated May 22, 2020. https://www.marriage.com/advice/physical-intimacy/experts-reveal-how-to-deal-with-incompatible-sex-drives/.

Montgomery, Heather. "How Often Do 'Normal' Couples Have Sex?" *Healthline.* June 11, 2018. https://www.healthline.com/health/baby/how-often-do-normal-couples-have-sex

SECTION II

Twist and Shout

The dance of the middle years of marriage and the
importance of partnership

*"The goal of marriage is not to think alike, but to think
together."*

ROBERT C. DODDS

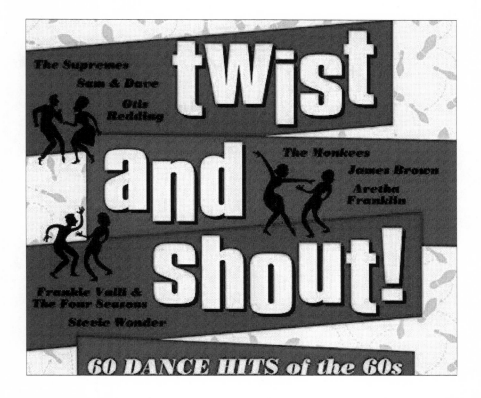

Recorded in 1961 by the Top Notes, "Twist and Shout" was written by Phil Medley and Bert Berns, who used the pseudonym Bert Russell. The Isley Brothers turned into a hit single in 1962. Two years later, the Beatles covered the Isley Brothers' version. The dance that came from the song is done with a partner, with rapid swiveling of the hips and intermittently throwing arms in the air. While there is minimal touching, "Twist and Shout" can be a very sensual dance.

The "Twist and Shout" is an accurate metaphor for this next stage of your marriage; one filled with fast-paced movement that feels chaotic at times. You are likely in the throes of your careers, raising children, trying to keep your house in order, meeting obligations in your community, church, extended family, and socializing with friends. You are both moving fast, but you may often want to throw up your arms and shout, "Stop the world, I want to get off."

Carving out time, alone and together, every day will be critical during this phase of your marriage. The commitment to your partnership is what will keep you both on the dance floor when the music slows down.

CHAPTER 23

Preventing Gray Divorce

*"Success in marriage is more than finding the right person.
It's becoming the right person."*

UNKNOWN

This stage of twist and shout can seem overwhelming. Amidst the chaos, it is easy to slip into habits that are not supportive of your marriage. These behaviors can have a negative and long-term effects on your relationship if they are not recognized and prevented.

The overall divorce rate has declined since the 1990s, while it has doubled for those couples over the age of fifty. Jay Lebow, a psychologist at the Family Institute at Northwestern University, explains: "'If late-life divorce were a disease . . . it would be an epidemic'" In 1990, only one in ten of all divorces involved people over fifty. In 2009, it was one in four, or 600,000 divorces. By the end of 2030, gray divorce is predicted to reach 800,000. The major increase is with couples fifty to sixty-four years of age, with 66 percent of those divorces initiated by women as found in an AARP survey.

I introduce this bleak statistic now because this is the time when you can prevent becoming part of this group in the future. Prevention is a critical factor in combating this rising divorce rate in the years that should bring a sense of fulfillment. During these twist and shout years, it easy to put your relationship on the back burner. With all the demands on your time and energy, you may minimize the need to attend to yourself and each other. The hopeful thinking may be "Let's just keep everything copacetic and we will be fine." This is the time when your marriage deserves the most attention because there are so many distractions.

The ability to recognize and address problems early allows a couple to take steps to ensure their future. The issues that lead to divorce later in life *do not* pop up late in marriage. They are more often the results of unhealthy habits and patterns rooted early in the relationship. According to Dr. John Gottman, the behavioral precursors to late-life or empty-nest divorce are no different from those for younger couples—criticism (demeaning the *person* rather than the behavior), defensiveness (asserting your position and not listening to your spouse), contempt (engaging in nasty and belittling behavior) and stonewalling (refusing to discuss an issue). If a couple does not get their dance in sync in the early years, repeating the same missteps is likely to continue throughout the marriage. When a couple has completed the job of raising the children, they may view the remaining years as limited, and one or both may feel the need to find a different dance partner. Interestingly, infidelity is not the leading cause of a marital split later in life; rather, the desire for self-fulfillment is cited as the motivating factor.

For men, the "gray years," can bring a sense of "Is this all there is?" Too often, personal needs and desires have been put on the back burner for decades. As they worked to provide for their family, men may feel their sacrifices were unappreciated. They have neglected time for themselves and social connections. Sometimes, any extra money was spent on the children or the house, with little left over for personal hobbies or fun as a couple.

For women, it is often boredom and potentially having more financial resources, which allows them to contemplate a life change. Issues they have resented for years no longer seem tolerable. For both spouses, a general lack of appreciation and being taken for granted is often cited as reason for this life change. They want out.

The breakup of his parents' 30-year marriage inspired William Nicholson to write the play *Retreat from Moscow*. Jamie, the couple's son and the play's narrator, states in the introduction, "divorce is the murder of a marriage." I think the definition is noteworthy because he does not say "death" but rather chose the grisly word "murder." There are no winners and many victims. Edward, the husband, has chosen to leave. He admits to his wife, Alice, that they did have an exotic honeymoon. Then, referring to her in the third person, Edward says, "She was a brilliant, dazzling girl. She could recite poems. She had passion. That is all gone now. I can't make you happy." He makes references to her criticism and nagging. He describes the newness and the nervousness of new love. He admits he has "fallen in love with another woman. She has no demands and no expectations. Just love." Alice accuses him of being a traitor: "It is not an accident. I have made an effort for 33 years. I feel I don't know what you want. You cared so much, but not now. You don't do things with me. This is your problem. Do something. Say something. I want a reaction."

You do not have to be a psychotherapist to recognize that such dialogue reflects problems that were not acknowledged over the many years of their marriage. They seemed to be doing the tango in the beginning, but when they started to step on each other's toes, they continued their missteps. Learning how to listen to each other, have fun together, and prioritize their marriage may have prevented indifference and apathy from seeping into their relationship and ultimately "murdering" their marriage.

Fun is the f-word that far too many marriages are lacking. The absence of enjoyment causes many couples to hit their 50s with the panic that the senior years are breathing down their neck and there is precious little time left for fun. Too often, fun keeps getting put off with the thinking that "We will do that later," or "We'll have more time when the kids are grown," or "We don't really have the money for fun right now." These thoughts and attitudes can kill a relationship. Marriage is not supposed to be all work, with years of drudgery, thinking that you are going to wake one day and suddenly know how to have fun. It must be built in during the marriage. There is no reason that a husband and wife cannot experience a sense of joy and fun as individuals and as a couple during these busy years.

Early in our marriage, before children, we read an article about cross country skiing. We were saving for a house and funds were tight, but this sport looked affordable. We hunted for sales and outfitted ourselves. Those skis provided a lot of fun and made winter fly by. Whenever it snowed, we just headed outdoors, sometimes in the street after a fresh snowfall or to the nearby golf course. We got friends interested who also enjoyed the activity.

With the longevity that many couples are now experiencing, it has been said that there are multiple marriages built into one union. In decades past, the life expectancy was in the 40s. With the advent of penicillin and improved medical care, people lived to be in their 60s. Now, with emphasis on eating healthy and physical fitness, the life span has extended well into the 70s, with many people living far longer into their late 80s and 90s. How does one prepare for being married to the same person for 60 or 70 years? I think the answer is *not being* the same person and not expecting our spouse to be the same person.

Over that stretch of time, there should be personal growth, new interests, hobbies, and knowledge. We should each take responsibility to pursue avenues that expand our mind as well as our conversations. That prevents boredom from draining the life out of a relationship. Sometimes you may share some of these pursuits and sometimes you will enjoy different ones. Whether activities enrich or divide you will depend on the freedom you allow each other and the interest and encouragement you offer your spouse. One couple I know, married for several decades, always sets aside one day a week to spend together in a mutually enjoyable activity. This keeps them connected and prioritizes their relationship above their separate interests but does not replace them.

Ignoring problems, dismissing the needs of your spouse, and allowing apathy to leach into your relationship, bodes poorly for a happy, long-term marriage. The effort you invest during these busy years will result in compound interest in the future. I love the cartoon I saw years ago where an older couple is seeing their last child off to college. The mother is crying, "George, you are all I have left." "Emma," the husband replies, "I am all you started with." It is a great reminder to stay focused on your primary relationship if you want to be there for the waltz years.

Experiencing an emotional connection during these demanding decades will require awareness, creativity, and sensitivity to each other's needs and interests, along with open communication, having fun, and compromise. A U.S. study published in the book *Social Networks and the Life Course: Integrating the Development of Human Lives and Social Relational Networks* reveals that couples married for at least 20 years are happier than newlyweds. How encouraging to know that putting in the effort early will pay off in the end as well.

Steps:

- Know and encourage your spouse's interests and dreams.

- Schedule time for fueling your marriage with fun activities.

WORKS CITED

AARP Research. "AARP The Magazine Study on Divorce Finds That Women are Doing the Walking - But Both Sexes Are Reaping Rewards in the Bedroom." May 2004. https://www.aarp.org/research/topics/life/info-2014/divorce.html.

Gottman, John M., and Nan Silver. *Seven Principles for Making Marriage Work*. New York: Three Rivers Press, 1988, 1999.

Petter, Olivia. "Couples together for 20 years or more are happier than newlyweds, study claims." *The Independent*. April 22, 2018. https://www.independent.co.uk/life-style/love-sex/marriage-happy-years-relationship-couple-partner-best-time-a8316506.html.

Nicholson, William. *Retreat from Moscow*, October 1999.

Smith, Michelle. "What is Gray Divorce? And How to Navigate One…" *Thrive Global*. https://thriveglobal.com/stories/what-is-a-gray-divorce-and-how-to-navigate-one/.

"Twist And Shout by The Isley Brothers." https://www.songfacts.com/facts/the-isley-brothers/twist-and-shout.

CHAPTER 24

Preparing for Parenthood

"Trust because you are willing to accept the risk, not because it is safe or certain."

ANONYMOUS

Pregnancy is a waiting game that can also be a rich time for connecting about the upcoming changes in your marriage. Since there is no training required for the vocations of spouse or parent, most couples find themselves repeating patterns they observed during their own childhood. For better or worse, your parents, or the primary caregivers in your young life, are the role models for your intimate relationships and parenting. If you have concerns about the examples you and/or your spouse experienced growing up, you are wise to discuss this now.

Open communication about sensitive issues from your childhood can be challenging. Avoiding a discussion of these topics, however, is asking for trouble down the road. There will need to be ongoing merging and reconciling of your different values and goals as you address the unending issues of raising a child. This period of your marriage requires flexibility in your dance routine and your willingness to learn new steps. It is important to realize that your childhood experiences are going to influence your parenting.

Questions to consider for discussion:

- What were the best things about my childhood?

- What were the worst things about my childhood?

- What mistakes do I feel my parents made?

- What were the best things my parents did?

- What do we want for our family?

As adults now becoming parents, you are free to define what you want as a couple, and as a family, and to do things the way you choose. You are not obligated to repeat the mistakes you may have witnessed. Recognize that you may have been raised with different styles of parenting. No one way is always the right way, but consistent expectations make life more predictable for a child. Talking about what style you encountered in your upbringing and what you would like to use with your child are important discussions to have.

How will you handle disagreements? Do they happen in front of the children? You may have been shielded from all marital discord growing up, leaving you believing that married people never disagree. Arguments may make you feel anxious. Your spouse, on the other hand, may have observed every argument, so disagreements are not a foreign concept. The decision on how to address emotional topics may depend on the issue, but when done with respect, settling disagreements can provide a valuable example to children on how to deal with conflict without demeaning the other person.

As you prepare for this parenting journey, it is wise to decide what techniques best match the hopes you have for your family. You could put the answers to the previously listed questions, along with other topics you come up with, and make your own grid. List the habits or behaviors from your own parents (include cultural practices along with discipline methods) you would like to *keep* and another column for those that you would like to *discard*. This exercise will require both compromise and learning on the job.

When you have experienced different upbringings, there will be some important adjustments. Acknowledging your spouse's views, especially as they differ from your own, will be critical to the best outcome. Respect and compromise are essential, as was the case with a colleague of mine. Barb was a woman I met through work who was raised by two parents who battled alcoholism. She moved away from home at 18 to attend the state university. A few years after graduation, she met a man whom she later married. He did not have a family history of alcoholism. Barb recognized that although she did not have a problem with alcohol, some of the coping behaviors she developed during her childhood could now affect her marriage and parenting. Her anxiety about impending events and a hypervigilance in routine situations resulted from growing up in an unpredictable environment. She did not want these traits to affect her marriage and parenting.

Such insight is important and powerful for initiating change. Barb and her husband were committed to being consistent, loving, and dependable parents, qualities Barb had not always experienced in her own family. She began attending a support group for Children of Alcoholics (COA) and learned new ways of dealing with old issues. Her husband supported her efforts with patience and understanding. Together, they have achieved a thriving 39-year marriage and raised two successful sons. They are an ideal example of partnership, adapting their dance, and working in sync for the benefit of their marriage. One spouse can be a great asset in seeing a situation more objectively than the one who is directly, emotionally affected. Taking time to share your concerns and listen to your spouse can be invaluable in determining the best way to deal with difficult situations.

Thinking about the upcoming changes can cause anxiety in the happiest of married couples. What will it all mean? Will our baby be healthy? Will we still have time for each other? Will I be a good mother, a good father? Will we ever sleep through the night again? Can I go back to my job? Will we be able to afford childcare? Will we have sex again? Will I ever have my wife back? These are among the endless worries prospective parents have and the answer to all these questions is "yes!" With subsequent children, many of these questions will be answered with experience, but with the first child, it is all about the unknown.

Your transition into these twist and shout years, may well define the essence of your partnership. *Preventing problems is much easier than fixing them later.* The habits you develop can be your best tools to navigate this new dance. How you communicate, how you deal with differences from your own upbringing, how you view issues of parenting, and how you take advantage of community resources (workshops, classes, expert speakers) will determine your success as you enter this stage of your marriage. Educating yourselves allows you to be proactive. Resources abound to strengthen your relationship during this transition. *Listen. Talk. Connect.* Fast foot work will be necessary for staying on the dance floor as you anticipate the reality of parenthood.

Steps:

- Share your experiences growing up, what you felt worked and what did not.

- Talk about your expectations and your worries about parenting.

- Identify the style of parenting you are most comfortable with and be prepared to revise it while on the job.

- Discuss those issues you disagree on, keeping the result in mind.

WORK CITED

Tashjian, Sarah. "Parenting Styles and Child Behavior." *Psychology in Action.* May 16, 2018. https://www.psychologyinaction.org/psychology-in-action 1/2018/4/23/k17ziyfqt1vy9tlytr9l9k48epdnur.

CHAPTER 25

Dispelling Myths and Adjusting to the First Born

"Having a baby dragged me, kicking and screaming, from the world of self-absorption."

PAUL REISER

I remember going to visit my niece, Karen, who was placed on bed rest awaiting the birth of her first baby. This is a difficult situation for any woman who is active but being in her third year of pediatric residency, confinement really threw her a curve ball. I gave her credit for using this unexpected gift of "downtime" for things she might not otherwise have had time for. In her case, however, it was like working from home.

Karen was propped up on the couch, a half-filled glass of water in one hand, her legs resting on a bolster pillow, and the other hand maternally placed on her protuberant belly. Scattered across the coffee table and nearby floor were a cadre of books all related to, what else, childbirth, breastfeeding, postpartum, infant care, and parenting. Of course, I added to this collection by bestowing the gift of yet another book of wisdom on how to survive this new turn of events which she and her equally intelligent husband, Paul, were about to experience. My gift was T. Berry Brazelton's classic *Infants and Mothers*, which is about the differences in infants' temperament during the first year. It should be named *Infants and Parents*!

Sitting with Karen, amidst all this published expertise, I was reminded how overwhelming the first baby can be, even for the best prepared. There is a definite perception by outsiders that for a pediatric physician, newborn care should come naturally. After all, she had completed four years of medical school and two years of residency in children's health, so what could possibly challenge her? As a pediatric nurse practitioner, I had spent my career examining infants and working with new mothers. Did that lessen my anxiety awaiting the birth of our first child? No.

I remember one evening in childbirth class when I was eight months pregnant. During a break, I walked over to the window and looked at the night sky, with lights twinkling over the city. Although it was a peaceful scene, I felt completely flooded with anxiety. The thought that I could not turn back, that in a few weeks I would give birth and become a mother swept over me like a tidal wave. I knew I had far more training than others who take on this role every day. With a loving spouse, I had more support than many mothers. All transitions are stressful, but this one felt overwhelming.

During the last weeks of pregnancy, a woman goes into "nesting" mode. In preparation for mothering, she centers her energies around her upcoming role and often needs to put everything else aside. I remember a woman calling me a few weeks before delivery and inviting me to become a board member at the Child Care Association where I had worked. I was a bit aghast, as I told her I was expecting my first child, and I could not do that. I am sure she was chuckling as she explained that it would not be for a few months, gently indicating that my life would be changing, but it would not be over. I later became a board member, and life did indeed go on. But right then, I needed to nest!

This is also a challenging time for fathers who have their own anxiety about their new role. Their presence in birthing classes and involvement in the delivery room connects a couple and promotes bonding between father and baby. Birthing classes educate husbands about the mood swings that their wife experiences during labor. This was helpful information when I lost it on Patrick as he stood at my bedside during active labor, vocally debating about whether 5:00 a.m. was too early to call his boss to say that he would not be at work that day. I finally yelled, "Stop the frigging talking and just go do it!" He then understood the "transition stage of labor." He never asked for my opinion during the three subsequent deliveries.

These moments served me well in the years ahead as I worked with new parents who were beginning this journey. As delightful and anticipated as the first baby may be, the addition is transformational. Amidst the joy, new couples should know that feeling overwhelmed is normal and be assured that the anxiety about the changes will abate. The reality of sleep deprivation and a new mother's erratic hormone levels can make even the routine activities challenging.

Among the many things I emphasized to new mothers was the importance of taking care of themselves by slowing down and not trying to be superwoman. Often, first-time mothers expect to return to a daily schedule, as if nothing has changed. Years ago, a mother would stay in the hospital for up to a week. Then, due mostly to cost and insurance regulations, the time frame was shortened to 24 or 48 hours. I hated that! It is not enough time to begin healing, receive assistance from the staff in caring for your newborn, and have your questions answered.

After delivery, parents benefit most from help. They arrive home to find it is business as usual: the laundry piles up, meals need preparing, dust balls accumulate. The phone is ringing, and well-meaning people stop in to see the baby. All this is happening while the new parents want to focus their energies on caring for their infant. It is all disruptive and exhausting. A supportive spouse can make the difference during this transition by giving mom important time to recover and taking over the duties she usually handles in addition to his own. This is a time for true partnership.

We have all seen an overtired toddler—not fun. There is only one thing worse, and that is an overtired mother! Mothers need their rest and should not apologize for it. A partner should grant and protect that request. The whole family will benefit. Parents do well to grab a nap when they can, to help deal with their interrupted nights. Ask would-be visitors to call before coming over, and then be honest if you two are not up for a visit. Disrupted sleep can make parents very crabby. Mom's body is healing, and she needs time and care. Hormones are in flux, and therefore, so is her mood. Rest and support for each other can cement a bond during this transition.

It is wise for both of you to be aware of what to expect after birth, in terms of mood swings. Most prenatal providers share information with expectant couples. Delivery nurses usually screen for postpartum depression and give guidance before discharge. With the too brief stay in the hospital, however, the symptoms may not be evident. *Postpartum blues* are normal, due to the rapid hormone swings that occur with delivery, and often cause a roller coaster of emotions. The moments when a new mother feels like crying for no apparent reason may catch her by surprise and totally baffle a new father. Postpartum blues are very common in the weeks after giving birth. This is normal and is helped with adequate rest, eating well, and talking about what each of you is feeling. Sleep deprived mothers will feel the postpartum sadness more acutely.

If the "baby blues" last more than a few weeks or seem to get worse, this should be addressed at the postpartum check-up, as well as with the infant's primary care provider. *Postpartum depression* is more intense and persistent. It can sometimes occur later, even months after birth. Postpartum depression is not uncommon and is treatable.

About one out of 500 new mothers experience a severe form of depression known as *postpartum psychosis*. If there is a dramatic change in mother's behavior or any thoughts of hurting herself or the baby, it should be treated as a medical emergency. Awareness and treatment can restore equilibrium and help a couple through this traumatic, sometimes life-threatening, experience.

Although I believe that it can benefit a couple to have the first few days alone with an infant to assimilate as a family, it is helpful to have support within reach. I was reminded of this when my 31-year-old daughter and son-in-law arrived home with their first child. They had been married four years and owned their own home. They were both healthy, college educated, and experienced. She had been in the Peace Corps for two and a half years in a village without running water or electricity, and he had been a medic in Afghanistan. They had both handled difficult situations. I planned to give them a few days alone to adjust as a family, and then go visit on day three. At midnight, the day of discharge, she called. No, nothing major was wrong. She just stated calmly, "I think it is wrong to send a couple home after three days and expect them to know what to do." After listening, I said, "Talk to hubby and let me know if you would you like me to come down in the morning." She immediately replied, "Oh, we talked about it, and believe me, it is okay." Here were two very capable people with a healthy newborn, but they needed some rest and reassurance. Friends and family need to be sensitive to new parents' needs.

As a couple, you should talk about how to ask for support, if it is not forthcoming. This can mean help with meals or household chores that allows you to get used to the tasks of feeding, changing, and bathing the baby. The chance to catch some sleep, while you adjust to the new schedule, is a great gift. As new parents, you are wise to screen phone calls and limit visitors, so you do not get over tired. It is an exciting time, but it is also good to remember that exhausted parents become irritable spouses. Tired mothers are often weepy. One thing I find that makes a difference for the inevitably sleep-deprived new parents is relieving each other, so you are not both awake with your baby. While one is on duty, the other sleeps. Few things are worse than having two exhausted parents at the same time.

The usual schedule for a new mother's check-up, following a normal, vaginal delivery, has been six weeks. I would warn new moms: "Do not evaluate anything in your life during this time" You will not like your body as it seems to leak from every orifice, the flab prevents you from getting into the clothes you are dreaming of wearing again, you will feel your spouse is not doing enough (even though you are both spent!), the house is a mess etc., etc. You get the picture. Nothing is right. You fear that is this is the way it is going to be forever. Not to worry.

The first six weeks are the postpartum period. Flush them! Do not pay much attention to the things that bother you as your emotions are ruled by hormones and the irritations will not seem so important later. I used to say the reason why doctors did not want to see new moms for six weeks was because they did not want to hear the litany of new-mother complaints. I do believe there was truth to that. Many providers changed the protocol to two weeks, and that is much more supportive for new parents. I think the change happened when the number of female obstetricians increased! If your appointment is scheduled for six weeks, it does not mean that you cannot call for an earlier appointment if there is a concern. Good medical care and loving support from family and friends can help make your transition to parenthood a positive one.

Amidst the excitement, this is also a time of adjustment in your relationship. I remember looking at Patrick with new eyes as he held our daughter, thinking he was more than my husband now. He had become a father. Sounds funny, but all these years later, I remember that "Aha!" moment. A new dance is emerging, and new steps are required. Your previously uninterrupted time will now be heralded by cries that you do not yet recognize. It takes about a month to differentiate the various cries for hunger, pain, wet diaper, or just the infant's need to be held. In years past, it would often be said that holding will spoil the baby. Do not believe a word of it! If you have fed and changed your baby, but the little darling seems fussy and calms when you hold her, then hold her. Remember where this baby spent nine months, all bundled up, cozy and warm, listening to mom's heartbeat. If that calms your baby now, enjoy it, and do not let others make you feel guilty.

That is not to say that letting a baby cry is bad. It is not. After holding and cuddling, do not be afraid to put the baby on his back to fall asleep in an uncluttered crib. The famed Dr. Benjamin Spock would tell parents, if all else was well with your infant, letting him cry for 20 minutes is perfectly fine. It is said that crying helps the infant make the transition from the stimulation of the day to going off to sleep. I found this to be true professionally and personally. It helps to get away from the crying by listening to music or reading in another room as 20 minutes can seem like an eternity. If the crying continues, intervene. This helps to establish good, safe sleeping habits you will come to appreciate when you do not have a toddler crawling into your bed every night.

Today's fathers are much more involved in childcare than in past generations and that is a healthy change for everyone. If dad is hesitant, one of the things that a new mom would be wise to do, is include the father right away. The reason is twofold. First, most fathers feel that they do not know what to do or are afraid of doing it wrong, like with holding the baby or changing a diaper. I taught the football hold to fathers, as many know how to do that, and it gives the baby the all-body support needed. Show a dad once how to change the diaper, and then do not correct him. If he puts it on backwards, or it is not as snug as it should be, he will learn soon enough, so back off. Secondly, mothers, do you really want to do everything? If dad feels incompetent, he will just abdicate, and the job will be all yours.

I remember one visit with first-time parents. Father had brought the infant in for the first several visits when mom was working, and he was doing a great job with the baby. One day, they came in together. Mom corrected him several times on how he was dressing the baby, so he just backed off and let her take over. I pulled her aside after the visit and suggested to her that encouragement would go a long way to foster his continued involvement, bonding with their infant, strengthening their own relationship, and provide her with more freedom. She got it!

When the baby is fussy, ask for help. Dad may be feeling more relaxed and able to rock the baby to sleep. Nothing will make him feel more confident than to solve the problem and soothe mom as well! A breast-feeding mom can pump an occasional bottle allowing dad to feed. This also can let the new mom leave the house for a couple of hours to get a haircut or have lunch with a friend. It provides you both with the belief there is a future with some normalcy.

Humorist, columnist, and author Erma Bombeck wrote about divvying up infant care. She inquired of her husband, "Do you want the top half or the bottom half?" Then she added "One of us can handle the feeding, burping, and spitting up and the other can change the diaper every three minutes." Sometimes there is truth in humor. Sharing the duties does not only lighten the workload for each of you, it also gives you both special time with your baby.

Back to my story: as I sat there with my niece, I remember how inept I felt when giving the first bath to our daughter in the hospital nursery, a place with which I was familiar. When my pediatrician colleague popped in, he casually asked, "So how's it going? This is old hat for you, hey?" Yeah, right! I was all thumbs trying to coordinate the water and holding the soapy baby, who felt like a slippery eel, all the while trying to remain calm. I was certainly not feeling at all like a pro!

About the mechanics of holding, feeding, and changing, not to worry, you will do fine. Remember, your baby has no one to compare you to. What infants do know is if they are warm, fed, changed, cuddled, talked to, loved, and protected. With that, and taking care of each other, there is nothing more important. Your baby will think you are doing a fine job. As the famed pediatrician Dr. Benjamin Spock said, "Trust yourself. You know more than you think you do."

Another recollection that was most poignant for me occurred a few weeks after delivery on a horrendously hot and humid July day. I placed our daughter safely in the bassinette, and I rushed to take a quick, cooling shower while Patrick was out on an errand. As soon as I shut the water off, I heard the baby wailing miserably. I ran naked into the nursery, grabbing a pad on the way that I irreverently slapped between my legs. I scooped the baby up, put her to breast, and taking a deep breath, I settled into the rocking chair as she began to nurse.

By now, the milk was dripping from my other breast. An infant's nursing often causes their sphincter to relax, so with that came an explosive noise from the little darling's diaper, immediately followed by an unmistakable warmth running down my leg. Startled at what was happening, I yelped, and made a lunge toward the changing table to grab a cloth. With my sudden move, she pulled off the breast, screaming, and my pad dropped to the floor, milk now squirting from both breasts, baby poop running down my leg and all with my wet, uncombed hair. It was at that precise moment that Patrick arrived home. On hearing the commotion, he stuck his head in the nursery. I looked up at him in utter amazement and a degree of disgust and said, "So this is motherhood?" Perusing the scene, he calmly responded, "Not like any magazine cover I have ever seen." Me neither!

This was a story I wanted to share with my niece to add some levity to the new role that lay ahead for her and Paul. I was hoping that she could forget her credentials and just take motherhood as it was meant to be. It is a unique journey for each woman, couple, and family, not to be compared with anyone else's, because there is nothing like having the first baby. This is the little being that takes a couple from what I refer to as "singlehood" to parenthood. Even though married, a couple is still aware of their individuality, and are used to doing things on their own schedules. A baby changes that. Remember, change is not bad, it is simply different.

This first baby is the one that makes you a mother and a father, creating your new roles as parents. Subsequent children, while a blessing, do not confer the same transformative power. By then, you have already earned the title, and generally know what to expect. The fatigue and interrupted nights are not a surprise to either of you. You know things will settle down. But with this first baby, it is all new. It does not matter if you have nieces or nephews or made a teen career of babysitting. This one you do not leave after a few hours. The responsibility is yours alone. The reality of it can feel daunting.

After childbirth, sex is often the last thing on a woman's mind. Her whole body is aching. She is wondering if she will ever feel normal again. Fatigue and soreness interfere with the desire for intercourse for the first few weeks and that is when the risk of complications is the greatest. Four to six weeks is usually recommended for better healing. The wise couple will realize there is more to intimacy than intercourse and employ other means to stay connected during these early weeks.

An article titled "Sex after Pregnancy: Set Your Own Timeline" on the Mayo Clinic website addresses these issues as you adjust to life with a new baby. They recommend that "If you're not feeling sexy or you're afraid sex will hurt, talk to your spouse." They go on to say, "Until you're ready to have sex, maintain intimacy in other ways. Spend time together without the baby, even if it's just a few minutes in the morning and after the baby goes to sleep. Look for other ways to express affection." Do not ignore the topic of physical intimacy. It is especially important during this major life transition.

First time parenthood brings many challenges. Your own experiences of childhood, your personality and temperament, and the different skills you each possess will be brought into your new role. This evolution from pregnancy, birth, and caring for an infant is a new dance that requires learning trickier steps than one might imagine. Your steps will not be perfect, but they will be good enough. Be kind to yourself and each other.

Steps:

- Learn what to expect during pregnancy, delivery, and newborn care.

- Keep regular prenatal visits and go together whenever possible

- Be honest about your own fears.

- Sign up for childbirth classes.

- Ask for the help you need.

- When someone offers help, accept it.

- Take turns caring for your infant so the other can rest.

- Do not criticize or correct each other on small issues.

- Show appreciation as your spouse learns their new role.

Suggestions for family and friends:

- Help new parents by making a meal or offering to do some housework.

- Offer to help with infant care to give parents a chance to sleep.

- If there are other children, take them for the afternoon, so parents can rest.

- Call before stopping in on new parents and make the visit brief.

WORKS CITED

Bombeck, Erma. *A Marriage Made in Heaven: or Too Tired for an Affair.* New York: Harper Collins Publishing, 1993.

Mayo Clinic Healthy Lifestyle. "Sex after Pregnancy: Set your own timeline." July 7, 2018. https://www.mayoclinic.org/healthy-lifestyle/labor-and-delivery/in-depth/sex-after-pregnancy/art-20045669.

Pearlstein, Teri, Margaret Howard, Amy Salisbury, and Caron Zlotnik. "Postpartum Depression." *American Journal Obstetrics and Gynecology.* April 1, 2009. https://doi.org/10.1016/j.ajog.2008.11.033.

Spock, Benjamin, and Robert Needleman. *Dr. Spock's Baby and Child Care.* New York: Simon and Schuster, 1945 and 2005.

CHAPTER 26

Valuing the Gift of Solitude

"I hold this to be the highest task of a bond between two people: that each should stand guard over the solitude of the other."

RAINER MARIA RILKE,
Bohemian-Austrian poet and novelist.

During these twist and shout years you may find it hard to stay in sync with all the responsibilities you are both carrying. You do not just want to survive this stage; you also want to enjoy the dance. Keeping emotionally connected during the chaos is the not-so-secret ingredient in preventing gray divorce. What can make the difference? Taking the time for personal solitude and encouraging your spouse to do the same can serve as one answer.

Solitude is that alone time where you seek quiet: no radio, TV, cell phone, computer, tweeting, blogging, reading, or talking. Shut out the world, the chaos of life, and center yourself. Nothing fancy, just a quiet place where you can focus—on nothing! It may be going for a walk without an iPod or cell phone in your pocket or sitting quietly in a room protected from distractions. In her book, *Listening Below the Noise*, author Anne LeClaire writes about finding a personal sanctuary where "you are drawn for inspiration and restoration, for solace or consolation." She shares that practicing silence has allowed her a sacred space for personal growth and inner peace. Begin with small steps.

Walking the dog became my place of quiet. Prior to having Duke, I admit I was not consistent with solitude. After establishing the daily walking habit, I became a believer. The time I took, with no devices or talking, made me appreciate the quiet. Talking to myself, praying, and thinking over different scenarios of a problem, provided me new ideas and insights.

The couples who are aware of the many benefits of solitude make it an essential aspect of their life and see the positive effects on their relationship. Quiet time has several physical and mental health benefits: calming your heart rate, lowering your blood pressure, and general de-stressing. Issues around work, marriage, parenting, politics, and community can be overwhelming. You are setting yourself and your marriage as priorities when you take time alone every day and encourage your spouse to do the same.

For those of you who live a yogic lifestyle, you may already be incorporating mindfulness, meditation, silent time, maybe even silent retreats into your life. Good for you. Strive to continue these healthy habits during the "twist and shout" years. This alone space may seem nearly impossible, given all the demands on your time and the continual input of technology. Designating 15 minutes each day to escape from devices and people requires a deliberate decision, but the benefits can be liberating. Listen. Be still.

Solitude helps your mind to relax, prevents stresses from accumulating, and allows you to determine what is really bothering you. Quiet space lets you focus on individual issues and how best to address them. Is there another way you could look at a situation? Are you reacting to someone, or some circumstances, because of a totally unrelated issue? Remember the "Preventing Contamination" chapter? Quiet often permits solutions to percolate that an assaulted mind cannot hear.

Then, who to talk to? In her book, *Help, Thanks, Wow: The Three Essential Prayers*, Anne Lamott talks about the "God Box." This is a physical container where she puts a note of request, frustration, or distress for which she has no answer and needs help. She folds the paper, places it in the box, and turns it over to God, asking assistance in knowing what direction to face so she'll have "a moment of intuition."

After churning an issue over, I like to pray. Asking God helps me accept my limitations in solving problems on my own. My personal feeling about prayer is that it does not change the circumstances I am facing, but it gives me the courage to do what needs to be done. Solitude can be a powerful and amazing tool for "hearing" feedback that may be impossible otherwise.

Give yourself the time to "listen" for answers. Do this daily and encourage it for your spouse. Solitude is an opportunity to gain self-awareness and build a stronger bond with each other. It can also spare your spouse from having to listen to the litany of issues that may well be troubling both of you. Taking time alone can allow you to process concerns, solve a problem, and perhaps be able to offer options to each other.

Even couples who recognize the value of time alone admit that making space is a challenge. Unfortunately, you cannot make the time, you must *take* the time from the 24 hours allotted you each day. Make this exercise a priority. Let something else go: a TV show, time on the web, checking social media. Solitude can bring solace, but you must recognize its value and assign the time, just as you should for physical exercise. This practice is a way to treat yourself and your marriage with care. The sense of renewal is a gift you give each other that helps you stay in sync.

Steps:

- Set a time every day for 15 minutes of uninterrupted quiet.

- Encourage the same for your spouse.

- Write down thoughts you gain during this time.

- Listen for possible solutions to an issue.

- Learn the techniques of mindfulness and meditation to de-stress.

WORKS CITED

"Getting Started with Mindfulness." *Mindful.* https://www.mindful.org/meditation/mindfulness-getting-started.

Kabat-Zinn, Jon. *Falling Awake: How to Practice Mindfulness in Everyday Life.* New York: Hachette Books, 2018.

Lamott, Anne; *Help, Thanks, Wow: The Three Essential Prayers*, Penguin Group, New York, N.Y. 2012.

LeClaire, Anne D. *Listening Below the Noise*. New York: Harper Collins: 2009.

Rilke, Rainer Marie. *Rilke on Love and Other Difficulties: Translations and Consideration*. W.W. Norton & Co. Inc. New York, N.Y. 1975, 2004.

CHAPTER 27

Raising Children

"One thing they never tell you about child raising is that for the rest of your life, at the drop of a hat, you are expected to know your child's name and how old he or she is."

ERMA BOMBECK

This book is about marriage and is not an instruction manual on parenting. The following chapters on raising children are meant to preserve and promote emotional and physical intimacy in your marriage, while also rearing well-adjusted, healthy, happy children. Taking care of yourself and keeping your marriage intact is the best way to provide a healthy and nurturing environment for your kids.

If there is a more challenging, rewarding, exhilarating, exhausting, joyful, heart-wrenching, humbling career than parenting, I am not aware of it. The word "career" seems to describe parenting more accurately than the word "job." A job is often temporary, and you may have several during your lifetime. Career implies a longer duration, perhaps transitioning to a lighter schedule, but often requiring your skills even in retirement. Similarly, parenting is a lifetime commitment. Raising children is a journey that can expand, enhance, and deepen your marriage or it can tax, deplete, and erode your relationship. Healthy habits and attention to your marriage are intended to prevent the latter.

When I think about raising children in the context of marriage, I think of my parents and my childhood. They had very different personalities and temperaments, which often made parenting a task for them. I benefited growing up the fourth of five children, sandwiched between two boys who were challenging adolescents. If my behavior stayed under the radar, I was afforded a lot of independence and freedom. Their focus was on keeping those two boys in line.

One day, when I was about 16, my mother, alluding to the stress, put her palms together and then separated them as she raised them high in the air saying, "Children do this to a marriage." She was confirming what research now shows that couples with children deal with more stress than couples without children. This finding could be referred to as "grandmother research," which are topics that have been scientifically proven that your grandmother could have told you for free!

Parenting is a vocation that will require work and compromise, but it has its rewards. It is remarkable that every day, couples unwittingly sign on for a 24 hour a day job, 365 days a year, with no pay, no vacations, no sick time, and no pension plan. Of course, there is no retirement because the job is never done! The only break parents may have when they are raising their children is when they can pay someone, or barter with family and friends, to give them a little time off. Staying focused on the prize—raising caring, independent, productive, healthy adults, with your marriage intact—can help keep you two on the dance floor.

Here are some considerations as you face the challenges and rewards of parenting.

The importance of self-esteem and self-confidence:

A good marriage begins with knowing who you are, and good parenting is no different. Having a strong sense of self will enhance your dance during these busy years. The steps you two perform will be fast and furious at times, and will require patience, confidence, and commitment. Parents who have self-confidence are better able to set boundaries, enforce rules, and model healthy behaviors for their children. They are more likely to be patient during the vicissitudes of their child's development. Parents with positive self-esteem do not feel put down when their children are not happy with the rules. It is important to recognize you are not meant to be your children's best friend. They will have many friends during their lifetime, but they will have only one set of parents who love them unconditionally. Be that for them.

Know that it is not unusual for young children to be upset when they do not get their way. Some parents have their self-esteem crushed when their little darling yells, "I hate you." They do not hate you; they are angry! Children can learn the power of how language can heal or hurt from your reaction. When you know why you have your rules, and have clearly explained the reasons to your child, you are modeling your values, morals, and expectations.

When you follow through with the consequences you have laid out, you are demonstrating predictability, consistency, and trust. *Do not be intimidated by your children.* They need to know you love them, what reaction to expect, and the consequences of their behavior. A lack of self-confidence in your rules will undermine your parenting and your marriage. If you find yourself falling into this trap, work to bolster your self-esteem and that of your spouse. Parents who know who they are as individuals and value taking care of themselves, each other, and their children, fare the best. Learn from the parenting resources available through community agencies, health providers, churches, libraries and online sites. Knowledge is power, and when it comes to raising children, knowledge is critical.

Nurturing your emotional intimacy while parenting:

Children certainly require attention during all stages of their development. To meet their physical, emotional, financial, social, and spiritual needs takes energy and resources. As adults, however, it is important to recognize your own needs and look to yourself and your spouse and not expect your child to fill those needs. When a marriage is suffering from a lack of support and intimacy, it may cause a parent to look to the child for the emotional connection that should be available from the spouse. This is an inappropriate and an unfair burden to place on a child and one that can result in emotional confusion. Children are not in your lives to meet your emotional needs. If your marriage is challenged by poor communication and lack of connection, you need to address this with each other and talk about what is needed. If you are unable to bridge this emotional gap, you should seek professional help for both individual and marital therapy. Your child's well-being, as well as your marriage, is at stake.

Awareness of your different parenting styles:

Since each of you is a product of your own upbringing and experiences, you may often find yourselves at odds as to how to respond to a child's behavior. Researchers have identified four types of parenting styles. Amy Morin wrote about these styles and their effects on children in her article, "4 Types of Parenting Styles and Their Effects on Kids." These styles are Authoritarian, Authoritative, Permissive and Uninvolved.

You may have been raised in a household that employed strict rules with a "because I said so" approach. This *authoritarian* style is very restrictive and misses the opportunity for children to safely make some decisions, take some risks, and learn from their mistakes.

One of you may have been brought up in a family with high expectations, a safe home environment, with specific rules and limits. This method is referred to as the *authoritative* style. I would prefer this be called democratic so as not to confuse these two styles, and I think it more accurately describes this approach. This style allows for give and take and reasonable decision making. If you grew up in a home with emotionally absent parents, you may have essentially raised yourself having few, if any, rules. This *permissive* style often does not provide the child with boundaries that help build emotional security. A fourth style is the *uninvolved* or disinterested or distracted parent, bordering on neglect.

In 2011, Amy Chua published the controversial book *Battle Hymn of the Tiger Mother*. Chua coined the term "Tiger Mom" to describe a mother who is a tough disciplinarian and brings up her children in what Chua describes as the traditional Chinese way. The apparent success of Chua's own strict upbringing and how she raised her children could make a strong argument for authoritarian parenting. Others would argue about the danger for children who feel they cannot or do not meet their parents' high standards.

Dr. Laurence Steinberg refers to studies over the years that address the correlation of the parent-child relationship to the child's psychological development. Steinberg notes the outcome depends on parenting style: "Responsive parents are warm and accepting toward their children, enjoying them and trying to see things from their perspective." Other "parents who are insufficiently demanding are too lenient; they exercise minimal control, provide little guidance, and often yield to their child's demands." Steinberg concludes that a child's "healthy psychological development is facilitated when the parents are both *responsive* and *moderately demanding* [emphasis added]."

For better or worse, your family of origin is your primary model for parenting. As unhealthy as the model may have been, you may find yourselves replicating it with your own children, even against your better judgment. Without new knowledge, it is very easy to slip into the parenting methods that you witnessed growing up. Talk about what you want for your child. Be respectful of your different approaches and try to find common ground regarding setting limits and consequences for behavior.

While you may not always agree, negotiating to present a unified front is the best approach. Even young children learn early how to manipulate parents. Children can become masters at the "divide and conquer" approach. Many parents have found that it is wise to not answer a child's request until they have talked with their spouse. This prevents undermining the other parent and strengthens your partnership. Frequent, effective communication, and compromise will help you provide consistent parenting.

The many demands in your daily life are no excuse to ignore what is most important. Maintain that private time every day to connect with each other. The physical, emotional, financial, social, and spiritual legs under your marriage table are fortified by the love, respect, trust you have built into your relationship. These need to be continually shored up during this child-rearing stage.

Avoiding parent burnout and choosing parent renewal:

There are some parents who pride themselves on running ragged for their children and focus their energy almost solely on them, to the exclusion of their marriage. I have rarely seen where this approach benefits either party. Parents inevitably end up exhausted and feel underappreciated. The children often end up over-indulged with a sense of entitlement. Parents who learn how to encourage independence in their children, with a gradual increase of responsibility have children who enter adulthood accountable for their own choices. They know how to problem solve, manage their money, and create their own lifestyle.

When I conducted groups for parents raising young children, I would share my Parent Burnout Cycle and my Parent Renewal Cycle. When you can identify where you are on this merry-go-round, you can decide how to change it into a positive cycle for yourselves.

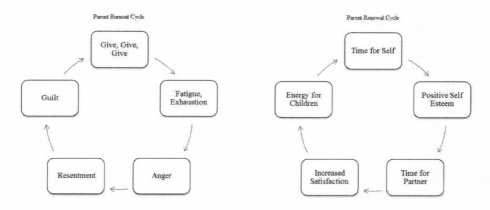

The Parent Burnout Cycle is easy to recognize. Because you love your child, you want to provide the best care you can. You do this by giving of yourself. However, if you do not set boundaries, you may find yourself giving until the well runs dry. Continually giving to your child, with little regard for your own needs, results in fatigue and exhaustion, which, in turn, can cause anger. Feeling deprived yourself, you may justifiably experience resentment. Then, as a "good" parent, you will feel guilty for resenting your child, resulting in giving even more, which continues the cycle.

"If Mama ain't happy, ain't nobody happy" is a well-known cliché that may sound sexist today, with many fathers doing the parenting and running the household. It could rightly be altered to say, "If the at-home parent ain't happy, ain't nobody happy." There can be a domino effect regarding parenting, which is to say, that as the main caregiver falls, so falls the family.

The Parent Renewal Cycle shifts the priority to the caregiver. You recognize the importance of taking time for yourself. Even if it is just an hour a week, self-care can elevate your self-esteem. Then you allot time with your spouse. Together these can give you a renewed sense of satisfaction. This in turn provides an increase in your physical and mental energy. With that sense of renewal, everyone benefits.

Everything you want to get done in a day as a spouse, parent, employee, and homemaker will not all get done, and none to perfection. The sooner you can accept that reality, the happier everyone will be. What items can you eliminate from your to-do list that could soothe your soul? Peace of mind is priceless. Do not set yourself to live up to someone else's standards. You can always clean up things later. Dust keeps.

Steps:

The importance of self-esteem and self-confidence:

- Watch your self-talk.

- Be predictable and consistent in your approach, not moody.

- Do not be intimidated by your child.

- Be your child's mentor, not their best friend.

- Express affection, verbally and physically.

Nurturing your emotional intimacy while parenting:

- Remember to take time to connect with your spouse daily.

- Seek emotional support from each other, not from your child.

- Prioritize your marriage and family over appearances.

- Appreciate and support what you each accomplish every day.

Awareness of your parenting styles:

- Appreciate and respect your different parenting styles.

- Compromise on different approaches about the rules and consequences.

- Support each other in your healthy attempts at parenting. It is never perfect.

Avoid parent burnout and choose parent renewal:

- Pay attention to your eating, sleeping, and exercise. Parenting takes energy.

- Know your own needs and express them.

- Ask for what you need from others.

- Take time for yourself.

- Make a reasonable (not a ridiculous!) to-do list before bed.

- Expect that the unexpected will interfere with getting it all done.

- Spend time with friends who understand and do not judge you.

WORKS CITED

Chua, Amy. *Battle Hymn of the Tiger Mother.* New York: Penguin Books, 2011

Morin, Amy; www.verywellfamily.com, "4 Types of Parenting Styles and Their Effects on Kids." May 16, 2019

Steinberg, Laurence. "Parent-Child Relationships: Infancy, Toddlerhood,

Preschool, School Age, Adolescence, Adults." *Psychology Encyclopedia.* https://psychology.jrank.org/pages/472/Parent-Child-Relationships. html, 2019.

CHAPTER 28

Picking Your Battles

*"Perhaps the soundest advice for parents is: Lighten up.
People have been raising children for approximately as long as
there have been people."*

GEORGE WILL

For me, these "twist and shout" years hit full-on when I realized I no longer had sole control of my own turf. When our oldest child started first grade, I came up against the first of several competing authority figures, namely Mr. Brown. It was a Monday evening in early September. The perfectly organized first child announced at dinner that Mr. Brown, the physical education teacher, told the children they all had to have their sneakers by Friday's gym class. We had already determined that she needed new sneakers after an active, growing summer. They were indeed too small and worn out; replacing them, however, was not high on the priority list.

Our children were six years, three years, and three months old. We had moved into our new house two months before (not smart postpartum planning!) and boxes were still not unpacked. The other house had not sold leaving us with two mortgage payments and a bridge loan. The three-year-old just started nursery school, Patrick was teaching and refereeing, and I was nursing the baby, trying to keep the business afloat, and working one or two days a week. Sneakers were not a pressing issue.

"Mr. Brown says we have to have them!" she announced.

"When is gym class?" I inquired, half listening, while serving dinner.

"Friday," she replied.

"Oh well, today is only Monday," I said with relief.

Then, the killer statement only a perceptive first child would make: "Well, you know how fast time flies around here!" I could not help but laugh, but part of me wanted to cry. How right she was.

Flash forward three nights. It is Thursday evening, bucketing rain, and I am serving dinner at 7:30 (way too late for young children!) when the oldest asks, "What day is tomorrow?"

Immediately, my mind registers the day. Damn that Mr. Brown. "It's Friday," I say pathetically.

"I knew it, I knew it. I don't have my sneakers," as tears welled in her eyes.

"Patrick, pull up her pajamas, throw on her boots and raincoat and get her down to the shoe store," I ordered. "It closes at 8:00, so there is no time to waste."

It is a funny scene now. It was not a funny then, only reflective of the chaos that was swirling in our household.

Dr. Linda Papadopoulos, a Canadian-born psychologist, who practices in England, wrote about the 20 most common causes of parental stress following a poll of 2000 parents. Five out of the 20 related to getting children up, dressed, ready with everything they need, and out to school on time. Mothers and fathers spend almost two hours a day feeling stressed with these tasks, along with trying to keep the house tidy and getting their children to behave well in public. Our situation certainly validated the results of that study.

I did not like appearing overwhelmed and looking like I was not on top of my duties. That is how I felt then. And it was just the beginning of a long stretch of years when most of the time I probably looked much more organized than I deserved. Actor, comedian, and father of five, Jim Gaffigan said it well for me, "I don't know what is more exhausting about parenting; the getting up early or acting like you know what you're doing." Somewhere along the way, I realized that it was important to be kind to myself and accept that I was indeed juggling a lot of balls and it was not unusual to drop one occasionally. Friends who accepted me "as is" were the best support during these years. Anyone doing a white-glove test at my house was no real friend.

Throughout these years, it is critical to be there for each other without criticism of what is not getting done. This is when a daily habit like teatime provides connection without interruption. During this stage of marriage, the time is likely to be after the kids are in bed. You will be exhausted but keep this routine anyway. You can both reiterate what you did that day to contribute to the well-being of your family. It is good to list even the miniscule tasks, so you can give yourself and your spouse full credit. Why not? No one else is going to. Some days I would add things to my to-do list I had already done just to have a complete record of my "accomplishments." Seeing the items scratched off on the paper helped me justify my existence some days and made me feel better. Feeling better is an okay goal.

These are the days when you realize other people have an influence on how you run your family. Teachers and coaches will pose as a higher-ranking authority figure to your child. While they deserve your respect, do not allow yourself to be intimidated! Do whatever it takes to keep dancing during these crazy days. Supporting each other is the name of the game. Consider these:

Picking your battles:

During the years of raising children, you want to remind yourself where to focus your precious, limited energy. One mantra that many parents have found helpful is "pick your battles." While many issues may frustrate you, far fewer will be worthy of your energy. A fun memory and a great example occurred when I was carpooling to nursery school. I pulled up to my friend Paula's house. As Paula waved to me from the door, four-year-old Becky raced out from behind her mother with colors flying. She was decked out in a polka-dotted blouse, a striped skirt, colorful leggings like Pippi Long-stocking, and an orange hairband. Paula, mother of three, just smiled as she rolled her eyes. She had long ago learned some battles are not worth fighting. Paula knew that no one would ever think she dressed Becky!

Rather than getting caught up in all of life's daily aggravations, you can categorize the situations by their importance. *Safety* is first and always a top priority: car seats, seat belts, helmets, no playing with matches, etc. Parents are responsible to set and consistently enforce such rules. There are no exceptions here.

Secondly, is *teaching good manners, courteous behavior, kindness,* and *empathy.* This is an ongoing and repetitive process. When teaching politeness, it is important not to be punitive, but to recognize children learn through repeated lessons and your modeling. Learning these attributes has a life-long impact.

The third category is to *recognize age-related behaviors* and keep your cool. These behaviors, while frustrating, usually represent a developmental phase (temper tantrums, a messy room, choosing clothes) rather than a serious issue. It is good to know the difference. More appropriate ways of reacting may be to talk with the child about alternative behaviors, redirecting them to another activity, or grab a camera and capture the moment.

Remember patience and a sense of humor:

Sometimes parents can find themselves a bit too serious about raising a good, decent human being when a little humor could help. Patience may be in short supply leaving you overreacting to some issues. There are no perfect parents out there and it is important to forgive yourself for your less-than-perfect behavior. The great philosopher, Mister Rogers had wise words to take to heart: "Just as it takes time for children to understand what real love is, it takes time for parents to understand that being *always* patient, quiet, even-tempered, and respectful isn't necessarily what "good" parents are . . . All children need to see that the adults in their lives can feel anger and not hurt themselves or anyone else when they feel that way."

A sense of humor during these seemingly endless years of child rearing can be a saving grace. I learned it was more helpful to take a picture of the toddler who unraveled an entire roll of toilet paper rather than lose my cool over an event that was unlikely to ever happen again. But rest assured, I did not always see the funny side of things.

One evening, I served up a pork chop dinner. The seven-year-old was not fancying pork that night and she kept moving it around the plate. Well, maybe it was fatigue, the heat, or just cooking one more dinner, unappreciated by children, but I'd had it! My patience was spent, and the well of humor had run dry. I told her to sit there until she finished as I walked out of the room. After she left the table, Patrick went to clean up the kitchen and found no remnants of a bone on her plate. He called me into the bathroom after finding the lone pork chop floating in the toilet, unable to be flushed. I went ballistic, worried that we were raising a deceptive human being with no moral compass. My humor was not to be found that evening, as Patrick had to peel me off the ceiling. A calm talk later with the offender about a better way to handle the situation (along with some humor about a pig being too big for the plumbing) would have been far more appropriate and helpful to everyone's emotional health.

Recognize the work involved and the importance of coordinating schedules:

Our four children were spread over 12 years. I took a picture of the four of them the week one started college, one high school, one junior high, and one first grade. Because they were at different developmental ages, Patrick and I were handling temper tantrums amidst adolescent meltdowns, checking out kindergartens on the weekdays, and doing college tours on the weekends. We limited each child to two activities: a sport and a music lesson. That made eight weekly commitments not including their social activities, birthday parties, special celebrations, and holidays. Most of the time, my head was spinning. Patrick worked full time as a teacher. After school, he refereed high school and college soccer and our children's teams on the weekend. He worked our business in the evenings with me. We never watched sitcoms during those years; we felt like we were starring in one. I posted a sign on the refrigerator that said "Having children is like installing a bowling alley in your head." The truth of that made me laugh and that was good.

Patrick helped with housework as time allowed, but as in most families, this more often falls to the one at home. I was not "Suzy Homemaker," much to my mother-in-law's dismay. The house was not a showcase. On a weekday, one could find my kitchen counter stacked with clutter and piles of laundry at various stages: dirty, wet, dried, and folded. It was the same way with food: grocery bags to be unloaded, food to be cooked, dirty dishes to be washed, and clean dishes to be put away. Tomorrow was the same show, same players. Nothing was ever completed.

Traditionally, household chores have belonged to the woman. Even though most women now work outside the home and many are the higher wage earner, they still perform more of the household tasks. According to a study by University College London of 8,500 heterosexual couples, "women do approximately 16 hours of household chores every week, while men do closer to six." The result is fatigue, and often a chronic source of friction in marriages.

One of the things I feel prevented my resentment for the inequity of housework that still permeates many marriages today is that, on my days at home, Patrick would ask, "How was your day?" rather than, "What did you do today?" I am sure there were many times he wondered, given the state of the house. I certainly had nothing monumental to report. I had not knocked down any walls or redone a bathroom. My time was spent repeating the multitude of mundane tasks from the day before. It helped our marriage a great deal that he did not ask. When one spouse is the stay-at-home parent and the other is the primary breadwinner, it is important that couples show respect for both roles. Providing support and appreciation for each other's contributions goes a long way to shore up your marriage.

For a few years, when our children were young, I worked one or two days a week, which allowed me to stay professionally connected. I called them my "mental health days," as getting out of the house kept my sanity intact. Running our business from our home, along with caring for the children, made for full days and a hectic schedule. There was a part of me, however, that thrived on the chaos. Such disorder would not suit everyone's temperament. This is another instance when it is important to know who you are and what you can handle, and plan accordingly. Not to do so can have a serious impact on your own stress level, the household, and your marriage. Talking with your spouse about the week ahead and who is doing what, can help alleviate misunderstandings and know that everyone and everything is covered. Patrick and I met twice a day for teatime: when we got home from work to touch base on the day and again after the kids were in bed to coordinate our calendars. Connecting with each other and drawing a deep breath, helped keep both of us in sync.

It is not always possible to stop the merry-go-round but look for ways you can give each other a break so that you are not both running on empty. One thing Patrick and I discovered that helped us was to give each other a free morning on the weekend. On Saturday morning, one of us would get up with the kids while the other slept in. We went to church on Saturday afternoon, so we could allow the other to sleep in on Sunday. The next weekend, we switched the days.

Staying connected as a family:

One way to stay connected in your marriage is to prioritize dinner time, or maybe breakfast for families where a parent works an evening or night shift instead. According to the Search Institute, "research shows that kids in families that frequently eat together tend to get better grades and are less likely to use alcohol, drugs, and tobacco." With the busy timetable you are keeping, this is not always easy but think about it. Does it not make sense that a family who comes together for at least 20 minutes daily would build more connections and bonding than those who rarely do? Talking about the "thorns and roses" of your day or having a stack of cards with questions to stimulate conversation can keep you connected about each other's lives.

Parenting and running a household require a lot of energy. The duties should not fall solely on the adults. Your children are part of the family. Assign age-appropriate chores so that each child is part of the team. Swap the duties so no one gets stuck permanently with an assignment they hate. Along with contributing to the household, your children are learning skills that will make them a better roommate when they are out on their own. Your efforts will make a positive difference!

Model behavior you want your child to emulate:

During the chaos of daily life, one of your primary jobs is as a disciplinarian. You want to remember that discipline involves teaching, as in imparting moral and ethical values and not punishing out of anger. It is the wise parent who remembers the importance of modeling the behavior you want your children to emulate. During the child raising years, I kept a sign on the refrigerator as a reminder, "Your behavior is screaming so loudly, I cannot hear what you are saying."

Learning about caring for others and instilling kindness and empathy is not taught by words but rather by action. When our children were young, we would take them to a local nursing home to visit some of the residents. They were not always enthusiastic about going, but they seemed happier after they went. The fruits of that were born out later when our older daughter chose a nursing home as her volunteer work in Junior High and brought me to meet one of her residents. To see kindnesses paid forward is among one of the greatest gifts a parent can receive.

Seek continuing education for parenting:

Anyone who has a professional license knows the necessity of continuing education to keep up their accreditation. There is no job, however, that will have more impact on your marriage or your children's lives than the role you play in raising them. Yet, there are no requirements for parenting. There is no orientation and there is no instruction manual. Attending childbirth classes helped you prepare to bring your child into this world, but what about after that, during all the different stages of their development?

Children are constantly changing as they move through childhood and parents are well-served knowing what to expect at each stage. Take the time to peruse the parenting section of your local bookstore to educate yourselves. Magazine articles, online posts, blogs, and podcasts about parenting can increase your confidence as you learn about their stages of development.

Your health care provider, church, schools, and community agencies often have speakers presenting on topics about the growth and development of children and teens. Such opportunities can allow you to parent in a proactive way. Patrick and I knew that, even as a teacher and pediatric nurse, we did not have all the answers. We took every opportunity to hear from experts about raising kids and implemented those ideas we found helpful. Knowledge is power. Use it to your advantage.

Parenting today is different than in past generations. Connect with the parents of your child's friends. Have the kids over to your house so you can get to know each other. Talk with other parents about the use of social media. Technology, access to a myriad of electronic devices, and differing values among families are some of the reasons that make your job more challenging. You must now be willing to ask some tough questions to assure the safety of your children. I learned this the hard way after the fact.

Our first child went to a sleepover for a ninth birthday party. When she arrived home, I asked what they did. She told me they watched five movies, one being *Psycho*! She said, "we were scared, so some of us just played with her dolls." After that, I never assumed. You are not dictating what should happen in another's home, only that you want to know for the safety of your child if you should let them attend. You may well find that you are giving another parent the confidence they need to do the same for their child under similar circumstances. Be supportive of each other in these actions so as not to undermine your marriage. You will feel comfortable about the decision you make, and your children will come to expect these questions as something they can count on when going outside your home.

I look back on those hectic days with few regrets. My mother had a saying about the busy years of raising a family: "The days may drag, but the years fly." With the children now grown, and on their own, Patrick and I understand what she meant.

Steps:

Picking your battles:

- Be the adult. Maturity matters.

- Enforce safety issues.

- Teach your children manners.

- Model kindness and caring.

- Be firm, fair, and consistent in your approach to rules.

- Remember that discipline means teaching.

- Discipline out of love, not anger.

Remember patience and a sense of humor:

- Take a deep breath and relieve each other when tensions are high.

- Use humor with each other and your children.

- Keep your phone camera handy.

- Have fun with your child.

Recognize the work involved and the importance of coordinating your schedules:

- Share parenting responsibilities.

- Share household chores and include the children.

- Communicate about your week so everyone knows what is happening.

- Be kind to yourself and each other. Parenting is a hard job.

- Look for ways to give each other a break.

Stay connected as a family:

- Keep your priorities in check.

- Make daily family mealtime a priority.

- Let your child know you love them unconditionally.

Seek continuing education for parenting:

- Educate yourselves on child development.

- Take advantage of community resources on parenting.

- Be a responsible parent. Check in with other parents. Ask the tough questions.

WORKS CITED

"The 20 Most Stressful Things About Parenthood Revealed." September 1, 2016. https://www.swnsdigital.com/2016/09/the-20-most-stressful-things-about-parenthood-revealed/.

Barr, Sabrina, "Women Still Do Majority of Household Chores, Study Finds." *The Independent.* July 26, 2019. https://www.independent.co.uk/life-style/women-men-household-chores-domestic-house-gender-norms-a9021586.html.

"Free Resources from Search Institute." *Search Institute.* https://www.search-institute.org/tools-resources/free-downloads/.

"The 20 Most Stressful Things About Parenthood Revealed." September 1, 2016. https://www.swnsdigital.com/2016/09/the-20-most-stressful-things-about-parenthood-revealed/.

Rogers, Fred. *The World According to Mister Rogers.* New York: Hyperion, 2003.

Yasinchuk, Jeff. "The Ideal Parenting Myth…Busted?" Getting Curious (blog). September 29, 2019. https://jeffyasinchuk.ca/2019/09/29/the-ideal-parenting-myth-busted/.

CHAPTER 29

Accepting and Enjoying Your Child as an Individual

"Allow children to be happy in their own way, for what better way will they find?"

SAMUEL JOHNSON

As a parent, you may expect to feel unconditional love toward your child but *liking* and *accepting* may not come as naturally. If you have more than one child, you may marvel at the differences in their personalities, temperaments, hobbies, intellect, humor, and mannerisms. If you have siblings, look at the differences in your characteristics. You may wonder where these traits came from, especially if they are so different from yours. Parents of adopted children expect differences, yet they may still find it difficult to accept the idiosyncrasies of their child.

Children are brought into the family, be it through birth or adoption, with parents' highest hopes and expectations. Birth parents likely believe their children will have related physical features and will likely have similar interests and values. Adoptive children, while they likely will not physically resemble their parents, are often expected to duplicate them in their values, religion, and habits. When a child's behavior, interests, and/or abilities, however, are vastly different from the parents' expectations, it can pose such a conundrum that some parents do not know how to respond.

Conflicts can arise when one of you holds fast to how you feel your child *should* behave, or what interests they *should* have. When a parent refuses to acknowledge and accept differences in their child, this can cause a rift, not only in the marriage, but can also pose a threat to the child's healthy sense of self. Attempts to mold a child who has interests different from a parent can have detrimental, lifelong effects on a child's emotional development.

An example of differences and the lack of a parent's acceptance of a child's nature stands out in my mind and occurred early in our marriage. While traveling across country, Patrick and I stopped to visit some family friends I had not seen in years. We had never met their adopted children. The father had a large physical presence along with a personality to match his successful career as a salesman. He enjoyed sports and was an avid fisherman and hunter. His 12-year-old son had a slight build and a pleasant, polite, and quiet demeanor. The boy was telling us about his stamp collecting when his dad managed to cajole him out into the yard. There, he tossed him a glove and proceeded to pitch fast balls at him.

This pubescent boy was no more interested in playing ball than he was in hunting or fishing. It was evident his hobbies were totally different from his father's. He was quite eager to tell us about his stamp collecting, while his dad showed little interest in his son's quieter pursuits. To this day, it is painful to recall watching that father hurl fast balls at a kid who had no interest in sports and recoiled with every pitch. During the visit, we never heard the dad share any pride about his boy. It was clear to me that this father could not accept the fact his son shared no interest in the pastimes he enjoyed.

The incident left an indelible impression on Patrick and me as we contemplated our future as parents. While the mother did what she could to soften the interaction by giving her son positive feedback, it was not likely to fill the void for a boy who feels he does not measure up to his father's expectations. When a spouse observes insensitive behavior, it is important to be alert to the detrimental effects on the child and discuss the issue. If unable to communicate openly, a couple should seek professional help to see the situation through a different lens, one that will benefit the child, family, and the marriage.

You will see traits in your children that come from family members you may have never met or may not like! They may have DNA from descendants who lived generations earlier. This is when you realize that children are not clones of you but rather carry physical traits and behaviors from many ancestors. If you can accept your child's individuality as an enrichment to your family, rather than trying to change it, everyone will benefit, as will your marriage.

My career as a pediatric nurse practitioner certainly educated me about the uniqueness of each child. Even in the first few weeks of life, an infant's individual temperament manifests itself by its cry, sleeping patterns, and the ability to soothe itself. During the school years, parents notice other differences by observing their child's behaviors and developing interests. Mom runs marathons and Dad was a college varsity soccer star. They are surprised when their child prefers art or dance classes over sports. When the time comes to choose a college, the teen may gravitate toward engineering, while Mom is a CEO and Dad is a social worker. After attending weekly church services throughout his childhood, the young adult may have no interest in practicing religion and may even question the existence of God.

My awakening to differences happened in the delivery room with the first child. What a surprise for us to be greeted by a baby with a full head of red hair! Neither Patrick or I, or our siblings, had red hair. It was not long before my in-laws informed us that several of their siblings were redheads. Even when the third of our four children emerged as a redhead, we did not fully appreciate how traits from distant family members would influence our family.

Some parents live vicariously through their children. This situation can happen subconsciously when a parent tries to direct a child to an interest or career that they were not able to pursue. Some parents may feel the need to see their child excel at a subject, sport, or field of study that the parent loves. The encouragement and support can be well received by the child who shares that leaning. Difficulty arises when it is the parent's push that results in excess stress for the child. Parents need to be the adults in this situation and check that their dreams do not override the child's needs.

The 2019 college scandal is a sad and extreme example of parents' desires taking precedence over the child's best interest. When parents surreptitiously paid to have their child accepted into a college of their choice, one must ask, "Whose need is being served?" Misdirected desires can come at a cost to the child, the relationship with their parent, and ultimately to the marriage.

Some parents wonder, "Where did I go wrong?" They react as if they are responsible for their child's individuality. Yet, differences in children can make parenting interesting if you can come together to recognize and embrace the uniqueness of your child. Connecting with each other to discuss your child's daily happenings will be important during this already busy time in your marriage. You will be best served if you learn to expect the unexpected regarding your child's personality and temperament.

Children can expose you to hobbies, music, sports, art, literature, and experiences that you never had or sought. Seeing your child pursue, and perhaps excel in, an area that is foreign to you can provide tremendous rewards as a parent. More importantly, however, it permits your child to expand their own boundaries and explore new things, while building their confidence, independence, and self-esteem.

Our children pursued interests that broadened our exposure as well as theirs: the Peace Corps in a third world country, volunteer work in the aftermaths of Hurricane Katrina and the earthquake in Haiti, collecting and delivering books for prisoners, success with a new genre of music, visiting with and expressing condolence to a bereaved parent who lost a child, maintaining a daily paper route for four years, and giving a eulogy for their piano teacher were among the experiences that surprised and enriched Patrick and me.

Other parents often complimented us on these accomplishments, as if we had done the good deeds. I would respond, "Thank you for your kind words, I will pass them on to our child." Patrick and I learned to not take credit for their achievements and not take blame for their mistakes. I am reminded of the saying about the job of parents: "Give your children roots and give them wings." And with those wings, they may fly in directions vastly different than parents expect. Our job is to love them.

Setting aside alone time with your child can be time well invested. Patrick recognized that working full time, and with all the children's activities, there was little one-on-one time. He decided that every Saturday morning, he would take one child out to breakfast on a rotating basis. It was interesting to notice how important this routine became to each of them. One week, when we realized that we would be away that weekend, Patrick told our younger daughter that breakfast would happen the following Saturday. She immediately responded, "Then we will just go out on Friday morning." Reminding her that this was a work/school day did not deter her. "We will just go early." And there she was on Friday morning at the bedside, fully dressed, with her backpack on at 6:00 a.m.! That was when we realized these outings were more special than we might have thought.

When you learn to accept, encourage, and enjoy the unique aspects of your child in the early years, you are setting the stage for open communication in the years ahead. As your child enters middle and high school, different issues will arise. Your child will greatly benefit from an accepting and non-judgmental attitude. How rich the child is who knows that their parents not only accept, but value and encourage their uniqueness. You want the best for your child, but who defines what is best? Those answers may well come from your own child.

Steps:

- Recognize your own and your child's personality types.

- Expose your child to a variety of activities: physical, intellectual, spiritual, musical, artistic, and allow your child to choose what activities to pursue.

- Ask your child to teach *you* something about an activity they enjoy.

- Recognize and support all your child's traits and strengths, not only athleticism and academics but kindness, generosity, and sensitivity as well.

- Plan one-on-one time with each child.

- Let your child take credit for their successes and responsibility for their mistakes.

CHAPTER 30

Enduring and Enjoying Adolescence

"When your children are teenagers, it's important to have a dog so someone in the house is happy to see you."

NORA EPHRON

The adolescent years can bring joy to parents watching their teens transition into young adults. It is also a stressful period for many parents dealing with the physical and emotional changes that accompany adolescence. The impact of hormones on the growing body seems to happen overnight: breast development forecasts the menses, while testosterone transforms voice and body hair. These are the visible changes. Then, there are the internal happenings that are every bit as startling.

The teenage brain is in a period of rapid and vulnerable growth that continues until the mid-20s, which explains why adults find some teen behaviors so confounding. Their pubescent choices are often not logical to the rational brain of the adult parent. These opposing views are the basis for much conflict between parents and teens. If ever parents deserved and could benefit from continuing education, it is during this tumultuous time of adolescence.

Adolescence, in some respects, is not unlike toddlerhood. Both stages present with a strong drive to explore independently and gain a sense of individual identity by challenging rules established by parents. However, that is where the similarity ends.

Watching a toddler stare down the parent, while assertively saying "no," and proceeding to do the forbidden activity, offering that coy "make me" smile, can leave even the most exhausted parent chuckling. That is rarely the case with the hormonally infused adolescent. Here stands a person, sometimes physically larger than you, with a mind which doubts your intelligence and wants no restrictions of any kind. The coy toddler smile is now replaced with adolescent eye-rolling and the feeling of general disgust that they are dealing with parents who are totally out of touch with reality.

Dealing with adolescent behavior can present challenges to a marriage. Some of the angst has to do with the age and stage of the parents. Couples in midlife are dealing with their own hormonal issues, job and financial stresses, and worrying about aging parents. This period is often referred to as "The Sandwich Generation." Couples are stuck between the issues of self-centered teens, and the health and economic demands of elderly parents. Having carefree time for themselves is hard to come by. Tempers are short, and kindness can be at a minimum. Exasperation often permeates the household. Parents must get a grip on themselves, each other, and their blossoming teenager.

This time of adolescence can bring up memories about your own teen years. If your teen years were relatively easy, you may find yourself bewildered by what you witness and the frequent conflicts that arise. If this was a difficult time, you might fight desperately to prevent your teen from experiencing the same. Differences in your pubescent histories can affect how you each feel about the way things should be handled. Your parenting styles may conflict regarding discipline. Early discussion can hopefully help you find a compromise about which you can both feel comfortable.

Raising teens today is more challenging than in years past. Thirty years ago, when I conducted parent groups on raising adolescents, the discussion focused on the physical, developmental, and emotional changes helping parents to better understand their teen. There was little, if any, talk of depression, substance use, or suicide, and certainly no discussion about social media, since it did not exist.

There are high points raising adolescents: seeing your teen learning new skills, achieving academically, having fun with good friends, and playing sports. The journey of watching adolescent romances and breakups, prom dates, and passing the driver's test can be bittersweet experiences. It is good to have positive expectations for your adolescent. You should also educate yourself on the changes and appreciate the stresses your teen may be experiencing.

Learn to Ask the Tough Questions:

You will now find yourself facing new issues: curfews, effects of social media, worries over alcohol, marijuana use, illicit drugs, sexual behavior, and more challenging schoolwork. Connecting with parents of your teen's friends has never been more important. It is dangerous to assume that your idea of supervision is the same as other parents. When your teen is going to a party or spending the night, you need to ask some tough questions. One way of approaching this may be to say, "Like you, I am concerned about my child's safety and I ask these questions of every parent whose home my teen is invited, so I hope you will not be offended." Ask about supervision. "There have been many parties where the parents are in their second-floor bedroom and never go down to the basement where the kids are to check on them. I am concerned about drugs, alcohol, and digital access to bullying and porn. Will you be home and physically checking in on them?" Ask about guns. "I know many homes have guns, so I need to ask, if you do, are they locked up and is the ammunition locked separately?" Explaining your reason for asking is for the safety of your teen and your peace of mind. Your teen will likely not appreciate this and will tell you that you are embarrassing them. So be it. Would you rather have your teen in danger or be embarrassed? By now, they should be used to you asking. You also may be providing a safe way out of an uncomfortable situation and your teen can save face.

Stress, Depression, and Suicide:

The stress that children and adolescents are experiencing today is a serious concern. Parents often find this a hard realization. Even when a child has a stable home, which is sadly not always the case, teens are feeling pressured to be the best, the coolest, the most popular, and get good grades. In 2017, suicide was the second leading cause of death among individuals between the ages of 10 and 34, according to the Centers for Disease Control and Prevention (CDC). According to the Jason Foundation, a suicide prevention organization, "more teenagers and young adults die from suicide than from cancer, heart disease, AIDS, birth defects, stroke, pneumonia, influenza, and chronic lung disease, combined. I share this dark statistic as a reminder to every parent who works so diligently to keep their child physically well.

The real dangers are often insidious and occur as emotional and behavioral health concerns and are not as evident as physical symptoms. These deaths most often come as a shock to parents who had no idea their child was suffering to such an extreme. Experts advise open and direct communication with your teen. Asking if they are depressed or if they have thought of hurting themselves does *not* plant the idea in their head. The conversation gives your teen permission to talk about a subject they may have thought was forbidden. Grief over the loss of a child in any circumstances is agonizing, but when it is felt to have been preventable, it is particularly heart-wrenching. Depression or a traumatic incident is the usual precursor to suicide and since untreated depression is a leading cause, it is imperative to tune into your teen.

- Connect your adolescent with an activity of their choice.

- Be direct in asking how they are feeling.

- Ask if they ever think about hurting themselves.

- If yes, ask if they have thought about how they would do it.

- Connect with a professional if you have any concerns.

- Have ALL medications, guns, and ammunition locked.

Connectedness and Social Media:

In the article "Teen Depression and Suicide: Effective Prevention and Intervention Strategies," authors Keith A. King and Rebecca A. Vidourek reference the National Longitudinal Study of Adolescent to Adult Health (Add Health). The study "found family connectedness to be the leading protective factor against teen depression and suicide, and school connectedness was the leading school-based protective factor." This study was done in the 90s, before texting and social media were ubiquitous. As a society, we have yet to determine the full impact of today's devices on relationships, but there are serious concerns.

There is little question that stress has intensified with social media. Teens send and receive messages that they, and others, might never express in person, leading to misunderstandings, bullying, sexting, and anxiety. Parents cannot possibly monitor the amount of social media interaction that their child is exposed to 24/7. This often leaves parents in the dark about what their child is dealing with outside the home environment, which is one that they are trying to keep healthy. What can you do as a parent to prevent being overwhelmed by your responsibility?

- Talk to each other early about social media and the limits you want for your teen.

- Pay attention to connectedness in family, school, church, and community

- Delay cell phone use until eighth grade.

- Have appropriate blocks on your teen's phone.

- Agree to some basic ground rules. Trust is essential.

- Educate your child on the *permanence* of what they put on social media.

- Take their phone at bedtime to prevent interference with sleep.

Sexual Orientation and Sexual Behaviors

Many parents are hesitant to talk about sexual orientation and gender issues with their teen. How you approach these important topics is vital to your child's well-being and can affect your long-term relationship.

If these are not personal concerns for your teen, they may well have a friend or classmate for whom it is an issue. Your openness in talking with your teen will give them permission to raise these topics. Society has made good strides in this area, and resources and support are more available than in years past. When an extended family member transitioned in late adolescence, the parents' willingness to attend the PFLAG support group helped provide information and support to the teen and family through that transition.

Direct discussions about sexual behavior is more needed than ever, especially if your value system is different than that portrayed in the media. Years ago, television shows could not display a toilet in a sitcom! Parents knew their children were not exposed to mores vastly different than their own. This is not the case today. Young teens are bombarded by overt sexual messages from the nightly news, radio broadcasts, sitcoms, and movies. A mistaken digital click can introduce them to pornography. This is happening at a time of raging hormones, a heightened sense of curiosity, and trying to figure out where they fit in. When your teen starts dating, they will benefit hearing from both of you about what defines a healthy relationship and the importance of respect. Sharing some of your angst when you were an adolescent and what you found helpful or not, may facilitate discussion with your teen. This open communication can bolster your adolescent's belief that they too can navigate the rough waters.

Suggestions:

- Talk with your spouse about how you want to address these topics.

- Ask your teen if they wonder about their sexual orientation. (It will *not* plant the idea.)

- Ask if they have any questions about sex.

- Talk with your teen about what defines a healthy relationship.

Drugs

If you tried drugs during adolescence and moved on to a successful clean adulthood, you may expect the same for your offspring. You may think "This is a normal phase, a rite of passage, and they will be fine." Research concludes differently. Your child may be genetically/biologically vulnerable. Know and respect your family history and share it with your teen. Remember, there are ancestors whose history you do not know.

If you are currently using substances, you may feel hypocritical disciplining your teen for the very behavior in which one or both of you are engaging. There is often a tendency toward denial or minimizing the problem, hoping that it is a phase that your teen will outgrow. Sadly, this is rarely the case. Because the adolescent brain is in a period of rapid growth, it is more vulnerable to the effects of substances. Since this is a time of curiosity, teens are at risk for experimenting. Dr. Mark Garofoli refers to data from the National Center on Addiction and Substance Abuse, which concludes that "adolescent substance abuse is America's #1 public health problem." He goes on to explain that "people are most likely to begin abusing drugs during adolescence." In an article from NIH titled "Adolescent Brain Development and Drugs" research shows that "the earlier the onset of drug use, the greater the likelihood that a person will develop a drug problem . . . Moreover, early age of onset rather than duration of use is a stronger predictor of the rapid progression of substance use disorders." When initial use is delayed until after 21, there is a marked decrease in developing a lifelong problem."

For the past 18 years, Patrick and I have facilitated a weekly peer support group for adult family members with a loved one with substance use. When we started, we were a group of parents of young teens smoking marijuana, skipping school, dismissing curfew, and not obeying house rules. In recent years, the picture has escalated to include adult children caught in the spiral of opiates, cocaine, methamphetamine, heroin, and serious alcohol use.

The first night a parent attends the group, they can best be described as "hemorrhaging." They are desperate for help and do not know which way to turn. No parent ever thought they would end up sitting with a group of strangers talking about their out-of-control child. Their disbelief is focused on "How has our darling infant, adorable toddler, happy middle schooler, now evolved into a disheveled teen who has been skipping school, hanging out with 'bad kids,' stealing from us, and even at times, been physically threatening?" The realization that their child is now the "bad kid," whom other parents do not want their teen hanging with, is too painful to bear. Many parents do not come to the group until their "child" is well into adulthood. The situation has posed enormous stress for the marriage as well.

Mothers more often attend the meetings initially, being the more proactive partner who recognizes that her child is in serious trouble. The fear of her child dying is intolerable to a mother and overrides any embarrassment about seeking support. Sometimes, the mother may admit to having been the enabler in the family, while the father felt further action was needed. Sometimes those roles are reversed. Yet, for fathers to seek counseling or walk into a group of strangers, it is like admitting defeat, and it is difficult for many men. Fathers seem to have a sense of failure at not being able to prevent or fix the problem besieging his family. Men who are not badgered, but allowed to come at their will, have been more likely to attend. When both parents work together to address the issue of substance use, it can result in recovery for their child and benefit the marriage and the family.

We have seen family members witness behaviors they, or their loved one, could not have ever imagined. We have also seen many who now lead clean and sober lives, return to higher education, marry, and raise children. I have called them miracles, but that is inaccurate. They are the results of successful treatment and commitment to recovery. According to a 2012 report by the Partnership for Drug Free Kids and the New York State Office of Alcoholism and Substance Abuse Services (OASAS), "there are 23.5 million American adults overcoming an involvement with drugs or alcohol that they once considered to be problematic." That is the hope we should all hold for individuals suffering with substance use disorder.

We witnessed one family whose home had become an unsafe place due to their son's drug activity. They lost their savings seeking treatment for him. The mother was a regular attendee to the group, while the father kept hoping things would get better on their own. The situation became worse. This mother, who greatly valued her marriage, made the very painful decision to seek her own apartment until her husband could make the tough decisions necessary to help their child get clean. It was a long and painful process but did result in the son's recovery. The father ultimately attended the group, and the marriage remained intact. Tough decisions are sometimes necessary to experience healing.

With the explosion of the drug epidemic in our country, parents are now dealing with a "child" who is 22 to 45 years old, who started with marijuana in their teens, when it may have seemed innocent enough. Then, it became evident that their child was the one out of six adolescents who, unlike his friends, found marijuana the panacea for his anxiety or depression. Due to the dramatic increase in the potency of marijuana and the lack of regulation, self-medicating becomes a dangerous habit.

Numbing the pain can escalate to daily, chronic use and put the teen on a trajectory different than their peers. Gradually, issues like homework, attending class, hanging with clean friends, can fall by the wayside. Later, the young adult may be introduced to pain pills by a provider who treated him for an injury, by a friend who had access to a narcotic prescription, or ones available in their home medicine cabinet. When those became too expensive, they moved onto heroin, cocaine, or methamphetamine, which were initially cheaper and easy to obtain. Cough medicine containing the suppressant dextromethorphan provides a high that ranges from mild euphoria to intense hallucinations and paranoia and is available without prescription. Spice, erroneously referred to as synthetic marijuana, and K2 are substances to which a teen can be easily exposed and provides a sought-after initial reaction, often leading to severe consequences.

When medications can be bought over the counter or online, it is hard for a parent to keep up with all that is available. Googling information on different drugs can help you learn the signs and symptoms of various substances. Stay vigilant of your teen's behavior and mood swings. Work to keep communication open and stay connected with their friend's parents. If you are concerned about anxiety, depression, or behavior changes, speak to your teen's primary care provider. Your adolescent would be better served by a provider who can prescribe and adjust medication to treat a diagnosed mood disorder than to self-medicate.

These days, Patrick and I are encouraged when parents of a young teen with issues around pot use and skipping school attend the group. It means that there is time for prevention and early intervention. As a parent, you still have legal rights to help your child and communicate with the professionals. This is not the case when your child turns 18 and may choose to deny that interaction. In addition to your child's health, this is a strong reason for you to think early about prevention, assessment, and intervention.

Some parents drink daily and smoke pot "recreationally" in their home. While they may view this as a harmless, and even a "cool," activity to share with their teens, research shows otherwise. What you model for your offspring sends a loud and clear message that even your preaching cannot override. This can be very confusing to your adolescent who is trying to find their way towards a healthy future among peers who are equally confused. When you try to befriend your children instead of holding them accountable, you do them a great disservice.

Children will have many friends during their lifetime. They will, however, have only one set of parents. That role carries a lot of responsibility and demands that you model healthy behavior. If you cannot find common ground, it is wise to seek professional counseling, to get a plan you each can support. Your ability to provide a united front and sticking to your decisions can result in a positive outcome for your teen and your marriage. Some things you can do to be proactive about substance use:

- Educate yourself about drugs in your community.

- Be vigilant about your teen's friends and their whereabouts.

- Connect with other parents and school personnel.

If ever there is a time to put my Marriage Hierarchy of Needs (found in the "Maintaining Your Marriages" chapter) into effect, it is in raising an adolescent. Teenagers can knock you off your feet if you do not guard your partnership and work to shore up your dance routine. You need to be very deliberate in keeping perspective on your individual well-being and your marriage. Take turns covering the home front and allow your spouse time to enjoy some individual pursuits to recharge their battery. Then, work with extended family or close friends to provide respite by taking your teen for an evening or weekend, so you can have a much-deserved getaway.

We close our weekly group by asking each parent what they are going to do for themselves this coming week and what they will do with their spouse or another adult. Initially, we get a blank stare and a "Who me?" or "Us?" When one couple announced they were going away for a weekend alone for the first time in 25 years, it came as no surprise why the marriage was under such stress. It had not occurred to them to nurture themselves while raising their three children. They had no practice in the early years to draw upon when their stress escalated from raising teenagers. Sadly, it was too little, too late, and their marriage ended.

When you carve out time for a date, or a brief getaway, whether it is for two hours or two days, there is one critical rule: there will be no talk about your teen and the issues you are facing. These situations can be addressed during daily connection time. Date times must be different. Patrick and I are very clear when working with parents; during these times of respite, you need to focus on one another. Your relationship is best served talking about what is good in your life and the things that you are looking forward to in better days ahead. This is a decision that takes effort but provides connection during this time of turmoil. Focusing on your needs as an individual and as a couple will keep hope alive for your teen and keep you two in sync.

Steps:

- Take care of yourself physically and emotionally and encourage the same for your spouse.

- Model the behavior you wish to see in your teen.

- Connect with other parents.

- Be willing to ask the tough questions.

- Talk proactive strategies before issues become a crisis.

- Have a regular, problem-free outings.

WORKS CITED

Centers for Disease Control and Prevention, National Center for Injury Prevention and Control. Web-based Injury Statistics Query and Reporting System (WISQARS) [online]. (2017). https://webappa.cdc.gov/sasweb/ncipc/leadcause.html.

Garofoli, Mark. "Adolescent Substance Abuse." *National Library of Medicine.* June 4, 2020. DOI: 10.1016/j.pop.2020.02.013

King, Keith A., and Rebecca A. Vidourek. "Teen depression and suicide: effective prevention and intervention strategies." *The Prevention Researcher* 19, no. 4 (2012): 15+. *Gale Academic OneFile* (accessed July 9, 2020).

The Parent Resource Program. *The Jason Foundation.*

http://prp.jasonfoundation.com/facts/youth-suicide-statistics/

"Survey: Ten Percent of American Adults Report Being in Recovery from Substance Abuse or Addiction." *Partnership to End Addiction.* March 2012. https://drugfree.org/newsroom/news-item/survey-ten-percent-of-american-adults-report-being-in-recovery-from-substance-abuse-or-addiction/

Winters, Ken C., Amelia Arria. "Adolescent Brain Development and Drugs." *National Library of Medicine.* https://www.ncbi.nlm.nih.gov/pmc/articles/PMC3399589/.

CHAPTER 31

Using Humor to Enrich Your Marriage

> *"It has been wisely said that we cannot really love anybody with whom we never laugh."*
>
> AGNES REPPLIER, 19th century essayist

I cannot imagine a marriage without mirth. From our dating days, Patrick and I always enjoyed a lot of laughter. Decades later, we still laugh about our wedding night when, with great enthusiasm, I announced that I wanted to write a book on marriage. With a look of disbelief, Patrick replied with his Irish humor, "Please don't base it on tonight, it might be a short subject!"

No marriage is immune to stress. Money, work demands, health issues, and raising children are among them. How can humor not help? A good place to begin is to lighten up on your seriousness, a principle well expressed in "Rule Number 6," as described in *The Art of Possibility* by Rosamund and Benjamin Zander.

Two prime ministers are conferring when they are interrupted three times by aides ranting about an issue. The resident prime minister calms each one immediately by admonishing, "Please remember Rule Number 6." Puzzled, the visiting dignitary asks about Rule Number 6. "Very simple. Rule Number 6 is: "Don't take yourself so g—damn seriously." 'Ah', says his visitor, 'that is a fine rule.' After a moment of pondering, he inquires: 'And what, may I ask, are the other rules?' To which the resident prime minister replied, "There aren't any."

Learning to keep issues in perspective can allow you to lighten up. In her book, *The Rough Patch*, Daphne de Marneffe refers to "the big picture." If you can keep in mind exactly what you want for yourself, your spouse, and your marriage, it can help you keep perspective on how important, or unimportant, an issue is. Is it worth the time, energy, frustration, and discord that it may be costing your relationship? Without avoiding addressing serious issues, are there times you could insert humor into your conversation? A well-placed one-liner can break the tension of an argument and help you move past minor frustrations.

There is physiology behind the benefits of laughter. It releases endorphins, a group of hormones secreted within the brain and nervous system that function to cope with pain, relieve stress, and provide a safe, natural high. They are the "feel-good" chemicals that soothe the mind. Laughing is an excellent way to reduce cortisol levels elevated by daily stresses. According to the article "Laughter Therapy as Stress Relief," "since our bodies cannot distinguish between real and fake laughter, anything that makes you giggle will have a positive impact. You do not need to be happy or have a sense of humor to benefit from a good laugh." You can release those endorphins by plugging into laughter yoga or watching laugh therapy videos on YouTube.

What helps to release endorphins in our body?

- Exercise

- Eating dark chocolate and spicy food

- Connecting with people you enjoy

- Spending time in nature

- Making love

- Meditating

- Playing music

- Laughing

When you look at this list, the only activity that does not take any time is laughter and it's free! That means that you have no excuse for not utilizing it. You can employ laughter at work to release stress while collaborating on a project. Lovingly teasing an irritated child can often distract their frustration. There can be many opportunities with your spouse to lessen tensions: sharing a funny story about what happened during the day, a joke you heard on the radio, or a humorous memory that was triggered while driving home from work.

Often, the most hilarious comedy comes from the ordinary events of daily life. One I recall happened when I was by myself amidst the routine chaos. It was a Sunday night in December. Patrick was out, and the four kids were in bed. I took a rare moment on the couch and picked up a Christmas catalog. I came across a contraption that I didn't recognize. When I read the description and learned it was a pasta drying rack, I started to chuckle.

I only needed to walk into the kitchen to see the dirty laundry waiting to be washed, the wet laundry waiting to be dried, the dried laundry waiting to be folded, and the folded laundry waiting to be put away, to wonder how the hell anyone could have the luxury of time to *make pasta and then wait for it to dry*! The very thought of it, contrasting with the scene I was looking at, escalated my chuckles into full belly laughs, with tears running down my cheeks. I can still giggle about that scene today, 35 years later! My married daughter called recently to report that she had just made pasta. Before I could comment, she added, "It wasn't worth it." Bless her heart.

Try to notice the humor in the mundane. There are a lot of things that happen during the day worth a good laugh. Laughing at yourself can give rise to many occasions for humor. I seem to be able to provide them all too frequently! Patrick and I were out for a ride in the country one day when I saw a hand-painted sign that read "lots for sale." Before I gave it a thought, I blurted out, "lots of what?" We have had recurring laughs from that unfiltered question!

The stuff that makes you laugh may be very different for your partner. It is important to know your spouse's type of humor. If your partner hates practical jokes, they will likely elicit annoyance. Pay attention to what your spouse laughs at and look for similar jokes or situations. Patrick can completely lose it over Gary Larson cartoons that often use reverse dialogue from humans to animals. Many "boys" in the family share that humor, so every Christmas I buy several desk calendars of his cartoons and a group of males sit together, hilariously telling each other what date to open. My own endorphins increase watching that scene unfold.

Probably no one demonstrated the positive effects of humor more significantly than Norman Cousins. He was "a longtime editor of the *Saturday Review*, a global peacemaker, the receiver of hundreds of awards including the UN Peace Medal and nearly 50 honorary doctorate degrees." After a stressful trip to Russia, he was diagnosed with ankylosing spondylitis, arthritis of the spine, leaving him in almost constant pain. His doctor told him he would die within a few months.

Cousins was not willing to accept that prognosis, and he rationalized that if stress could precipitate negative health effects, the opposite should be true. Believing that humor and laughter would promote healing, "he checked himself out of the hospital and into a hotel across the street and began taking extremely high doses of vitamin C while exposing himself to a continuous stream of humorous films and similar 'laughing matter.'" The laughter allowed him two hours of pain free sleep when even morphine could not.

I had the opportunity to meet Norman Cousins and hear about his experiences captured in his book, *Anatomy of an Illness*, which was later made into a TV movie starring Ed Asner. I attended the talk with a friend who was a two-time breast cancer survivor. She was familiar with his work and wanted to hear him. Here was a man who sensed that the mind and spirit each played a role in wellness. Cousins maintained his respect for medicine, but he believed in the human body's ability to heal and regenerate itself. After six months of treating himself with laughter, "he was back on his feet, and within two years he was able to return to his full-time job at the *Saturday Review*, . . . [which] baffled the scientific community." Cousins' experience and resulting studies confirmed the physiologic benefits of humor.

In his *Psychology Today* article, "How Humor Can Change Your Relationship," Dr. Gil Greengross refers to several studies on the relationship between humor and marital satisfaction. In one study of 3,000 couples, "both husbands and wives were found to be happier with a humorous partner." Notably, wives experienced greater satisfaction than the husbands even while they both agreed the husband was funnier. Ultimately, "married couples overwhelmingly say that humor has a positive impact on their marriages."

Dr. Greengross notes another study of 60 newlywed couples that explored the use of humor when things were not going well in their marriage. These couples initially completed an exercise that measured "life stress" and researchers "coded on how much humor was used in [a problem-solving] conversation." When the follow-up happened 18 months later, "in couples that reported high stress, the *more* the husband used humor, the greater the chance the couple would separate or divorce." Dr. Greengross concludes that "for men, humor might serve as a way to distract from dealing with problems in the relationship, perhaps in an attempt to reduce their own anxiety."

Humor can reduce stress when it is not used to avoid serious discussion. To gloss over tough issues with a joke can cause resentment over time. Caustic humor or laughing at one's spouse will never be helpful to a relationship. According to that same article, research also found "that couples with fewer children laughed more." Having four children, I am not surprised by this finding. Couples with more children must be more deliberate in laughing at chaos, keeping perspective on what is important, and finding humor in the ordinary. When we learned that we were expecting our fourth child, Patrick's immediate response was "Well, 10,000 more laughs!" What a great reaction.

Steps:

- Don't take yourself too seriously.

- Be willing to laugh at yourself.

- Look for humor in everyday situations.

- Know your spouse's type of humor.

- Watch funny shows or movies when experiencing stressful times.

- Deal with important subjects directly and employ humor when appropriate.

- Consider using laugh therapy as a stress relief.

WORKS CITED

Berry, Jennifer. "Endorphins: Effect and how to increase levels." *Medical News Today.*

February 6, 2018. https://www.medicalnewstoday.com/articles/320839.

Cousins, Norman; *Anatomy of an Illness*. New York: W.W. Norton & Co., 1979.

de Marneffe, Daphne. *The Rough Patch*. New York: Simon & Schuster, 2018.

Gendry, Sebastian. "Norman Cousins Anatomy of an Illness" *Laughter Online University*. https://www.laughteronlineuniversity.com/norman-cousins-anatomy-of-an-illness.

Greengross, Gil. "How Humor Can Change Your Relationship." *Psychology Today*. November 17, 2018. https://www.psychologytoday.com/us/blog/humor-sapiens/201811/how-humor-can-change-your-relationship.

"Laughter Therapy as Stress Relief." *Skills You Need*. https://www.skillsyouneed.com/ps/therapeutic-laughter.html

Levy, Jillian, "What are Endorphins?" *Dr. Axe*. June 19, 2017. https://draxe.com/what-are-endorphins.

Zander, Rosamund Stone and Benjamin Zander. *The Art of Possibility*. New York: Penguin Books, 2002

CHAPTER 32

Blending Families

"Marriage is a lot like the army, everyone complains, but you'd be surprised at the large number that re-enlist."

JAMES GARNER

If you are divorced or widowed and looking to marry, you are wise to embark on this journey with your eyes wide open. Unlike a first marriage, where you can initially focus on each other, blending families often requires addressing parenting issues *and* attending to your marriage. Even if the children are adults, they will have an influence on your relationship. Remember, regardless of age, they are your spouse's children, and there are strong emotional ties that existed before your relationship began.

Second marriages have proven to be at a higher risk for divorce than first ones, but that does not mean that yours cannot succeed. Having experienced a loss, you are both in a good position to want this relationship to thrive for you and your children. Since I cannot share first-hand knowledge on blending families, I relied on the insight of couples whom I interviewed, the anecdotes of others, and research.

In their article "Blending Family and Step-Parenting Tips," Dr. Jeanne Segal and Lawrence Robinson recommend waiting two or more years after divorce or the death of a spouse to give time and space for your own grieving. Learning from your past marriage and seeking counseling can help ensure future success in blending your families. More time may be necessary for your children depending on their ages and their emotional needs. As one couple advised in my interview with them, "do not rush into marriage to deal with loneliness. If that's how you're feeling, get a dog." Another couple noted that if you can wait to marry until the kids are adults, it is easier. There will be less interaction with the former spouse, and young adults can now make their own decisions. Love may not allow you to wait that long, however!

Take dating slowly and allow children to get to know their pending stepparent and stepsiblings in different situations. It is wise to make sure that every gathering is not structured around a fun outing. Rather, include routine daily activities that are more representative of real life. The stepparent initially playing the role of friend or listening ear is less likely to cause friction than one who acts like they may be replacing the absent parent.

You will want to discuss important issues with your new partner *ahead of time*. The topic of finances will be especially critical, as this is a major cause of marital friction even without the complication of merging families. How holidays will be spent should be addressed to avoid additional stress at an emotional time of year. The discussion of how you want to parent, given the different parenting styles, will be especially vital when you have younger children and teens. You will need rules that are basically consistent for all your children, so favoritism does not interfere. Some couples find it helpful to deal with their own children regarding behavior and not involve the stepparent. Others want to give the message of marital unity. Whatever you decide, having rules that are straightforward and communicated directly can help the child to accept discipline from both parents. You might find it helpful to have them posted. Allow yourselves to evaluate how things are working and be flexible enough to alter the rules when necessary.

As the adults, you need to be realistic. The children, regardless of age, are not going to instantly love and accept you in this new role as a stepparent. You likely will not instantly love your spouse's children. Relationships take time and you need to allow for assimilation. When a child has become accustomed to having a parent to themselves, there can be jealousy about sharing their parent. Making sure you allow time alone with each of your children can provide the sense of love and security during this period of change.

As you work through blending your families, it is important to be the adults and take responsibility for your own behavior. If your children are not living with you full time, it will help them feel part of your new family if they have their own space for personal belongings. This way they do not have to bring those items each time they stay with you like a visitor would. Many parents suggest that if you can establish a new living environment, instead of either of your previous homes, this provides a fresh space to launch your new family. When children can have their own rooms, it helps to ensure their privacy. Be aware of boundaries, especially for teens who are stepsiblings of the opposite sex. Feeling protected will be central to their well-being.

When you discuss rules with your kids, it is important to give the clear message that your marriage is a top priority. Children can quickly determine how to divide and conquer if you allow it. Respect and civility need to be the keystone of communication between all members of the household. You will want to set that expectation and example as fundamental for your new family. Establishing some routines and fun rituals can help family bonding without forcing your children to form instant friendships. "Be patient" was the consistent advice offered from experienced couples. They noted that small investments can yield good results over time.

When you, as the parents, acknowledge the different stages of development of your children, as well as their individual needs, they will have an easier transition into your new family. Work to understand and honor their personality and temperaments. It is helpful to remember that as mentioned in the article, "Blended Family and Step-Parenting Tips" children in a blended family have the same basic needs as children in any family:

- A safe and secure environment

- Feeling loved unconditionally

- Being valued as a person

- Listened to and having a sense of belonging

- Appreciated and encouraged

- Age appropriate limits and boundaries

- Consistent consequences.

Without a solid marriage, there will be no blended family. You will not have the luxury of having that childless time to adjust to your life as a couple. Rather, you are both coming into your relationship with one another's children. There will be many different temperaments and personalities involved, making your new life an experiment in process. Review the earlier chapters to see what healthy habits you can introduce to your blended family to ensure that your dance is a smooth one for your marriage and for your children. As the 18*th* century English writer Samuel Johnson said, "A second marriage is a triumph of hope over experience." Go forward with great expectations.

Steps:

- Talk early about how you want to parent.

- Respect the needs of each child, giving private space when possible.

- Plan time alone with each child.

- Be patient in letting your child adjust to the stepparent.

- Monitor and protect teenage stepsiblings.

WORK CITED

Segal, Jeanne and Lawrence Robinson. "Blending Family and Step-Parenting Tips." *HelpGuide*. Updated November 2019. https://www.helpguide.org/articles/parenting-family/step-parenting-blended-families.htm.

CHAPTER 33

Dealing with Spousal Substance Use

"If there's one thing I learned in Al anon, it's that you got to face the music because it just grows louder when you ignore it."

VICKI COVINGTON, *Bird of Paradise*

Few issues will fracture a marriage and family life more dramatically than problems with substance use. While it is very difficult to have any loved one affected, it is especially painful when the individual is your spouse. This person is your partner whom you love, have committed yourself to, and rely on for support in dealing with life's situations, along with the task of raising your children. When one parent is shouldering responsibilities alone, it often shatters a marriage and family. Even when a couple stays together, it alters the family dynamics for every member.

You may have sensed a problem early in your relationship, hoping that it would improve after marriage or starting a family. This is not an uncommon belief. Diseases, however, are rarely controlled or cured without treatment. When you realize that nothing is changing in a positive way, you are wise to address the issue to prevent further erosion of your relationship and detrimental effects on your children.

Substance Use Disorder (SUD) often coexists with untreated mental health (MH) diagnoses like depression, anxiety, bipolar disorder, personality disorder, and history of trauma. The desire to lessen emotional pain by self-medicating is often what initiates the use. Overprescribing of pain medication has also played a significant role in people becoming dependent. It can be argued that first-time use is a choice, but for those individuals who have a family medical history, biological vulnerability, and find relief from physical and/or emotional pain, that choice is short lived. The substances act on the reward center of the brain and affect the chemical receptors, often resulting in unexpected dependency. Repeated use physiologically alters and eventually hijacks the brain, leading to a chronic, relapsing, and often terminal illness, if not treated.

It is a rare person who does not know someone suffering from SUD (the term addict is no longer used). These conditions do not discriminate and can happen in any family regardless of age, race, religion, economic, educational, financial, or social status. If someone in your home is not affected by SUD or MH issues, you only need to look to extended family, friends, neighbors, colleagues, or coworkers to find someone who is. Unfortunately, there remains a stigma attached to these brain diseases. This discrimination has interfered with the general public educating themselves about how this illness alters brain function. The resulting ignorance contributes to perpetuating the stigma. There needs to be universal dissemination of material to inform society and promote open dialogue about these disorders.

Years ago, cancer was a disease that no one felt comfortable talking about. The diagnosis was held in secret. Two decades ago, HIV and AIDS were heavily stigmatized and considered fatal. We have come a long way in a relatively short period of time. There is now targeted treatment for these once terminal illnesses. Medical advances now allow people to live longer and healthier lives. Support, understanding, and acceptance has given people the ability to speak openly about these conditions. Society has not yet made the same successful strides with substance use or mental illness. Part of the reason may be the societal impact when these disorders remain untreated and the individual engages in illegal activity to self-medicate. Many people feel that SUD is a moral issue, not a medical one. They believe that the one who suffers should be jailed or left to die from an overdose. Research proves otherwise.

As previously mentioned, there are over 23 million people in our country who are currently in long-term recovery from SUD. They are living proof that treatment works and should provide hope for a marriage when a spouse is willing to seek treatment. Until your partner agrees there is a problem and wants help, you need to be vigilant about the impact SUD has on the family, particularly children. If there is any physical, emotional, sexual abuse, or domestic violence occurring, this requires immediate intervention for the well-being of the individual and every family member, especially children. A crisis intervention team should be called (911) to help manage the situation and find resources that provide a safe environment and follow-up care. If these emergency situations are not present, and substance use poses a more chronic condition for the family, a plan can, and should, be implemented to help treat the entire family.

Stella is a friend who was married to her husband for 25 years until his death from complications of alcoholism. I asked about her reflections living with a spouse with SUD and the impact on their marriage and raising their two children:

> At some point, there is the realization that you cannot count on your spouse for anything. Every plan has to have a plan B. Every day begins with listening for clues as to the condition of your loved one, so plans can be formulated to make the day go as smoothly as possible. Then, there are the feelings of embarrassment when your loved one shows up to a function, private or public, under the influence. Even knowing the behavior has nothing to do with you, the looks you get from others, or the pain/embarrassment in your child's eyes, can still make you feel you should have done more. Your own behavior may become compromised until you don't recognize yourself or your "crazy" reactions to incomprehensible situations. The merry-go-round speeds up, each spouse blaming the other for his/her behavior, until you both realize that the only person you can control is yourself. YOU are responsible for YOUR behavior. How can the unimaginable forcefulness of the emotions of living with a spouse with SUD be conveyed in one chapter?

The answer to her concluding question is, it cannot. But Stella agrees there are steps that can help take care of you and your children when you recognize what you *do* and *do not* have control over. When your spouse refuses to recognize the problem and is not willing to seek help, what can you do? Begin by taking physical and emotional care of yourself. Just like flight attendants instruct you to put the oxygen mask on first, you need to support you and your children before focusing on your spouse. Continually remind yourself that you are the only person you can control. You cannot affirm or visualize behavioral changes for your spouse and expect that the situation will be different. Changing your reaction to your loved one's behavior, however, can make a difference. A new dance lesson is needed; a dance you will have to perform alone while you formulate a strategy.

A good plan begins with acknowledging the problem. Admit it. State it. Learn about SUD and how it affects the brain and behavior. Connect with individual counseling to help you focus on your own needs and set up a plan. This is no time for embarrassment. You are not the cause. If you could fix it, you would have already done so. And you are not going to control the situation without more information and support.

A counselor can be found through the behavioral health service number found on your insurance card. Both MH and SUD issues are covered by insurance with the same coverage afforded to all chronic, relapsing illnesses that your plan covers. The Paul Wellstone and Pete Domenici Mental Health Parity and Addiction Equity Act of 2008 assures this equal coverage. If you do not have insurance, your church, or the local mental health center can connect you with free or sliding-fee scale providers. Do not be deterred.

Find a local support group that addresses your issues. This can provide a non-judgmental atmosphere where you can learn about SUD and the resources that have helped others. For three years, I worked with local communities setting up support groups around the state that could be accessed by calling 211—a resource support line. Check out what your state has to offer. Al-Anon, Nar-Anon, and SMART Recovery groups are available throughout the country and have helped millions of people living with loved ones with these disorders. These groups, along with your individual counselor, can provide information, resources, and support.

Beyond Addiction: How Science and Kindness Help People Change is an evidence-based resource offering practical skills to help a loved one with SUD. This book has been endorsed by some of the leading professionals working with substance use treatment. There is no quick fix when it comes to these issues, and families need to have a compassionate, comprehensive plan that they understand and know how to implement. The chapter on *Positive Communication* is a must-read and study for anyone helping a loved-one with SUD to connect to treatment. Some of the points they address in detail are:

- Be positive (not easy when you are hurt and angry)

- Be brief (difficult for those of us who tend to preach)

- Be specific (challenging when there are so many issues needing attention)

- Label your feeling (avoiding blaming and finger pointing)

- Offer an understanding statement (helps reduce defensiveness)

- Accept partial responsibility (sharing in the problem fosters collaboration)

- Offer to help (phrase as a question, ask permission)

Loving someone with SUD becomes a very lonely dance. The lack of partnership and isolation can feel devastating. If there are children, they can experience the loss of both parents when the one affected is physically and/or emotionally not present and the spouse is so focused on the illness they are not available to the child either. This emotional absence can result in childhood trauma, causing physical and mental health issues later in their adult life, including SUD.

Parents, wanting to protect a child, often do not discuss the situation, thinking the child does not know what is happening. Nothing could be further from the truth. Children are incredibly perceptive and often view the circumstances as even worse than they are. The sober spouse must take responsibility to intervene and connect with family counseling. Younger children often feel they are responsible for the turmoil happening in the family. Depending on the age of your child, you want to communicate in a developmentally appropriate way. Professional guidance can help you provide the trust and security your child needs to handle issues over which they have no control.

Learning to care for yourself, your marriage, and your family, while dealing with a spouse with SUD or MH issues, may be one of the more intricate dances you will need to learn. It is critical to remember through this journey that treatment and recovery work. When you master positive communication skills, and your spouse is willing to address their issue, they can be among the millions of people living a clean, sober, and productive life and be able to again join you on the dance floor.

Steps:

- Recognize the problem.

- Learn about substance use and mental health disorders.

- Seek individual counseling. Don't go it alone.

- Involve your children in family therapy.

- Join a support group with others who have similar issues.

WORKS CITED

Foote, Jeffrey, Carrie Wilkens, Nicole Kosanke, and Stephanie Higgs. *Beyond Addiction:*

How Science and Kindness Help People Change. New York: Scribner, 2014

Henson, Priscilla Henson. "How to Help an Addict who Doesn't Want Help." *American Addiction Centers*, Updated June 1, 2020. https://americanaddictioncenters.org/how-to-help-an-addict-who-doesnt-want-help

CHAPTER 34

Lovemaking Interrupted

"Marriage has many pains, but celibacy has no pleasures."

SAMUEL JOHNSON

In every loving marriage, there are periods when your physical intimacy seems to take a nosedive. Back in the passionate tango years, sex used to be front and center in your thoughts. Then, the line dancing years brought some cooling off as you became engulfed by your careers, homeowning, and perhaps parenting. By the time you usher in the twist and shout years, you may feel like your love life is on the back burner. Distractions, fatigue, and/or lack of interest seem to hold center stage. Understanding this is not unusual can help alleviate the panic that your marriage is in a decline. Small acts of kindness and attention can offer a protective buffer and serve to reignite your emotional intimacy.

Be alert that times of transition are periods of the greatest stress and may disrupt your sex life. Even happy events, like a move to a new home or landing the sought-after job can be very taxing. Whatever the event, the effect on your sexual relationship will likely be temporary and need not derail your marriage.

Even in the absence of any major incidents, you may feel that physical and mental exhaustion rule the day. You can find yourself speaking and behaving in ways that even you do not like. Fatigue is a real problem during these busy years. You both are likely working full time, may be caring for a baby and/or young children, juggling household chores, paying bills, trying to keep up with friends, extended family, involvement with church, and fitting in some fun. Sometimes it looks like a scene from a circus.

When Patrick injured his back after the birth of our first baby, he spent seven months sleeping on the living room floor. After surgery, there were four months of recuperation. Add that ordeal to the last month or two of pregnancy and you don't have to be a math whiz to calculate our sexual intimacy was in dry dock for a long time. We also bought and moved into our first home that year. If all we had going for us was lust, our marriage would have been a bust!

When the physical relationship is unavailable, it is the "stuff of substance," as I like to call it, which can keep emotional intimacy alive. The ability to focus on the attributes that you love about your mate is what forms the foundation of a relationship that endures through the years. Demonstrating affection, without expecting anything more, can go a long way in comforting your partner and supporting you both through difficult times. Offering a back rub, a cup of tea, running an errand, or sending a loving text can serve to keep you connected. It is kindnesses such as these that offer the emotional intimacy to connect you when your physical intimacy is interrupted by life's events.

Couples who have endured separation during military duty know the hardship this puts on a marriage. Our son-in-law was deployed six months after he and our daughter were married. This physical disconnection is a challenge when you are in the throes of adjusting to your new life together. Finding ways to connect and keep intimacy alive when the physical aspect is not possible is critical to reconnecting when deployment is concluded. The technology of Skyping and FaceTime, in addition to handwritten letters and personal care packages, can help you both stay emotionally connected until you can be together again.

During demanding times, one spouse may find sex a stress reliever. The other may view it as one more thing on the to-do list. What a turn off for both parties! An often-told tongue-in-cheek story may capture the feelings (or at least a chuckle) for some couples during this stage when both fatigue and chaos may be running rampant over your libido.

A husband was ready to make love when he hears the dreaded words, 'I don't feel like it. I just want you to hold me.' When he asks why, she responds,

'You're just not in touch with my emotional needs as a woman enough for me to satisfy your physical needs as a man.

'Can't you just love me for who I am? Does it have to be for what I do for you in the bedroom?' They go to sleep.

The next day the husband takes the day off work and they go out to a nice lunch and shopping. She chooses some expensive outfits and jewelry.

She was almost nearing sexual satisfaction from all the excitement and says, 'I think this is all dear, let's go to the cashier.'

Suddenly, the husband blurts out, "No, honey, I just don't feel like it.

I just want you to HOLD this stuff for a while. You're just not in touch with my financial needs as a man enough for me to satisfy your shopping needs as a woman. Why can't you just love me for who I am and not for the things I buy you?"

Apparently, they did not have sex that night either.

This tale may to be funny to some and yet may ring true for other couples during these twist and shout years. The scenario does not reflect the openness, sensitivity, and equality expected in a healthy marriage. Communication is as important a skill in your sexual life as it is in your discussions about money, children, and household chores. Talk about what your needs are and listen to your spouse's. What do you like and what is bothering you? To avoid talking about your feelings can result in resentment. Resentment, not addressed, festers over time and can be destructive to your emotional intimacy. Men and women think, feel, and communicate differently and your needs will not be perfectly aligned. One is not right or wrong, better or worse than the other. When you can listen and respect these differences, you can respond in ways that convey caring and unconditional love and offer a path to better communication and intimacy.

Children can pose an impediment to a spontaneous sex life. Because you love the little darlings, you may not like to admit to each other how things have changed. Before they were on the scene, you had the freedom of time and more energy. Since their arrival, however, keeping the spark alive requires some deliberation. You are wise to plan how to prevent children from taking precedence over your love life. In her article, Colleen Meeks writes about five ways to protect the sexual intimacy of your marriage: "get a babysitter," "enforce a 'back to bed' policy," "lock the door," "get in bed early—or at least on time," and "talk about something other than the kids." Yes, having a couple of trusted babysitters whom your children enjoy is a marriage saver. And do not share their names with friends! Overnight sitters were not readily available to us as our families were not nearby, and funds were tight, so we would swap an occasional weekend with friends who had children and give each other a break.

Our children had their own beds and we expected them to sleep there. Even as infants, I would nurse them in their room and not bring them into our bed, so it did not become a habit we had to break. Strangely, our bedrooms doors did not come with locks, but we had an "always knock" policy. Patrick and I stayed up long enough to have teatime while waiting for them to fall asleep. Having music and soft lighting (and no TV!) made our environment seem less chaotic than the reality. Taking deliberate steps helped keep our love life alive.

When needing to address sexual issues in your marriage, set up a time where you can relax without distractions or interruptions from the children or technology. Talk about some strategies that can help. Listen without judgment or criticism. Instead of pointing out what your spouse is not doing right, share what *you are feeling* and what *you need*. Relaxing with a sensual movie may help you both feel more amorous. And lovemaking does not always have to happen in the bedroom. Keeping a sense of humor can serve to lighten things up. We had a small brass sign hanging by the fireplace as a reminder to pay attention to the flue. It read "Damper Open" on one side and "Damper Closed" on the other. One evening, when life was especially crazy, I came out of the bathroom in a black negligee with the "Damper Open" sign hung around my neck. Moments like that kept us dancing!

I heard a speaker once say that our most important sex organ lies between our ears, referring to the fact that the desire for sexual intimacy is dependent on how we *think* about our spouse. If you, as a partner, are kind, caring, and maintain good hygiene, does it not make sense that your spouse is more likely to be attracted to you? You might think that foreplay happens in the bedroom, but it is much more likely to start in the kitchen. How you greet each other first thing in the morning often sets the tone for the day. How about arriving home after a frustrating day at work? Helping to cook? Cleaning up after dinner? Putting in a load of wash? Random acts of kindness and thoughtfulness comprise the best foreplay, like dropping off her car for an oil change or taking the kids so he can play golf with friends. For many couples, showing an interest in sex rather than acting like it is a duty, can make a spouse feel desired. Doing a task usually done by your partner can be the best aphrodisiac. The statement shared by a friend of mine says it directly, "If you want to score, do a chore." There is a lot of truth in that advice!

With most women now working full-time, co-sharing of household tasks is how it should be. In some relationships, however, there remains an imbalance in sharing parenting and household chores. This may persist with couples who carry traditional roles from their family into their marriage. When the heavier load falls on the woman, fatigue can rule the day. When not addressed, this exhaustion can build resentment. Resentment is often the basis of an unsatisfactory love life. Feelings of anger or bitterness can markedly interfere with the desire for sexual intimacy. The healthy marriage works to avoid these negative, harmful emotions. Be open about your concerns and your needs.

To be critical, impatient, and selfish toward each other and expecting there will be joy in the bedroom is the expectation of a fool. Why would you desire intimacy with someone who does not show interest in your life, helps with chores, treat you with kindness, and forgets basic manners? You are likely to find that what happens in the bedroom is a direct result of what happens throughout the day.

If you want to have a responsive, satisfying sexual life, be nice to your spouse. When bedtime rolls around, your physical intimacy becomes an extension of the emotional intimacy you have shared during the day and is then truly making love. You each have a role in ensuring that your sexual life remains a vital part of your marriage. Learning to live with the daily demands and acquiring the skills to deal with the upheavals can keep the spark alive at the end of the day.

Steps:

- Understand that a change in your sex life is normal and need not be permanent.

- Pay attention to the little things: a compliment, a hug, an affectionate pat.

- Talk about how you are feeling, (e.g. sad, tired, worried) and what you need.

- Be nice to each other: daily interactions, basic manners, and use of humor.

- Plan an occasional get-away weekend alone.

- If you are missing sex, say so.

WORK CITED

Meeks, Colleen. "5 Ways to Protect Your Sex Life from Your Kids." *Parents*. September 26, 2012. https://www.parents.com/parenting/relationships/sex-and-marriage-after-baby/protect-your-sex-life-from-your-kids/.

CHAPTER 35

Averting Infidelity

"The grass is not always greener on the other side of the fence.
The grass is greenest where it is watered."

ROBERT FULGHUM

To prevent infidelity, a good place to start is for you both to spell out your definition. Defining fidelity ahead of time can prevent any misunderstanding of the behavior that is expected. If you witnessed affairs in your own parents' marriage, the subject is likely to carry strong emotions. Couples in a monogamous marriage would agree that engaging in physical and/or emotional relationships with another person will cause great pain and disruption to your marriage. Some individuals consider infidelity to include having intimate discussions with someone other than a spouse, particularly when they include topics about one's own marriage. By most standards, "having sexual relations" includes oral sex as well as intercourse, even when some prominent figures may infer differently. Any excuse given is likely to pale next to the pain and sense of betrayal that a spouse endures. Does one partner's definition of infidelity serve to justify an intimate act? Don't count on it. Infidelity, however expressed, can stop your dance.

When you began your married life, you both vowed to be faithful to one another. Marital fidelity is based on trust. Your love, stability, and partnership are the threads woven to strengthen your bond. Infidelity is a break in that bond. Without trust, experiencing physical and emotional intimacy, the key ingredients to a fulfilling marriage, is impossible.

Even knowing that marriage is not a straight shot to nirvana, no couple wants their relationship to result in hurt and betrayal. Asking what leads to infidelity is asking a complex question. Wise is the couple who recognizes an affair is often not about sex at all. Rather, it can be a misdirected reaction to daily stresses, sense of boredom, resentment, indifference, feeling unappreciated, career worries, financial issues, grief, desire for change, feeling unloved, inadequate, and/or unlovable. Identify these emotions *early* and talk about them. It is not your spouse's responsibility to compensate for these moods. Rather, you must recognize these emotional states yourself and communicate your feelings. Talk *together* about how best to address them and do what you need to do to ameliorate them.

Is there a person who, at some time, has not longed to escape the grind of their daily routine and fantasized what life would be like "if I had only chosen another career, married so-and-so, decided to live elsewhere etc., etc.?" These feelings are not unusual and occasional daydreaming hurts no one. Dwelling or acting on these thoughts, however, can result in a totally different and destructive outcome.

The reality is there are challenges in all relationships. The mature person has the integrity and character to accept the responsibility for addressing troublesome issues, instead of pursuing someone else. If one of you is not happy with the physical and/or the emotional aspects of your marriage, likely the other is also unhappy. It takes a person with integrity to admit when they are having problems in their relationship and address the issues before seeking solace elsewhere. An affair will never be the answer to emotional or sexual problems in your relationship.

Author and therapist, Daphne de Marneffe, in her book, *The Rough Patch*, defines the meaning of integrity as "the capacity to withstand the impulse to come apart in the face of confusion and pain." Can you face the reality of your problems and make choices that allow for growth without hurt? The person without integrity seeks self-gratification without regard for the other. An unfaithful partner may declare, "it just happened," but as de Marneffe writes, "healing from an affair is tied to the recognition that our actions have to align with our values." She writes about the personal way of relating to the excitement and fears we attach to our desires and the meaning we give to them. She poses the question, "Do we call to mind and keep in touch with the big picture in just those moments when we are vulnerable?" Having integrity makes a difference.

In his book, *Marital Tensions*, Henry V. Dicks, a British psychiatrist who studied marital interaction, described marriage as "a mutual affirmation of the other's identity as a loveable person." An affair obliterates this feeling for both partners. The one violated no longer feels lovable, and the unfaithful partner is tormented by their decision. Additionally, de Marneffe notes that both parties need to be reinstated as lovable. She describes that even though a couple would like to turn back the clock, "Their life together and their story are now broken apart, and something different has to be constructed in their place. How they find their way through their feelings of loss—of trust, of their story of their marriage, of closeness—will determine whether they can find a way forward that works for both people."

The sense of deception and the loss of trust that results from infidelity are profound. The spouse who is the victim of an affair tries to piece together when and where it took place, consumed with why it happened and how they missed the signs. Feelings of unjustified guilt and speculation about what they did or did not do often occurs. Self-confidence is shaken to the core. The sense of grief, loss, and sadness can affect the spouse's physical and mental health, sometimes to a devastating degree. There can also be incredible distress about possible sexually transmitted diseases to which the innocent partner may have been exposed. The initial sadness is often replaced by anger, which can be equally corrosive to one's mind and body. The effects on children, extended family, and friends can be deep and permanent.

Marriages that survive infidelity may never be the same. Trust is rarely fully reinstated. While some couples may report improved communication after working through the pain, how much better to have had the skills to avoid the affair in the first place. It is dangerous to think the odds of improving your marriage with an affair are in your favor. A betrayal has occurred that may be forgiven but will not be forgotten. For the adulterous partner, forgiving oneself has its own trauma and often is as difficult as earning forgiveness from the spouse. It is better to prevent an affair from happening in the first place.

Patrick and I were friends with Kendra and Rob, a couple with whom we shared many good times. I can remember, on one visit, how upset and angry Rob became as he explained to us that his sister-in-law had an affair which left his brother distraught. Our friend's reaction seemed to reflect the high value he placed on fidelity in marriage. However, several years later, when their children went off to school and his wife was pursuing an advanced degree, Rob began an affair with a co-worker. Did he find midlife, empty nest, and boredom too much to deal with? The marriage ended, as did our friendship with him, one I know he valued. It was also the last he saw of his in-laws, with whom he had enjoyed many happy years. Could it have been less painful if he communicated his concerns to Kendra and faced the issues together? If there were irreconcilable differences, how much better to accept the dissolution of their marriage and avoid the added pain of an affair.

In her book, Not "Just Friends", the late psychologist, Dr. Shirley Glass, suggested that people who choose to have affairs do not differ from others "in their feelings, but rather in their choices." She talks about her theory on "walls and windows." She describes the "windows" as openness, transparency, and information that can flow between married couples, and "walls" as opaqueness, privacy, and limits that they construct with others. In the case of an affair, these walls and windows are reversed. The metaphorical window is constructed with the new attraction, while a metaphorical wall is built between the spouses through clandestine behavior.

The ability of a marriage to survive an affair may, to some degree, relate to the specific circumstances: who it was with and how long it lasted. If a spouse becomes intoxicated while attending a conference and hooks up for a one-night stand, it is likely to cause a cascade of emotions for both partners: anger, sadness, shame, a loss of self-confidence, feeling of inadequacy, and hesitancy with future physical intimacy. When the violation was a brief escapade and lacked emotional involvement, the marriage may be able to survive with counseling, rebuilding trust, and dealing with any underlying substance and sexual issues.

A secretive affair often has different complications, especially if others know about it, but the innocent spouse was unaware. If the duplicity has happened with a friend of the couple, it smacks of a double betrayal, as a trusted friendship is destroyed as well. Laurie was a colleague whose husband finally confessed about a lengthy affair he had with her close friend. The families had shared a long friendship, including vacations with their children. The couple remained married, but it forever changed their relationship and resulted in the loss of the friendship for her and the children. Laurie shared with me that she never again felt the emotional and physical intimacy she hoped for in their marriage.

There have been affairs where a spouse may claim to have no knowledge of the goings-on, but that raises the question of denial. Sometimes, given stresses in a marriage, one partner may focus too much attention on the children or on a career. They refuse to notice their life, and indeed the marriage, is seriously out of balance. The popular 1987 film *Fatal Attraction* starring Michael Douglas and Glenn Close portrayed how the husband's unplanned adulterous liaison resulted in a frightening set of events. With the fear of destroying a marriage and family, the film served as a sobering reminder of the possible repercussions of an illicit marital affair. One pastor I know said the film did more to curb adultery than all the sermons he had ever given!

In another film, *Unfaithful,* starring Richard Gere and Diane Lane, the marriage of a couple takes a turn for the worse when the wife indulges in a torrid affair. Both movies are noteworthy because of the very innocent and subtle way the affairs evolved, as do many in real life. Since a marriage may not always seem vulnerable, it behooves couples to be alert to the insidious danger signs. They may be as basic as boredom, the feeling of "is this all there is?" and finding yourself infatuated by attention. Allowing yourself to meet one-on-one with a co-worker or acquaintance to discuss a project may seem innocent enough, but if it becomes a more exclusive meeting, out of the confines of work, conversation may too easily stray to more personal topics. Meeting in private is a risky choice. Keeping your discussions on professional and impersonal topics makes it less likely to be construed as an invitation. Office parties without spouses, singles' bars, online dating sites, cruising chat rooms, and hunting for old flames on Facebook are *never* smart ideas.

Couples who have experienced infidelity know how much work is involved in rebuilding a marriage. Prevention is easier. Your marriage will be supported by the healthy habits you establish: setting a time every day to connect with one another without the interference of technology or children, having a regular time alone, getting away overnight two or three times a year, knowing and using your love languages, and *talking* to each other about your *feelings.* It is these rituals that will strengthen your emotional connection and will open the "windows" of your marriage rather than constructing "walls" that interfere with intimacy.

Since children suffer greatly from divorce, it is worth exhausting every avenue to work out your adult issues and not leave your children dealing with the emotional fallout. Look at how you can support each other to feel worthwhile and loved. Work with a counselor, if needed. While leaning on your faith and each other, you can build a stronger more emotionally intimate connection and keep your four feet on the dance floor together.

Steps:

- Spell out your definition of fidelity and your expectations.

- Talk openly and frequently about your emotional and physical needs.

- Watch for warning signs, your own and your spouse's.

- Refrain from intimate conversations about your marriage with others.

- Seek individual and couple counseling to address concerns early.

- Consider the impact of your decisions on your children.

WORKS CITED

de Marneffe, Daphne. *The Rough Patch*. New York: Simon & Schuster, 2018.

Dicks, Henry V. *Marital Tensions: Clinical Studies Toward a Psychological Theory of Interaction*. New York: Basic Books, 1967.

Glass, Shirley, and Jean Coppock Staeheli. *Not "Just Friends": Rebuilding Trust and Recovering Your Sanity after Infidelity*. New York: Free Press, 2003.

CHAPTER 36

Identifying Loneliness Early

"I can't think of anything lonelier than spending the rest of my life with someone I can't talk to, or worse, someone I can't be silent with."

MARY ANN SHAFFER

In the 2012 movie, *Hope Springs*, Meryl Streep's character, Kay, and Tommy Lee Jones' character, Arnold, play a couple living a ritualized, daily routine in a dull 30-year marriage. They are sleeping in separate bedrooms and bored with their life. In desperation, before calling it quits, Kay takes a proactive stance and pays for an intense, week-long session for couples counseling to work on their relationship. Arnold is resistant, but ultimately, and reluctantly, agrees to participate. Her statement, "it would be less lonesome living alone than staying in this marriage," is a telling description of how empty a relationship can become. By acknowledging the loneliness and working with each other and a counselor, they address what needs to change. Laugh-out-loud humor is woven into many poignant messages that married adults can fully appreciate.

A friend of mine, Sarah, now happily married for over 40 years, shared that she avoided a marriage that she felt was likely to have resulted in loneliness and ultimately divorce. Prior to becoming engaged, she and her long-term, serious boyfriend were out on a lovely summer evening in a bustling beach town. They stopped in a bar to enjoy a drink. After a few minutes, he asked if she minded if he played a game of pool, to which she agreed. Shortly, a young man sat down next to her at the bar and engaged her in comfortable conversation. She said that it was nothing out of the ordinary, but when her boyfriend returned, she found herself somewhat disappointed. She commented that the incident had a profound effect on her. She realized something was missing. If she was enjoying a stranger's routine conversation more than her boyfriend's presence, it was not a good sign. Engagement never happened and neither did regret. Unfortunately, not everyone is lucky enough to see the handwriting on the wall. Preventing these feelings from seeping into your marriage is the next best step.

Loneliness is not aloneness. The latter can be a healthy solitude. Loneliness is feeling a lack of connection with someone you love. This feeling of isolation in a marriage evokes a sadness that rivals few others. Here are two people living under the same roof, physically occupying the same space, passing in the halls, skirting around each other in the bedroom, and hiding behind the newspaper, while sipping their morning coffee. There is a physical presence without an emotional connection. Each person is dancing alone.

There need not be serious or chaotic problems like substance use, an affair, or domestic violence that lead to an emotional divide. These problems are destructive to a marriage and require treatment to have a positive outcome. Loneliness, however, can take hold in a marriage when there are no major difficulties. The relationship seems to be devoid of any real emotion. There are often far more subtle issues that have been ignored for too long: simmering resentment, an absence of fun, avoiding conversation about your day, and not sharing feelings.

How does such disconnection happen? Getting to this point does not occur overnight. Boredom can set in like mold in a damp basement. Symptoms can be insidious. Times of transition are vulnerable periods: having a baby, moving to a new city, a death in the family, facing a job change, children leaving home, or retirement. These stresses may cause one spouse to emotionally retreat, pushing the other away. It is important to pay attention to these potentially life-altering events if symptoms of depression present themselves. The length of isolation during times of transition may vary, as you each process what the impending change will mean. If this turns into more than a few weeks, with no improvement, you want to acknowledge how you are feeling and address what to do. If your spouse refuses to seek help, you should be assertive in connecting yourself with support.

In a marriage where loneliness is germinating, each partner may be doing their own thing, with little time spent on a mutual activity. You may spot red flags when there is more involvement with endeavors outside the home. Are you pursuing a hobby with greater intensity and time commitment? Is the act of chairing community boards providing a greater sense of purpose than is found at home? Are after-work gatherings with colleagues more satisfying than seeing your spouse at the end of the day? Is volunteer work requiring extended periods away from home? Sports, coaching, shopping, and even church activities can be a concern if they are more important than spending time with your spouse and family. Some groups are gender specific and do not involve spouses, thereby causing resentment for the one who is not included. While some activities are worthwhile endeavors, they can prove to be escapism from dealing with what is missing in the relationship. Be alert to the distraction of social media if there is more time spent online. The mounting lack of communication increases the isolation.

Couples who ignore these warning signs are the ones likely to experience an emotional loneliness in their marriage. Emotional satisfaction is sought elsewhere. Some couples remain married and are even physically faithful to one another. They care about each other, yet they cannot connect on an emotional level. They seem to lack the desire or even the energy to seek a divorce. When asked what makes a lasting marriage, one colleague who has been married for 50 years replied, straight-faced, "inertia." Almost unconsciously, they move through their daily routine, missing out on the most rewarding and intimate part of what *could* be a fulfilling marriage.

We all know of marriages that end in divorce after 25, 30, or 35 years and witness the visible shock from friends. "We thought they seemed happy," is the common reaction. Then, one partner is apt to share something like, "We were so busy raising the kids, working, and all the other commitments, it just masked the loneliness that I have been feeling for years. Now that those responsibilities are gone, I just can't do it anymore." When I wrote this chapter, I shared it with Bonnie, a writing colleague, who was a successful professional, married for more than 35 years and had raised two independent children. The response, much to my sadness, was, "I want you to know this piece is extremely insightful. Unfortunately, it describes my marriage all too well."

As many long-married couples will attest, there can be periods of loneliness in every marriage. According to a *Psychology Today* article, "studies show that as high as 40 percent of marrieds complain of feeling lonely sometimes or often." The difference with happily married couples is that the emptiness was recognized early and not allowed to fester and turn to indifference. When the pattern of the relationship begins to change in a discomforting way and persists, it is time to talk about what is happening. The willingness to act and have an open, non-accusatory dialogue can allow for positive change.

Couples need to think creatively about staying connected. Sharing your insights and feelings can prevent loneliness from taking root in your marriage. Having one community activity where you can both be involved can give a supporting connection: volunteering at the soup kitchen, a political activity, or a church committee. It was serendipitous for Patrick and me that we ended up in social service careers with children and families. Our overlapping work provided many topics for conversation that, in turn, evolved into community and political issues. For couples in diverse fields, which is often the case, taking time to understand your partner's work not only makes conversations more interesting, but also shows respect for your spouse's chosen career.

Couples busy raising children, taking little time for each other, are the most vulnerable. Having our four children over a 12-year spread made life dizzying at times. I recall the months leading up to the oldest leaving for college as a very stressful period (time of transition!), giving Patrick and me little time to focus on ourselves. One evening, I told the children that Mom and Dad needed to get away. We left the oldest one in charge and went to stay overnight at a hotel in the next town! It did not eliminate all the impending stress, but it did give us time together, which we both needed and helped to remind us of our priorities.

Recognizing stress is the first step in addressing the problem. This is when isolation and loneliness take seed. Learning to be *proactive* is critical to a healthy survival. Do not put your marriage on the back burner. Identify signs of isolation early and address them together. This can prevent loneliness from seeping into your marriage and sweeping you off the dance floor.

Steps:

- Celebrate your partner's strengths.

- Connect with a community activity you both enjoy.

- Have special time alone.

- Express gratitude to your spouse for the ordinary blessings of your life.

- Connect with a professional if your situation is not improving.

WORKS CITED

Chapman, Gary. *The 5 Love Languages: The Secret to Love that Lasts.* Chicago: Northfield Publishing, 1992, 2015.

Frankel, David, dir. *Hope Springs.* 2012; Culver City, CA: Sony Pictures.

Lancer, Darlene. "Are You Being Emotionally Abandoned?" *Psychology Today.* October 29, 2017. https://www.psychologytoday.com/us/blog/toxic-relationships/201710/are-you-being-emotionally-abandoned.

CHAPTER 37

Finding (A Relative!) Balance in Your Life

"Find the right balance in life. Man is body . . . mind . . . spirit. Give the right amount of attention to each."

ALFRED A. MONTAPERT

One of the first medical terms I remember in my nursing education was homeostasis: "the ability to maintain a relatively stable internal state that persists despite changes in the world outside." Striking a balance between physical and emotional needs can help your biological and psychological health. A certain degree of anxiety is healthy, in that it acts as a motivator to accomplish a goal. High anxiety, however, can affect your functioning and, ultimately, your health. Inertia or total stasis can interfere with personal growth. Finding the balance between the two can be an asset in your daily life and positively affect your marriage.

The article "The Perfect Balance" in *Tricycle: The Buddhist Review* describes equanimity, one of the most sublime emotions of Buddhist practice, as remaining centered in the middle of whatever is happening. It is a "form of balance comes from some inner strength or stability. The strong presence of inner calm, well-being, confidence, vitality, or integrity can keep us upright."

One means to assess the various aspects of your life when striving for equanimity is a balance wheel that looks at the seven aspects of life: social, emotional, spiritual, environmental, occupational, intellectual, and physical. The balance wheel is often used by life coaches during sessions to assess how well (or poorly!) the different aspects of life are working for their client. There are many models available online.

The basic wheel consists of several spokes. The spokes I have found helpful for me are spiritual, health, marriage, family, work, emotional, physical, social, financial, and community. You can draw the number that is essential for you. Do this exercise separately and then share your findings.

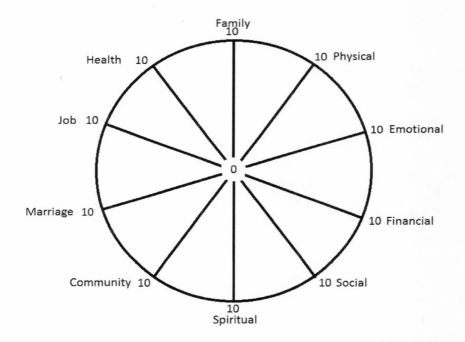

After drawing your circle and labeling your spokes, place a zero in the center and a 10 on the outer rim. To use the tool, go to each spoke and ask how you would mark yourself; with zero meaning no attention to 10 being heavily involved. For example, starting with **marriage**, if you are having a hard time connecting daily and your date nights have dwindled to three times a year, mark that spoke with a two. If you are chairman of five community boards, you would likely rate that a 10 on your **community** spoke. If you are attending church and are also in the choir, you might rate yourself a five or six on the **spiritual** spoke. You used to have friends over regularly, but that has not happened for months, so you might consider a one or two on your **social** line. If your **job** is demanding and taking up a lot of time and energy, mark that line closer to nine, due to intensity. Feeling overwhelmed by student loans, credit card debt, and a mortgage may place your **financial** line at a one. Good income, but with overspending and no strong investment plan, may put you at a nine. If time with **family** is a getting a lot of attention with the kids' hockey and soccer games, it may rate as a 10. If you are keeping up with your regular health screenings, log your **health** at a five. Your **physical exercise** spoke may come in at a three if you have not been getting to the gym regularly or missing your daily walk. On your **emotional** spoke, consider how you have been feeling. If your mood has been down lately or if you have been feeling anxious, mark it closer to a one, but if you are feeling happier and more content, mark it a five.

Now, when you have a dot on every spoke, connect the dots. Rarely is the "circle" round. This lets you know, at a glance, where things are out of alignment. Ask yourself how long you want to ride on this wheel. Do not be surprised if your spouse has a wheel that is out of balance in a different way than yours. That represents your individuality and perspective. Now, you want to each try to balance your own wheel. It does not have to be perfect, just closer to a circle. When you can each recognize the adjustments that are needed and can talk about how best to do that, you will find your wheels better aligned

During our twist and shout years, with child-rearing and careers, Patrick and I found it helpful to check on our balance wheels every few months. I recall, all too clearly, moving into our new home with a newborn and the older two starting nursery school and first grade. Complicated by the house fiasco, Patrick and I were sleep-deprived and financially stressed. After a period of juggling the demands, we recognized we were burned out. The social spoke was registered as a zero. We could not remember when we last had fun. For us, that meant that we were not getting together with friends and enjoying the benefits of socializing. Our brains needed refreshing. We were then able to deliberately make a change and put in the effort to invite people to dinner. That motivated us to clean the house, which also resulted in feeling better about our environment, a double win!

As you review each of your spokes, examine how you are *feeling*. Completing this exercise requires introspection. The importance of knowing yourself cannot be overstated, and it is an ongoing and ever-changing process (remember the first chapter!). This balance wheel exercise can give insight into the different aspects of your life and how they are affecting your marriage. Listen to your spouse's feelings, without becoming defensive. This is not all about you. Dr. Gottman's research notes that when men take counsel from their wives, the marriage has the most positive outcome. Women's intuition, insight, and logic are attributes that have often been overlooked. A husband who can listen and value his wife's input is often better able to see the broader picture in a situation, thus allowing for a more balanced plan. Two heads are better than one.

The balance wheel may prompt discussions that shed light on the needs of your partner you had not recognized. Economic needs aside, some women need the challenge of the workplace. Some fathers need more time to enjoy their children. It is important to note if the imbalance is a temporary situation, or if it has become a lifestyle pattern that needs concerted action to change. Wheels chronically out of balance may leave each of you asking, "Is this what I want for the rest of my life?" If this dissatisfaction becomes chronic, it is a red flag that change is needed.

Making even one adjustment to your wheel can make a difference. Recognize that exercise, a yoga class, better financial planning, going to lunch with a friend, signing up for spiritual retreat or participating in a community fundraiser may bring more balance to your life. No one can balance your wheel for you, but your choices can be invaluable to your marriage.

Remember that no one's life is always in balance. Couples who can keep their individual wheels in relative symmetry experience greater marital contentment. Striving for balance during these twist and shout years requires deliberation, but your effort will keep you on the dance floor.

Steps:

- Draw out and label your own balance wheel.

- Share your feelings and insight with your spouse and be supportive.

- Think about what needs to be tweaked, being alert to red flags.

- Work to make one change at a time.

- Set up a time to evaluate your efforts.

- Use the wheel as often as needed to seek a relative balance.

WORKS CITED

Fronsdal, Gil, and Sayadaw U Pandita. "A Perfect Balance, Cultivating Equanimity." *Tricycle: The Buddhist Review,* Winter 2005. https://tricycle.org/magazine/perfect-balance/.

Lanese, Nicoletta. "What is Homeostasis?" *Live Science.* July 15, 2019. https://www.livescience.com/65938-homeostasis.html.

"7 Dimensions of Wellness (And How They Form a Path to a Healthy, Happy, and Balanced Life)." *BestSelf.* https://bestself.co/blogs/articles/7-dimensions-of-wellness-and-how-they-form-a-path-to-a-healthy-happy-and-balanced-life.

CHAPTER 38

Caring for Each Other

"Neglect the whole world rather than each other."

UNKNOWN

The secret to a long and happy marriage lies in your ability to truly care for each other. Your spouse will have more impact on your physical, mental, emotional, financial, and spiritual health than any friend, acquaintance, or co-worker ever will. You want that impact to be a positive one. Knowing there is someone by your side out of love, not obligation, is one of life's greatest treasures. The partnership, support, and compassion that you offer to each other are the priceless gifts and the critical ingredients in a fulfilling marriage.

Over your years together, however, there will be times when those gifts are hard to offer. Finances, health, work, sex, religion, in-laws, raising children, and household responsibilities pose challenges to the strongest marriages. Your goal is to address them with healthy, honest, open communication to avoid simmering resentment. Unresolved resentment corrodes a relationship, and destroys the love, appreciation, and passion that a long and healthy marriage requires.

Taking responsibility for tending to your own physical, emotional, and spiritual needs is a gift that you give not only to yourself but to your spouse and to your children. Never feel guilty about self-care. Take time for solitude, physical exercise, socializing with friends, and opportunities for personal growth. A well runs dry when it is not replenished with new water. A car cannot run without fuel. Good maintenance is critical for your car, for you, *and* for your marriage. Are you encouraging and supporting your partner to take the time and energy to meet their own needs and replenish their own well? Some people need permission to take care of themselves. Provide that for your spouse.

There will be times when your partner will need your energy and support more than usual. Emotional setbacks can happen with a job loss, issues with extended family, or financial stress. There may be minor illnesses with a cold or flu, or a more prolonged impact with a chronic illness. Most couples do not picture these scenarios when they gaze lovingly into each other's eyes at their wedding, but it is times like these when the unconditional love you committed to each other needs to be demonstrated. Challenging times often heighten your emotional intimacy and forge an even deeper bond. The ability to be there in the good times, the bad times, and the mundane days of life reveals the depth of your love for each other and the respect you hold for your marriage.

Keep your home fires burning by taking care of each other. Your spouse will keep you warm, long after children and other people have moved out of your life. Pay attention to this most precious gift so you can remain on the dance floor together.

Steps:

- Place your spouse before other commitments.

- Guard against resentment by addressing issues when they arise.

- Be there for each other—always.

Afterward

"Happiness is a journey, not a destination. So, work like you don't need the money, love like you've never been hurt, and dance like no one is watching."

UNKNOWN

I was never able to interview the professor and his wife of 50 years, as they had long passed. I have, however, tried to learn what fosters the love they demonstrated. The stories others have so willingly shared with me, my observations on healthy relationships, the research on marriage, and my reflections on our years together have enriched my life.

Marriage is a unique journey that comes with no road map. When one thinks about living intimately with one person for decades, it is amazing anyone makes it. Writing this book has allowed me to think more deeply about love and explore the many unions that do happily endure. Marriage can bring the greatest joy and the greatest heartache.

On our honeymoon in Bermuda, we passed the hotel lobby where there was a bingo game going on. We decided to stop in and take a card. The last game was for the jackpot of $125. As we yelled "Bingo!" and went to claim the prize, an elderly woman said, "I think we won too." She and her husband were there on their 50*th* anniversary. Wow, that is such a long time, I thought! We split the winnings and took it as a good omen.

As we are in our 50*th* year together, I am stunned this time has passed. I am happy to get this book to you during your years of juggling careers, kids, and chaos and working to keep love alive. Every generation has new challenges, but as I was taught in nursing, the institutions where you work may vary, but the principles remain the same. I believe that is true for marriage also. Getting the basics down, will enrich your journey.

- Make God a partner in your marriage. It is hard to do it alone.

- Take responsibility for you; know who you are and what you need.

- Learn healthy communication skills and use them.

- Be nice to your spouse. Be kind and respectful.

- Help your partner be the best they can be.

Marriage is the foundation of your family and a cornerstone of society. The quality of your marriage can be the best legacy you leave to future generations. After the gifts of faith and health, there is no greater joy than loving and being loved by one person; that most precious gift you want to protect every day.

Have high expectations for your marriage. Do not accept mediocrity. A strong and loving union provides a profound sense of security and emotional intimacy. You two do not have to be the best dancers to remain on the dance floor, but neither does it happen by accident. Your chance of having a great marriage begins when you refuse to hang up your dancing shoes and commit to improving your footwork every day. There are no guarantees in life and certainly none for marriage and parenting. The one guarantee is that it will be an adventure. The twist and shout years can be busy, brain-boggling, and beautiful, as you head into the years of the cha-cha and the waltz. Love deeply and keep dancing.

Acknowledgments

This book was started during my years with my trusted writing group: Herb Pence, Kathy Fortin, Joanne Lahiff, and Marcy Lyman. I thank you for your insight, encouragement, and the helpful critique at our weekly gathering. This book was completed during graduate school, as I was earning my Master of Fine Arts at Southern New Hampshire University. Thank you to my classmates who kept me energized and gratitude to my published faculty mentors who helped shape and improve my writing: Katie Towler, Rick Carey, Jo Knowles, and Justin Taylor.

Thank you to the many friends who shared their thoughts and experiences. Your willingness to discuss the difficult times and what helped you and your marriages will provide support to couples facing similar challenges.

I appreciate the team at Atlantic Publishing Group for their editing skills and helpful feedback.

A special thanks to Andriana Skaperdas for her invaluable help with social media skills.

Thank you to my children for educating, inspiring, and enriching my life and providing enough challenges to make me a better person. And, of course, Patrick, without whom I could never have written a book about marriage! Your love, support, and encouragement have made this journey the one I wanted for us. I love you all.

S.M.

About the Author

Susan McKeown APRN (ret), CPS, is a graduate of St. Anselm College with a B.S. degree in Nursing and Northeastern University's Pediatric Nurse Practitioner Program. She worked with families as a nurse practitioner for over 40 years. As a Certified Prevention Specialist, she educates and advocates on issues of mental health and substance misuse. For the past 18 years Susan has co-facilitated a weekly support group for families with a loved one with a substance use disorder. In 2015 she was selected as Prevention Specialist of the Year by the Prevention Certification Board of New Hampshire.

In 2020, she earned her MFA in nonfiction writing from Southern New Hampshire University. *Beyond the Tango* is her second book. Susan speaks to groups on healthy relationships and strengthening marriages to prevent the trauma of divorce for couples and their children. She can be contacted through her website *Beyondthefirstdance.com* where you can sign up to receive her biweekly blog.